Children With Autism

of related interest

Autism – An Inside-Out Approach
An innovative look at the mechanics of 'autism' and its developmental 'cousins'
Donna Williams
ISBN 1 85302 387 6

Children with Language Impairments
An Introduction
Morag L. Donaldson
ISBN 1 85302 313 2

Children With Autism

Diagnosis and Interventions to Meet Their Needs

Colwyn Trevarthen, Kenneth Aitken,
Despina Papoudi and Jacqueline Robarts

Jessica Kingsley Publishers
London and Bristol, Pennsylvania

Based on a research report funded by the Scottish Office Education Department

First published in the United Kingdom in 1996 by
Jessica Kingsley Publishers Ltd
116 Pentonville Road
London N1 9JB, England
and
1900 Frost Road, Suite 101
Bristol, PA 19007, U S A

Library of Congress Cataloging in Publication Data
Children with autism : diagnosis and interventions to meet their needs
/ Colwyn Trevarthen ... [et al.].
p. cm.
Includes bibliographical references and index.
ISBN 1-85302-314-0 (pbk.)
1. Autism in children. 2. Autistic children--Rehabilitation.
I. Trevarthen, Colwyn.
RJ506.A9C453 1996
618.92'8982--dc20 95-23994
CIP

British Library Cataloguing in Publication Data
Trevarthen, Colwyn
Children with Autism: Diagnosis,
and Interventions to Meet Their Needs
I. Title
618.928982

ISBN 1-85302-314-0

Printed and Bound in Great Britain by
Cromwell Press, Melksham, Wiltshire

Contents

6 Brain Abnormalities in Autism 56

7 Brain Embryology and Autism 66

8 Where Development of the Communicating Mind Goes Astray 78

9 Communicating and Playing with an Autistic Child 98

10 What Can Be Done? 116

11 Music Therapy for Children with Autism 134

12 Psychoanalysis and the Management of Pervasive Developmental Disorders, Including Autism 161

13 Education for Autistic Children 172

References 179

Glossary 218

List of Tables

List of Figures

Preface

In the old story, a man looked under a lamp post for his lost keys. When asked where he thought he had lost them he said he wasn't sure, but he was looking under the light because it was much easier to see things there.

We wrote this book because all the authors had come to the conclusion that lately autism research has been looking under one particular lamp post because the light there is bright. Interest in language and thinking in autism may have missed evidence that these aspects, which can be measured only in individuals whose mental abilities are functioning at a relatively high level, are facets of a disorder which begins to affect the mind at a far more fundamental level. There are motives and emotions underlying words and reasons that make it possible for human beings to be conscious of one another, and to communicate. We believe that language, and the processes of thought based on language, are affected in autistic individuals because deeper and earlier developing functions are disturbed. Our evidence comes from observations on how infants communicate before they understand language, and on the expressions of feeling and interest by which all persons can make sympathetic contact. Developmental psychology has information that can lead to a more complete and coherent view of the experiences and feelings of an autistic child, and better interpretation of his or her behaviours and thinking.

Biases of interest also develop in research that is trying to identify what goes wrong in the brains of autistic people. Time and again parts of the picture are illuminated by measurement of one kind of physiological response or one kind of anatomical change for which there is a handy technique. But, that said, there is a great team work now among brain scientists, with rapidly increasing technical power to see how brains work. In time the various bits of information do lead to a larger picture. Above all, we are gradually realising that to understand this or any other kind of disorder in the human minds we have to have a concept of how the brain grows.

So, we have to make an effort to perceive the lie of the land, even the parts that are out of light, if we are to find what we are searching for. We will have to make some reconstruction of events that happened before the key was lost.

Most people reading this book will have ideas about autism. Very few will have personal experience of living with or teaching an autistic person. Even the average British GP will see but a single autistic child in his or her working lifetime. For the rest of us knowledge might have come from seeing a film such as 'The Rain Man', in which an actor played an autistic person, or a TV documentary on an autistic individual such as the artist Steven Wiltshire who has wonderful, and exceptional, gifts. The preconceptions about autism that we have picked up will be very incomplete. There is much that is mysterious about the problems autistic people have in sharing the world with us, even for the experts, and efforts to help them to realise the potential they all have for some development may seem like groping in the dark. Nevertheless, we hope to give an optimistic picture. A variety of the methods we review do bring improvements in the lives of autistic persons and in the lives of those who care for them or those who attempt to teach them.

Autism, properly identified, is a rare disorder. It affects only about 1 in 2500 people. Less severe problems that resemble autism more or less closely, called 'autistic spectrum' disorders, affect around 1 in 400 people. As there is an association with both cognitive and communication problems, most autistic children have serious learning handicaps and many are non-verbal. It is a pervasive condition affecting most aspects of a child's life, and our understanding of what it is like to be autistic is far from complete.

We will elaborate a model of autism that draws on developmental psychology, developmental neuropsychology, and neurobiology to document what is known about autism as a neurodevelopmental disorder. Most of all, we will situate the age-related changes in an autistic child's behaviour in relation to the way a normally developing infant gains understanding of the world and of people – how he or she learns to speak and act as a knowledgeable member of society. And we will approach our review of methods to help autistic children in therapy or teaching from this understanding of normal development.

Just about everyone has chatted to a small baby, or watched the wonderful mutual interest that sparks between a mother and her infant. As early as a few minutes after birth we were all capable of responding in that way. We sympathised and the rhythms of our gestures and vocalisations interplay with those of our affectionate partner to make a conversation. We sought for eye contact when our mother spoke to us, moved in time with the melody of her speech and took our turn. These responses and initiations are a part of a basic human repertoire carried in every newborn baby's brain. As we live and learn and grow stronger and wiser in our actions on the world, our innate sympathy for the feelings and interests of other persons remains as the guide to our consciousness and its increasing conventional sophistication.

Autism is a condition which affects the development of this inborn prelinguistic interactive system, which is the teacher of social understanding. Present knowledge of the maturation of brain systems involved in motivations and learning agrees with the evidence on emergence in the young autistic child of a pattern of increasingly abnormal behaviour. Responses to people become strange, apparently as a consequence of abnormalities of specific steps of brain growth coming to maturity at that time, about one or two years after birth, just as language normally begins rapid development. Families note differences in some autistic children within the first year, and in all such children clear symptoms can be seen by the middle of the second year of life, if there is sufficient understanding to recognise them.

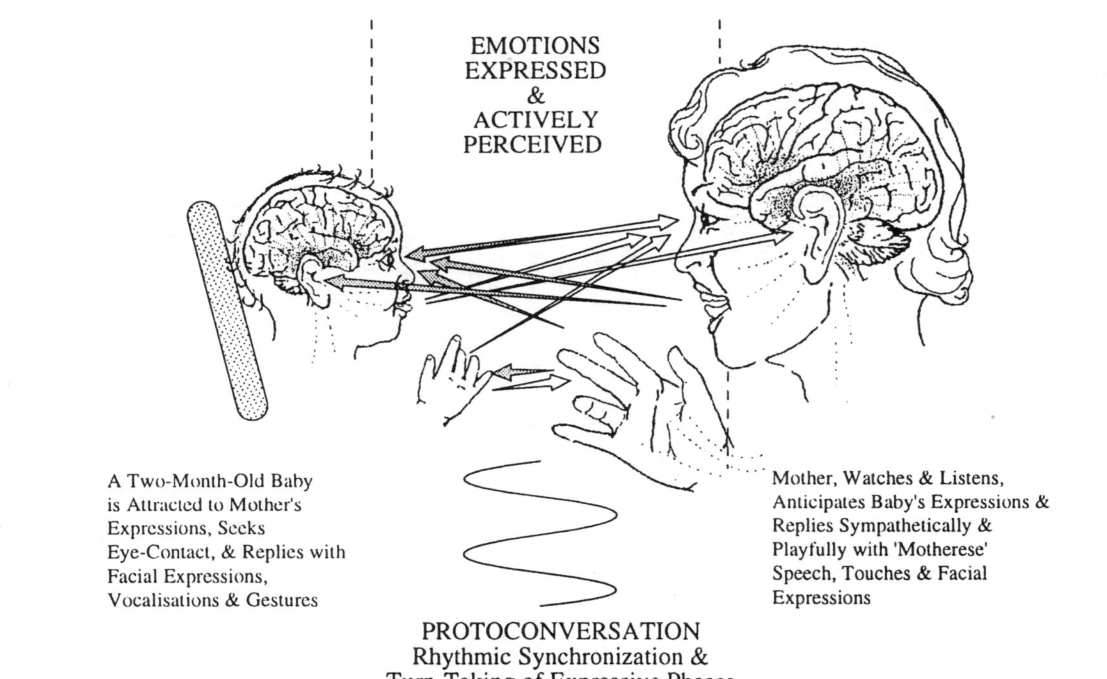

Figure 1: Illustrating the many channels of expression that bring the mind of a young baby into communication with a mother's mind in the first communication games

It is a major practical problem that in many places the typical age at first diagnosis for autism is around six years of age. Doctors and clinical psychologists even know of a significant number of cases for whom diagnosis was not arrived at until the individual was well into adult life. On the basis of current evidence, it would be relatively easy to set up routine population screening for autism and autistic spectrum disorders as part of normal preschool developmental monitoring at 18 months. There would be a high degree of specificity in diagnosis and a fairly low false hit rate. We hope that our account will make it easier for this to be achieved, because we also know that the best results of treatment or special education are achieved if they begin while the child is young, and this is also the time when parents urgently need sympathetic support and informative advice.

This book has grown from a report we were commissioned to make for the Department of Education of the Scottish Office in 1992. Ken Aitken, a clinical psychologist at the Sick Children's Hospital in Edinburgh has taken responsibility for the clinical and diagnostic review and for the explanation of methods of treatment. Despina Papoudi, who completed her PhD in the Psychology Department at the University of Edinburgh in 1993 and now is a lecturer in the Department of Psychology at the University of Rhodes, wrote the sections on play with autistic children and the development of communication and language. Jacqueline Robarts is a music therapist attached to The Nordoff–Robbins Institute in London. She draws on her experience of work with autistic and emotionally disturbed children to give us an explanation and history of improvisatory music therapy, with a case history to illustrate in detail the difficulties and progress of an autistic child drawn into communication by this non-verbal technique. Colwyn Trevarthen is Professor of Child Psychology and Psychobiology at the University of Edinburgh. He has incorporated knowledge of how infants and young children normally develop mastery of cultural understanding and language into an account of the ways an autistic child's motives and understanding go astray. Writing has been a cooperative effort motivated by an intention to offer an up-to-date account of both neurobiological and psychological knowledge of autism and yet present a picture of the whole child with his or her motives.

To underline this approach we invited Olga Maratos, a developmental psychologist and psychoanalyst, to write an account of her experience in helping autistic children and their parents in a special school she founded in Athens. Interpretations of psychoanalysts, taken too far, have undoubtedly spread confusion and anxiety in the past for autistic children and their parents. We believe that a new level of understanding in developmental psychology that acknowledges the importance of motives and their communication in development of human consciousness has led to a correction in the psychodynamic approach, facilitating the expression of important insights into the autistic experiences and how they may be assisted by therapy.

CHAPTER 1

Introduction

A Rare and Baffling Difficulty in Communicating and Learning

Every year about 350 children in the United Kingdom develop a disorder that will permanently affect their communication with other people and their ability to learn. For the first years the problem, which began months before birth, is hidden in the emerging complexity of the brain. Parents sometimes remember that in the first year these children were undemanding and placid babies who did not seek to 'chat' in play. Perhaps they had rather weak muscles and restricted or unstable attention, but they were not really significantly different from other babies at this stage, and no cause for concern. By about one to two years after birth, however, at a time when infants usually become acutely aware of other people and what they are doing, full of playful imagination and eager for new experiences, these babies became strangely self-contained or isolated in their own world and increasingly unresponsive or irritable, and difficult to understand, their movements often seemed repetitious and pointless, and their gestures and postures were also odd. Throughout their childhood they continued to express themselves in ways that made parents, teachers and other children feel unable to make contact.

The children are not insensitive to others or unaffectionate, and they can show strong likes and dislikes for particular people. Sometimes they imitate or seek to interact, but never in a free and easy way. Strange postures and movements and a need for sameness, combined with obsessional interest in certain objects and experiences, cut them off from others. At times they seem to be in a trance, 'floating off', 'looking' or 'listening' when nothing is there, often making strange flapping of the hands and an enigmatic smile with unintelligible baby-like vocalisations. They may get into inexplicable panics and seem very distressed, anxious or terrified, especially when forced to have close contact with people and in strange environments. In general they do not like unfamiliar places or routines. Some may injure themselves. Most of the time, however, they are content to amuse themselves, repeating favorite actions over and over. Their behaviours can be frightening and distressing to parents who need help to understand what is wrong and how to cope.

About half of these children do not speak at all when they are older. Others who become fluent, or even exceptionally articulate, make inappropriate use of language – echoing what others say, including questions addressed to them, or repeating phrases automatically without obvious sense, mixing up personal pronouns and using pedantically rigid, 'concrete' language with 'odd', idiosyncratic and distracting expression or prosody, the 'music' of speech. Those that can speak and understand language find reversals and negatives particularly difficult. They tend to take utterances literally, missing jokes or metaphors.

Most are distinctly subnormal in attention and intelligence. A few seem very bright and persistent in certain areas, especially in solving visual puzzles or working out and remembering series of events. In rare, but fascinating and theoretically intriguing instances, made famous by the film 'Rainman', a child with this condition may acquire an extraordinary highly specialised or focused ability to draw, to imitate musical performances or to calculate with huge numbers making seemingly miraculous deductions. An autistic girl called Nadia made wonderful drawings of horses from memory when she was four (Selfe 1978), and Stephan Wiltshire has become famous for his ability to draw, often from memory, most difficult architectural subjects and city-scapes, capturing space and perspective with a freedom that a professional artist must envy (Wiltshire 1987, 1989). The memory of more gifted autistic people for intricate details of whatever interests them may be astonishing (Luria 1969). These, of course, are 'one in a million' cases, often benefiting from exceptionally sensitive support from carers or lucky opportunities to persue their obsessions.

In general the children are not aggressive, but they may fly into tantrums and struggle or scream if forced to do what they do not want to do. Sometimes they cry out for no apparent reason. Even though they are 'distant' and avoid intimate turn-taking cooperation, they frequently show affectionate recognition of familiar people who are kind to them, and respond happily to cuddling and rough-and-tumble play. But, unless they are given special and patient encouragement, they do not 'mix-in' and share with brothers and sisters, may imitate but do not try to join in play with other children at preschool and are separate and uninvolved in classroom motivation at school. Imitations tend to be automatic or delayed so they serve no communicative function, and attempts to join in play may be awkward and easily misunderstood by others. As adolescents, though sometimes more oriented to others than when they were younger, trying to make friends, they tend to be 'odd' and may act in quite inappropriate, sometimes over-familiar ways, careless of other persons' feelings or customs.

These are the children, known as a special group for 50 years, who are described as 'autistic'. Though rare, about one in 2500 births, they are well-recognised and distinct from other handicapped emotionally disturbed children, but baffling to medical and psychological science, and they present very trying problems for their families. They need special education because they cannot fit in with normal school work or keep up in class, but most do respond to carefully adjusted communication and teaching or therapy that fits their individual needs, and they can improve in their responses to people and in their learning. Their condition is not just a mental handicap or learning disability and their development cannot be simply described as 'delayed'. They have very specific failure of responses to other people, and they need care that recognises and compensates for this.

These characteristics mean that parents and teachers need expert help to understand autistic children, and teachers need specialised training in their behaviour and how best to invite the autistic child's communication and motivate cooperative learning. Schools need professional support and psychologists and teachers must be aware of the ways in which autistic children are unlike other children with special needs.

In level of cognitive ability or intelligence, perception, use of language, degree of withdrawal, excitability and self-injury and physical appearance autistic persons vary greatly. Nevertheless, the core of their motivation for relating to other persons is always characteristically 'absent' or inaccessible. How can we explain the baffling responses of the autistic child? The consensus now is that we should look at autism in comparison with normal development with careful attention to the changing motives for communication that help children learn from other persons, both adults and peers.

It seems that the primary cause of autism is related to the 'instructions' for brain development that control the way a child's mind grows and learns from experience; that is by investigating the world, especially the world of other people and their ideas. Autism is one of a much larger group of related disorders that affect the development of motivation and learning in the brains of approximately one child in three hundred. It is the most puzzling because it so obviously affects the basic human capacity for sympathetic thinking and feeling.

There is no known cure for autism, and indeed a search for a cure may well be misguided because it is not a sickness in any simple sense, but our knowledge of its causes and how to intervene to help the child and family is growing rapidly in a period of unprecedented research activity and public interest. Autistic children have much brighter prospects now than in the past. Years ago they were often left to languish in a mental hospital or a home for severely retarded children and given little therapy or teaching, and indeed little opportunity for human life. Nevertheless, creation of the right support services and education will take time and commitment, and to succeed it must involve parents in an organised way, responding to their difficulties and worries.

CHAPTER 2

The 'Discovery' of Autism

First Description and Changing Explanations

The word 'autism' is a compound of two Greek words – 'aut-', which means 'self', and '-ism', which implies 'orientation or state'. So, autism could be defined as the condition of somebody who is unusually absorbed in him or her self (Reber 1985). This captures how autistic children fail to act with interest in other persons, but misses many other features of their behaviour.

The first accepted clinical paper describing the psychological features of children described as 'autistic' was published by Leo Kanner (Kanner 1943). Many earlier descriptions of unusual children such as those of Victor, the 'Wild boy of Aveyron' whom Itard studied (Itard 1801), and of Kaspar Hauser reportedly discovered in 1828 (see Tredgold and Soddy 1956), insofar as they can be taken as reliable accounts, are suggestive of the condition which Kanner so lucidly described (see Frith 1989 for discussion and further examples).

Kanner, who called the condition he recognised 'early infantile autism', concluded that the essential characteristic is a disturbance of affective contact. The term autism had already been used, in a somewhat different sense, by Bleuler (1913). He described the thinking of schizophrenics as autistic because it corresponds not to reality and logic, but to fantasy. It is important to point out that autistic thinking, in Bleuler's sense, is quite normal when people are being imaginitive and creative, trying to understand; it also has an assimilatory role, fitting reality to the fabrications of imagination and what is retained in memory. Only if the balance between autism and realism is lost does a pathological form of behaviour emerge. Autistic children cannot be said to have normally creative imaginations. In one 'microsociological' analysis of the logic of their thinking and interactions with other persons (Durig 1993), autistic persons have been said to lack creative induction (reasoning that moves from specific premises to general conclusions), while retaining deduction (arriving at specific conclusions from specific premises) and abduction (taking general premises to specific conclusions). But these very abstract or ideal rules of reasoning must be reflections of more fundamental disorders in the dynamics of the human motives of autistic individuals.

Kanner's and Bleuler's descriptions also differed in the assumed innateness (or not) of the cause of social withdrawal in autism. This has been a point of contention all through the last 50 years. Only now can we be sure that Kanner's first conception is essentially correct, and by far the most useful. Autism is the consequence of a complex disorder of brain development affecting many functions. As we come to understand this disorder and its effects better, we will be more effective in assisting autistic childrens' development.

The term infantile autism was taken by Margaret Mahler to imply both an assumed normal phase of the development of self-awareness and a type of childhood psychosis (Mahler 1952). During the phase of what Mahler calls 'normal autism', from birth until the second month of life, the infant is described as being unable to differentiate between him/herself and the outside reality, and unable to relate to the mother as a separate 'object' distinct from the 'self'. Pathological autism (infantile autism) is then described as being caused by the fixation or the regression to the primary 'normal autistic stage'; the child who is stuck in this stage or has slipped back into it cannot orient to anything outside, so is restricted to his or her own self-centred world. Anthony (1958) also argued that autism occurs in infancy as a normal phase, and the psychopathological form emerges only if the child is arrested in or returns to the 'normal autistic period'. Tustin (1981), a distinguished child psychiatrist, took a similar approach, explaining autism as a normal phase in infancy in which the child cannot yet differentiate between the sensations of the 'self' and those of the 'not-self' (mother). Recently, however, (Tustin 1991; 1994) she concluded that this is manifestly an incorrect interpretation because normal infants do not in fact behave at all like autistic children; '...there is not a normal infantile stage of primary autism to which the pathology of childhood autism could be a regression' (Tustin 1994, p.3). Tustin reports that Mahler also changed her interpretation of the nature of autism, in response to the new information in Daniel Stern's book (Stern 1985) on what young infants can normally do in communication (see Tustin 1994, p.5).[1]

Infants can freely and sensitively seek to communicate from birth, as we shall describe. Tustin was led by her clinical observations, which we shall discuss more thoroughly later, to relate autistic hyper-sensitivity to bodily stimulation, and avoidance of others' 'intrusions', to the observation that a baby is often much involved with feelings of his/her own body and with contact to the mother's body. She initially thought that if a serious emotional disturbance occurs in early life, the infant reacts by developing pathological autism. She subsequently took evidence on the complexity of normal mother–infant communication in early months as evidence that autism must be a disturbance in the innate mechanism for relating to persons; that it relates to a *pathological* state of the infant.

---

1 In Chapter 12 Dr Olga Maratos explains how she uses a modified psychoanalytic approach to helping autistic children and their parents.

Thus, the more extreme psychoanalytic ideas about a normal autistic phase in infant development, based largely on findings with adult patients and older children with psychiatric illness, are now called seriously in question by evidence from research on communication in very early infancy, from birth in fact, which shows that babies are born with the capacity to distinguish themselves from other persons, and that newborns can communicate by imitating reciprocally (Kugiumutzakis 1993). Normally developing infants may be building new motives and new cognitive abilities for communicating with persons and for manipulating objects, but they are not at any age like an autistic child (Trevarthen 1993a). Nevertheless, the relation of autism with pathological conditions in adults where the self is poorly or inappropriately demarcated remains a significant problem (Hobson 1990a, 1993a, b).

The Swiss child psychologist, Jean Piaget, who was primarily interested in intellectual development from a Cartesian perspective, also thought the infant and young child had an undifferentiated 'egocentric' consciousness and could not take the view of the 'other' into account until an 'object concept' had developed which could 'represent' an outside object, event or cause. Some suggest that this supposed 'egocentricity' can also be interpreted as 'normal autism', but in Piaget's theory the emphasis is definitely on the mechanism of general cognition or perhaps on perception, rather than on the the interpersonal 'object relation' and its subjective and emotional regulation. Piaget's theory, too, requires modification in the light of our present understanding of infants' early competence for communication with the motives and feelings of other persons, and how this competence contributes to cognitive development, in collaboration with different motives for investigating objects.

New, and Not So New, Ideas About the Thinking and Communicating of Autistic Children

Much argument in recent years has revolved around conflicting clinical concepts of autism reflected in lack of agreement between US and European diagnostic systems and a succession of revised systems, described below. There has been considerable dispute among psychologists over the extent to which the primary disorder is emotional, social, cognitive or 'meta-cognitive'.

Kanner's original idea was that the autistic child was born with an '...innate inability to form the usual biologically provided affective contact with people' (Kanner 1943). As we have said, he perceived autism to be a biological disorder of affective functioning.

More recently, Rutter, who, in reaction to psychoanalytic theories of an emotional pathology, has for years maintained the view that autism is primarily a disorder of 'cognitive processing', has, apparently reluctantly, conceded that it is primarily a deficit in social and emotional functioning. He expresses the turn-about in his thinking as follows:

> ...we are forced to the conclusion that autistic children's social abnormalities do stem from some kind of 'cognitive' deficit if by that one means a deficit in dealing with social and emotional cues...it appears that the stimuli that pose difficulties for autistic children are those that carry emotional or social 'meaning'. (Rutter 1983)

The view that autism is essentially a cognitive disorder that interferes with social functioning has, however, been restated in more sophisticated form in recent years by Baron-Cohen, Leslie and Frith (1985). They describe the condition as stemming from a primary disorder of 'meta-cognition' or 'interpersonal perspective taking' or 'thinking on thinking', especially *thinking on other persons' thinking.* This analysis of the condition applies meaningfully only to 'high functioning' autistic children, the tests or demonstrations of theory of mind failure being usefully applied only to autistic individuals who understand language and speak.

The cognitive view is to a large extent based on the assumption that emotion must always be the lower-level output organized by some form of higher cognitive–perceptual processing system that responds to information from both the environment and the self. This premise has itself been under considerable scrutiny and today seems largely untenable, it being clear that emotions are communicated directly by mechanisms of an integrated and intrinsically active self, and that they do not involve the kind of cognitive or 'inner language' processes assumed to be essential for a person to possess 'meta-cognition', or a 'theory of mind' (Barnard and Teasdale 1991; Hobson 1993a; Izard 1993; Trevarthen 1993b).

A number of researchers and clinicians, while agreeing that the social deficits are central in autism, have argued that these are not to be seen as consequences of cognitive deficits that lead to problems in thinking about social and emotional information, but that they are primary deficits of an essentially non-cognitive (non-rational) nature (Fein, Pennington and Waterhouse 1987; Rogers and Pennington 1991):

> It is our contention that the social deficits in autism cannot be reasonably attributed to more primary cognitive deficits, but should be regarded as primary manifestations of the neurological disorder. (Fein, Pennington and Waterhouse 1987)

Thus 'autism', indeed a fascinating and confusing condition, remains as enigmatic and provocative today as when first described some half century ago, having given rise to a myriad of clinical descriptions and theoretical views as to its genesis on the way. Obviously the controversies stem from the incompleteness of the various competing theories of the nature of the mind.

For many years after 1950 the psychogenic (psychoanalytic) view that autism arises from cold emotionless parenting, refered to by Kanner as 'refrigerator parenting', was the predominant theory (Kanner and Eisenberg 1956;

Kanner 1973). Recent times have seen a major shift towards recognition that in virtually every case, even if there are other aggravating problems in the interpersonal world of the child, evidence of organic abnormality in the child will be found if adequate examination can be carried out (Steffenberg 1991). (See Chapter 5 on Causes.) Advances in developmental psychology are leading to a new approach that seeks to relate the progressive isolation of the autistic child and his or her failure to learn in communication to normal stages of social or interpersonal development and learning (Sigman 1989; Rogers and Pennington 1991; Nadel and Peze 1993). The new comparative-developmental view is discussed fully in Chapter 8.

Seeking a Standard Description

The term 'autism' has been used in so many different senses, identifying so many different levels of abnormal function, that a descriptive approach that covers all aspects without prejudice is needed to dispel confusion. 'Autistic infantile psychosis' (Mahler 1952), 'childhood schizophrenia' (Wolff and Chess 1964), 'autism' (Tustin 1981), 'autistic disorder' (DSM-III-R 1987) are used as synonyms of the syndrome that Kanner first described as 'early infantile autism'. What is the whole child like whom these different terms are attempting to describe?

According to Kanner's original paper (1943) the main characteristics of an autistic child's behaviour are these:

(1) an inability to establish social relatedness,

(2) a failure to use language normally for the purpose of communication,

(3) an obsessive desire for the maintenance of sameness,

(4) a fascination for objects, and

(5) good cognitive potentialities.

Furthermore

(6) these characteristics appear in the child before the age of 30 months.

It is noteworthy that in subsequent descriptions Kanner reduced the main features of the autistic syndrome to two, which identify qualities of *motivation* for relating to other persons and to the shared environment (Eisenberg and Kanner 1956):

(1) aloneness, and

(2) obsessive desire for sameness.

Ornitz and Ritvo (1968), taking an approach influenced by conventional categories in experimental psychology, which subdivides the functions of the subject in relation to discrete stimuli and the responses to them, classified the symptoms of early infantile autism into five sub-clusters, identifying disturbances of:

(1) perception

(2) motor behaviour

(3) relating

(4) language, and

(5) developmental rate and sequence.

The inability to maintain constancy or coherence of *perception* (sub-cluster (1)) was considered to determine all the others.

Rutter (1978) proposed the following diagnostic criteria:

(1) onset before 30 months

(2) impairment in social development

(3) impairments in language development, and

(4) insistence on sameness.

As we have explained, he believed then that these effects stemmed from a fundamental disorder in *cognition or intelligence.*

These typify the varied understanding of the disorder before the effort of the last 15 years to obtain a standard of diagnosis that can serve as a basis for research and treatment. There is agreement about the social detachment and obsessional behaviour of autistic children. The ritualistic, stereotyped exploration of objects and insistence on sameness seem to be defensive, protecting from invasive and novel experiences or situations that the child cannot understand or predict. They may point to a motivational fault that is most in need of attention. They indicate the importance of carefully measured response by any person who is attempting to gain the autistic child's confidence, affection and cooperation.

Clinical Recognition of Autism

> We may conclude that there is no doubt that autism constitutes a valid and meaningfully different psychiatric syndrome; indeed the evidence on its validity is stronger than for any other psychiatric condition in childhood. (Rutter and Schopler 1987)

Despite acceptance that autism is a distinct and clearly recognisable medical condition, there is still considerable debate over the most useful diagnostic criteria (Aitken 1991b). Autism remains a useful clinical entity, but evidently there is a range of autistic conditions that requires sub-division (Gillberg

1991a). Classical Kanner's autism is but a part of this range, and it is becoming increasingly rare. The refined definition and the reduction in number of cases identified as autistic have come about from the following:

- There is increasing knowledge of a variety of biological causative factors, with clearer perception of differences between the conditions that develop from them.
- The number of cases caused by the genetic disease PKU, or by the infectious disease rubella, has been reduced.
- It is recognised that Asperger's Syndrome (Ghaziuddin, Tsai and Ghaziuddin 1992) and the mental retardation known as Rett's syndrome (Hagberg *et al.* 1983; Hagberg 1989) are distinct and separable clinical conditions (see below).

This is the medical view of autism, but the same condition may equally well be defined as a disorder of psychological development affecting learning. Indeed, for educational purposes it is more appropriate to view autism not as a psychiatric illness requiring therapy, but as one form of mental or emotional disability that will require special teaching and guidance. There are many different kinds of disorder in human psychological abilities that can arise in childhood either from a congenital change in the way the brain develops or as a result of imposed damage to the brain or from a mixture of genetic and environmental effects in the brain. Some affect intellect or language rather discretely. Autism comprises a subgroup that affects motives deeply, and within autism there is a range, mind functions, communication and learning being affected to differing degrees. We speak now of a spectrum of empathy disorders (Gillberg 1991a).

Medical Diagnostic Systems Since 1978

Two well-documented and internationally accepted diagnostic systems – the World Health Organization's International Classification of Diseases (ICD), now in its tenth version (ICD-10, WHO 1992), and the American Psychiatric Association's Diagnostic and Statistical Manual (DSM), currently in its fourth edition (DSM-IV, APA 1994) – are now widely used to classify autistic children. Prior to the widespread medical acceptance of these systems there was a large and confusing variety of accepted diagnostic criteria.

Diagnostic systems developed since 1980, including ICD-10 and DSM-IV, incorporate the notion of a triad of impairments which are taken to be characteristic of autistic individuals; affecting their **social relatedness** to other persons, their **communication skills**, and the richness of their **imagination** (Wing and Gould 1979). This triad, of behavioural failings in social skills, language and cognitive flexibility, reflects an historical preoccupation with testable disorders that are important in the development and education of school age children.

The Wing model does not incorporate recently gained insight into the innate motivating processes of the infant and preschool child that, from the first year, regulate mental development, preverbally and emotionally, in interpersonal contacts. We claim that these aspects of the intrinsic motivation for behaviour are more fundamental, more easily related to evidence on abnormalities of brain development, equally amenable to sytematic assessment and a better guide to an integrated programme of treatments.

International Classification of Diseases: ICD-9 and ICD-10

The WHO International Classification of Diseases has been widely adopted outside the USA. ICD-8 placed autism under 'schizophrenia'. The two most recent revisions of this system, ICD-9 and a draft of ICD-10, were published in 1980 and 1987 respectively, and the final form of ICD-10 appeared in 1993. Both categorise autism among 'the psychoses with an origin in childhood'.

ICD-9 distinguishes among 'Psychoses with Origins Specific to Childhood' as follows:

(1) Typical autism, onset before 30 months (**Infantile Autism**-299.0)

(2) Social impairment and stereotyped behaviour after a few years of normal development (**Disintegrative Psychosis**-299.1)

(3) **Atypical Autism** (299.8)

(4) **Remainder** (299.9)

Four major criteria are specified for Infantile Autism:

(1) Onset before 30 months

(2) Deviant social development

(3) Abnormalities of language development

(4) Restricted and abnormal stereotyped patterns of behaviour.
The clinical diagnosis excludes Asperger's syndrome (or 'autistic psychopathy').

ICD-10 defines a number of separable categories under the general heading of pervasive developmental disorders:

> **Childhood autism** (F84.0): impaired or abnormal development must be present *before* three years of age, manifesting the *full triad* of impairments:
>
> (1) in reciprocal social interaction,
>
> (2) in communication, and

(3) in restricted, stereotyped, repetitive behaviour.

Atypical autism (F84.1): onset of impaired or abnormal development is seen *after* three years of age, and is shown in *one or two* of the above triad of impairments.

Rett's syndrome (F84.2) (see discussion below)

Other childhood disintegrative disorder (F84.3) (see discussion below)

Overactive disorder associated with mental retardation and stereotyped movements (F84.4) 'An ill-defined disorder of uncertain nosological validity.' This diagnosis is used to identify individuals who show prepubertal hyperactivity, stereotyped movements and problems with attention in association with severe mental retardation.

Asperger's syndrome (F84.5) (see discussion below)

Other pervasive developmental disorders (F84.8)

Pervasive developmental disorder, unspecified (F84.9)

When ICD-9 and ICD-10 are compared, the main differences are seen to follow from the introduction in ICD-10 of clear definitions for a number of conditions which previously had been grouped with 'infantile autism'. Most important, explicit criteria are given for distinguishing Rett's syndrome and Asperger's syndrome. This provides a more precise clinical definition of 'childhood autism', and one which corresponds well to the DSM-IV definition of criteria for 'autistic disorder'.

Diagnostic and Statistical Manual: DSM-III, DSM-III-R and DSM IV

The American Psychiatric Association Diagnostic and Statistical Manual (DSM) has been revised several times (APA 1980, 1987, 1994). In the United States literature, four distinct periods may be distinguished – (1) pre-DSM-III (up to 1980), when there was little consistency in criteria employed in different research centres, and autism was not included as a diagnostic category in DSM; (2) DSM-III (1980–1987), (3) DSM-III-R (1987–1994), and (4) DSM-IV to the present. The three more recent systems are summarized in Table I.

In DSM-III-R, 'autistic disorder' was classified as a 'pervasive developmental disorder'. Diagnosis required the presence of at least eight items from three groups of criteria:

(1) *Qualitative impairment in social interaction* (five subsets, scoring on two of which was required for diagnosis)

Table I American Psychiatric Association DSM systems for diagnosis of autism

	DSM-III (1980)	*DSM-III-R (1987)*	*DSM-IV (1994)*
Name of Disorder	Infantile autism	Autistic disorder	Autistic disorder
Onset	Before 30 months	During infancy or childhood	Onset before 3 years of delayed or abnormal function in at least one of: social interaction, language for social communication, symbolic or imaginative play
Social Behaviour	Pervasive lack of responses to other people	Qualitative impairment in social interaction (5 mutually exclusive criteria)	Qualitative impairment in social interaction (at least 2 of 4 criteria)
Language and Communication	Gross deficits in language development. Speech, if present, has peculiar patterns	Qualitative impairments in verbal and non-verbal communication and in imaginative activity	Qualitative impairments in communication (at least 1 of 4 possible criteria)
Activities and Interests	Bizarre response to various aspects of the environment	Markedly restricted repertoire of activities and interests	Restricted repetitive and stereotyped patterns of behaviour, interests and activities (at least 1 of 4 possible criteria)
Exclusion criteria	Absence of delusions, hallucinations, loosening of association and incoherence, as seen in schizophrenia	None stated	Rett's disorder; Childhood disintegrative disorder; Asperger's syndrome

(2) *Qualitative impairments in verbal and non-verbal communication, and in imaginative activity* (six subsets, scoring on one of which was required)

(3) *Markedly restricted repertoire of activities and interests* (five subsets, scoring on one of which was required).

Onset during infancy or childhood was to be noted, but this was not required as a diagnostic criterion, as it is in all other DSM systems.

With older and more able subjects it was, in most cases, possible to evaluate the full set of sixteen features. However, the criteria were scored as 'present' only if developmentally inappropriate, which led to far greater difficulty in reaching a diagnosis if the child was very young, developmentally delayed or mute. For a positive diagnosis with young or delayed children, the eight criteria for diagnosis often had to be drawn from as few as nine possible features (Aitken 1991b). This was a serious defect in DSM-III-R, given the importance of early diagnosis for effective intervention, which we discuss below. Furthermore, the DSM-III-R was highly redundant, many of the items adding little to the diagnostic power of the system (Siegel, Vukicevic and Spitzer 1990). Its use since 1987 led to high rates of reported comorbidity – that is, autism was often identified by this system as co-occurring with other diagnoses in the same person. Altogether, the period in which DSM-III-R was used is a step back. Autism was not clearly defined, early diagnosis was unlikely, and high rates of occurrence were reported because the discrimination from other developmental disorders was poor.

There has been such variation in the criteria used over the past half-century, especially since the introduction of DSM-III-R, that care needs to be taken in comparison of research studies which have used different systems. DSM-III-R classified twice as many children as autistic when compared to DSM-III (Hertzig, Snow, New and Shapiro 1990) and described a much more heterogeneous and less severely impaired clinical population (Demb and Weintraub 1989).

DSM-IV was heralded as the most rigourously constructed system to date (First *et al.* 1992). It has been validated against both previous versions of the DSM system and against the ICD-10, and has resulted in a return to the diagnostic stability that characterised the period of DSM-III. The major advance over previous versions is in its use of a three-phase empirical approach in its development and its validation, incorporating a literature review, reanalysis of data from previous versions and, finally, field trials. It has achieved its explicit goals of high compatability with the European ICD-10 system, and low levels of co-morbidity between autism and other conditions.

The term 'autism' now identifies a specific subgroup of individuals with empathy disorder and cognitive deficits, who will be likely to have stable characteristics throughout their life. In other words, they will have a stable behavioural description or 'phenotype'. Both systems identify Asperger's syndrome, Rett's syndrome and Childhood disintegrative disorder (Heller's syndrome) as separate entities. Thus, for the first time, we now have closely comparable and concordant systems in use worldwide.

Questionnaires and Checklists for Behaviour and Psychological Functions

Many checklists or questionnaires have been developed for psychological or behavioural assessment of autistic children diagnosed on the ICD or DSM criteria, and for further discrimination of autism from other developmental disorders. The aim of such further assessment may be to elucidate the specific nature of the problems for the individual case, or to provide a more discriminating diagnostic tool.

A review of questionnaires and checklists by Parks (1983) summarises the Rimland's Form E-2, the BRIAAC, the BOS, the CARS and the ABC giving details on topics such as inter-rater reliability, internal consistency, test–retest reliability, content validity, concurrent validity and discriminant validity. The instruments for assessing autism are here presented in chronological order of their first versions.

The **Diagnostic Checklist for Behaviour-Disturbed Children, Form E-1**, first developed in 1964 by Rimland to be answered by parents for children up to seven years old, aims to diagnose early infantile autism and to differentiate it from other childhood psychoses. It is based on Kanner's description (1943), on studies of childhood schizophrenia, and letters and reports from parents. It consists of 76 questions about the child's birth history, symptoms, speech characteristics and age of onset. The Form E-1 had to be revised because the parents reported that important changes occur at around the age of five and a half years, and the **Form E-2** (Rimland 1971) was developed with an earlier cut-off age. It is a 109-item questionnaire completed by the parents of the index child that seeks information about the child's development from birth to the age of five.

Data are collected about social interaction and affect, speech, motor and manipulative skills, intelligence and reaction to sensory stimuli, characteristics of the family, development of any illness, physiological and biological history. A child is assigned plus points for indications of early infantile autism and minus points for non-autistic behaviours. The major advantage of the E-2 is that the results obtained are compared to a large continuously updated computerised database of over 16,000 cases. Systematic analysis of E-2 data has been instrumental in the assessment of a range of dietary and behavioural treatments. Thus, for example, the effects of supplementation of the diet with high dose vitamin B6 in combination with magnesium have been monitored (see under Treatments, Chapter 10).

The **Behaviour Rating Instrument for Autistic and Atypical Children (BRIAACC)** (Ruttenberg, Dratman, Fraknoi and Wenar 1966; Ruttenberg, Kalish, Wenar and Wolf 1977) was developed to complement a psychoanalytically-oriented approach to intervention. It is an observational measure derived from clinical practice and it consists of eight scales:

(1) relationship to an adult

(2) communication

(3) drive for mastery

(4) vocalisation and expressive speech

(5) sound and speech reception

(6) social responsiveness

(7) body movement, and

(8) psychobiological development.

Each scale can be scored on ten developmental levels. Factor analysis yields a single main factor 'resistance to realistic participation in various activities' (Wenar and Ruttenberg 1976) and the individual scales correlate from 0.54 to 0.86. Cohen *et al.* (1978) also found one primary factor on principal components analysis which accounted for 69 per cent of the variance in the BRIACC. Of more practical importance, however, is the finding of this study that the BRIACC failed to discriminate among diagnostic groups when comparing primary and secondary autism, schizophrenia with onset in childhood, developmental aphasia and mental retardation without autism.

The **Behaviour Observation Scale for Autism (BOS)** (Freeman *et al.* 1978; Freeman, Ritvo and Schroth 1984) is intended to differentiate autistic from normal and mentally retarded people, to identify subgroups among autistic individuals and to develop an objective instrument for the description of autism in the fields of behavioural and biological research. It consists of 24 behaviours divided into 4 groups: solitary behaviour, relation to objects, relation to people and language. The child is filmed playing on his own with age appropriate toys. The observer reviews the videotape and codes the occurrences of specific behaviours. The data are evaluated with a computer. The BOS was tested on a sample of 137 children. They included both autistic children with IQ above 70 ('high autistic' or HA) matched with normal children, or autistic children with IQ below 70 ('low autistic' or LA) matched with mentally retarded children. The mean chronological age of the groups is between four and five years. Differences were found between both autistic groups and their controls. 'Repetitive solitary behaviours' and 'specific sensory use of objects' differentiated HA and LA from their controls, but they were more important for the HA group. All autistic children showed less 'purposeful use of objects' and more 'non-purposeful use of objects'. 'Relating to the examiner' was found to score higher for the LA group, but the HA group had more language.

The **Autism Behaviour Checklist (ABC)** (Krug, Arick and Almond 1980) was developed to differentiate autistic from severely mentally retarded, deaf–blind, severely emotionally disturbed or normal people. It is completed by professionals and weighting scores are assigned to each behaviour descriptor. Its behaviour descriptors have been selected from seven articles including Kanner's (1943), Form E-2 of Rimland (1964), Creak (1964) and BRIAAC (Ruttenberg *et al.* 1966). It consists of 57 behaviour descriptors which have been distributed into 5 symptom areas: sensory, relating, body and object use, language and social. The analysis was based on 1049 completed checklists of individuals ranging from 18 months to 35 years.

Schopler and his colleagues developed the **Childhood Autism Rating Scale (CARS)** (Schopler, Reichler, DeVillis and Kock 1980), which was intended to broaden the classic conceptualization of autism by including Kanner's criteria (1943), the nine diagnostic points of Creak (1964) and the National Autistic Society's definition. It consists of 15 scales, which are: impairment in human relationships, imitation, inappropriate affect, bizarre use of body movement and persistence of stereotypes, peculiarities in relating to nonhuman objects, resistance to environmental change, peculiarities of visual responsiveness, peculiarities of auditory responsiveness, near receptor responsiveness, anxiety reaction, verbal communication, nonverbal communication, activity level, intellectual functioning and general impressions. There is a continuum of 7 scores for each of the above 15 scales, ranging from normal to severe abnormal behaviour. The rating depends on the child's age and the peculiarity, frequency and intensity of each behaviour. The development of CARS is based on direct observations of the children's behaviour rather than on a theoretical baseline. The test was constructed on assessment of 537 children, who were distinguished into three categories: non autistic, mild to moderate autistic and severe autistic. The CARS is highly reliable and has good validity.

The **Behavioural Summarized Evaluation (BSE)** was developed by LeLord to evaluate the severity of behaviour problems in autistic children. It has been used for evaluations in educational contexts (Barthélémy, Hameury and LeLord 1989) and in drug therapy (Martineau, Barthélémy, Cheliakine and LeLord 1988), and has proved to be a sensitive clinical instrument that specifies autism well in relation to other disorders (Barthélémy *et al.* 1992).

The **Autism Diagnostic Interview (ADI)** (Rutter *et al.* 1988; LeCouteur *et al.* 1989) is an investigator-based interview which does not rely on forced choice responses. Successive probe questions build up a detailed picture of development in three key areas:

(1) language and communication

(2) social development, and

(3) play.

The ADI was validated against ICD-10 criteria by psychiatrists' blind rating of 32 videotapes of unstructured interviews with mothers of autistic and non-autistic mentally handicapped children aged 7–19 years, matched for IQ. Inter-rater agreement was 81–89 per cent.

The **Autism Diagnostic Observation Schedule (ADOS)** (Lord *et al.* 1989) is a developmental test rather than a diagnostic rating scale. It focuses on the qualitative expression of the communicative and social behaviours. It was created in order to standardise observations of communicative and social behaviours regarding individuals with autism and related disorders, and to form a diagnostic instrument for differentiation of autism from mentally handicapped and normal developing people. The examiners behaviour has to be standardised during the administration of the test which lasts 20–30 minutes. The examiner interacts with the subjects using eight tasks to elicit certain behaviours. The tasks and their corresponding target behaviours are:

	Task	*Target Behaviour*
(1)	a construction task	asking for help
(2)	an unstructured presentation of toys	symbolic or reciprocal play; giving help to the examiner
(3)	drawing games	taking turns in a structured task
(4)	demonstration of tasks	descriptive gesture and mime
(5)	a poster task	description of agents and actions
(6)	a book task	telling a sequential story
(7)	conversation	reciprocal communication
(8)	socio-emotional questions	the sophistication of language for emotion.

The behaviours are coded during the interview and the score is assigned at the end of the interview. In most cases, the ratings range from 'normal' to 'definitely abnormal'. The ADOS was formed on a sample of 80 subjects from 6 to 18 years – 20 autistic children and adolescents with mild retardation, 20 mentally handicapped children and adolescents, 20 autistic without mental retardation and 20 normally developing individuals. It cannot be used for children having a MA of three years or lower. Although satisfactory inter-rater and test–retest reliability was found for some items, further study is needed.

The **Infant Behavioural Summarized Evaluation (IBSE)** (Adrien *et al.* 1992) is a recent adaptation of the BSE for younger children that has been used in a pilot version comprising 33 items for assessment of subjects from 6 to 48 months of age. Results with 89 developmentally disabled children, including 39 given a clinical diagnosis of autism, have been published. Statistical analysis demonstrated significant differences between the autistic children and the remainder in scores on a subset of 19 items.

The **Checklist for Autism in Toddlers (CHAT)** (Baron-Cohen, Allen and Gillberg 1992) is a scale of nine 'yes'/'no' questions to parents and five observation items to be completed by the health visitor or GP. It was used as a screening test at 18 months to assess 41 children at high genetic risk (approximately 3 per cent risk of family recurrence of developing autism) and 50 randomly selected control toddlers. Over 80 per cent of controls passed on all items, none failing on more than one of the following:

- pretend play
- protodeclarative pointing
- joint-attention
- social interest, and
- social play.

Four of the high-risk children failed on two or more of these key items. On follow-up at 30 months, all of the children were developing normally with the exception of the four children who had failed two or more items, all of whom received a diagnosis of autism.

The **Pre-Linguistic Autism Diagnostic Observation Schedule (PL-ADOS)** (DiLavore, Lord and Rutter 1995) is a new scale based on a 30 minute semi-structured observation of the child engaging in 12 activities involving free play, imitation, joint-attention, social routines, requests and responses, response to distress and separation from and reunion with the mother. It is designed for use with preverbal children, up to age six years, who are suspected of being autistic. It appears to have acceptable inter-rater reliability from blind rating of videotapes, and it correlated well with clinical judgement of diagnosis in the sample of 20 children of whom 12 were autistic, upon which it is based.

The Earliest Appearance of Autistic Symptoms and their Development

The first attempt to describe the early development of autism was by Wing in 1969. Parents of children from 4 to 16 years of age completed retrospectively a schedule about the children's development from birth until the time of the study. The schedule comprised five main categories: 'auditory perception and speech', 'execution of skilled movements', 'visual perception and related phenomena', 'social behaviour','non-verbal skills' and 'interests'. Each item was scored as occurring 'always', 'sometimes', 'never', or 'don't know', and the age at which the particular behaviour first appeared and then disappeared was to be noted, as far as could be recollected. Behaviours of autistic children were compared with children having congenital receptive aphasiapoor hearing of speech, congenital performative aphasia (poor production of speech), congenital partial blindness combined with partial deafness, children with Downs syndrome and normal children. Her conclusions were as follows:

> The comparison showed that autistic children are multiply handicapped, combining problems of comprehension and use of speech, and right–left, up–down, back–front disorientation similar to those found in the congenital aphasic syndromes, with abnormalities in the use of vision, difficulty in understanding gestures, abnormal bodily movements and preference for the proximal senses as in congenitally partially blind/deaf children. (Wing 1969, p.21)

Ornitz, Guthrie and Farley (1977) created an inventory for parents to complete retrospectively, seeking information when the children were less than four years old about their motor and perceptual development, speech and language when in their first and second year of life. The results showed that young autistic children, compared to a group of normal children of comparable age, were delayed in motor and communication skills, and to a minor degree also in perceptual responses.

In another retrospective study (Dahlgren and Gillberg 1989), a control group of mentally retarded individuals was included. Questionnaires of 130 items were completed by mothers, seeking information about the early development and the typical symptoms of autism. Autistic, mentally retarded and normal individuals were matched on sex, chronological age (CA) and measured intelligence (IQ). However, the groups' age at the time the questionnaire was completed ranged from 7 to 22 years and doubts are raised about the reliability of the study because of the time elapsed since the child was an infant, and in view of the mother's knowledge of the child's diagnosis. The results showed that the following 18 of the 130 items discriminated autistics from other non-autistic mentally retarded individuals:

- difficulties with imitating movements
- strange reactions to sounds
- severe problems with sleep
- play only with hard objects
- bizarre visual inspection of objects, patterns and movements

- lack of play with other children
- isolation from surroundings
- dislikes to be disturbed, in own world
- suspicion of a hearing deficit or deafness
- occupation with self when left alone
- empty gaze
- odd attachments to odd objects
- over-excitement when tickled
- no reaction to cold
- variability of behaviour
- content when alone
- lack of attracting adult's attention, and
- lack of smile when one would normally be expected.

The same questionnaire was used in a prospective study (Gillberg *et al.* 1990) of 28 children 8 to 35 months of age who were identified as autistic. The aims of the study were to find symptoms specific to autism, to relate these to underlying causes, and to follow up children for confirmation of the diagnosis. It was found that the crucial characteristics of the autistic disorder in young children are abnormalities of play, aloneness and peculiarities of gaze and hearing.

> The clinical picture is usually such that a diagnosis can be made on the basis of interview with the mother and observation of the child in the 1–3 year old age range. (Gillberg *et al.* 1990, p.933)

The CHAT questionnaire, described above, has successfully screened for autism from a high risk group at 18 months. It will be recalled that the key items discriminating infants who developed autism from those who did not were pretend play, protodeclarative pointing, joint-attention, social interest, and social play.

Adrien and colleagues (Adrien *et al.* 1993) have published the results of retrospective studies of home movies. Films of 12 infants under 2 years of age who developed autism were rated by two diagnosis-blind psychiatrists in comparison with films of 12 normal infants taken at the same ages in similar everyday circumstances, birthdays, etc. using the Infant Behavioural Summarized Evaluation (IBSE) scale. Pathological behaviours were found in the first year relating to socialisation, communication, motility and attention and these same behaviour problems were present and more intense in the second year. They conclude that poor social response, lack of smiling, absence of appropriate facial expression, hypotonia (muscle weakness) and unstable, easily distracted attention can be indicative of autism in the first year, but that all these become more marked in the second year, with excessive calmness and inactivity, unusual postures and absence of emotional expression, appropriate gestures and eye-contact with other persons. This supports the view that autism first becomes a serious failing in development in the second year. Degree of mental retardation and developmental delay varied, but were not controlled.

The above studies agree. All confirm that early recognition of autism and its discrimination from other developmental problems requires attention to a number of subtle indications. It is not easy to detect autism in a routine medical examination, and, indeed, most cases are first picked up by psychologists or teachers who possess knowledge of the important social features. The signs of abnormal motivation for interpersonal contact are particularly important, and these may escape medical attention. Parents are usually aware that something is wrong, but clinical assessment may lead to the child being pronounced *not* autistic after a hospital visit. Instruments of observation that collate results over a number of sessions and in a number of settings are most reliable. As we shall see, the manifestations of autism in early preschool years give strong indication that early diagnosis and early remedial education are highly desirable. Social interaction, imitation, play and non-verbal communication, to all of which parents are normally very sensitive, are more reliable indicators of a positive diagnosis before four years than an insistence on sameness and preference for fixed routines (Stone, Hoffman, Lewis and Ousley 1994). Frustration brought on by difficulties in social understanding, and common, if occasional, problems in the behaviour of all infants, such as displays of irritability, temper tantrums and self-injury, tend to be seen as abnormally intense and persistent by around 2.5 years in children who later develop unmistakable autism.

While recent research has made some progress in defining early behavioural indicators that a child is likely to be developing autism, it is important to add that many of the preconceptions concerning the pathogenesis of autism and what its first manifestations will be have been cast into doubt by more systematic study of early development. The practice of focusing on one or two aspects of early behaviour previously assumed to be strongly suggestive of autism, such as abnormalities of early **attachment** and absence of **joint-attention**, is now being systematically questioned.

Much of the literature to date has made the assumption that autistic preschool children will be likely to show weak emotional attachment. An autistic one-year-old has been expected to be indifferent to the mother's presence and free of distress in her absence. However, in a recent study (Capps, Sigman and Mundy 1994) in which security of attachment was examined in 19 autistic children aged 3–6 years, it was found that the relationship was not always weak. Fifteen of the children proved classifiable in the Ainsworth Strange Situation, and of these some 40 per cent were rated as securely attached. The same group has looked at the relationship between assessed IQ, developmental level, and joint attention in autistic preschoolers, mental age matched normal controls and IQ matched developmentally delayed controls (Mundy, Sigman and Kasari 1994). In contrast to the expectations of current cognitive models of autism (e.g. Baron-Cohen, Tager-Flusberg and Cohen 1993), the joint attention differences seen in the autistic subjects proved to be largely accounted for on the basis of differences in IQ and/or developmental level. Absence of joint-attention, as it was defined in this study, could not be used to discriminate the children with autism.

Towards a Synthesis – Current Concepts of Autism and an Up-to-Date Description

Autism is now much more difficult to understand than it is to recognise. We know consistent features that are peculiar to the condition. However, autism is both complex and rare (see Chapter 10). Presumably this is why it was not identified until much later than the classical mental illnesses of adults.

Kanner's description captured the characteristics now accepted to describe a coherent abnormality of brain development. Autism is a defect in psychological development that directly affects the way the expressions and actions of other persons are perceived. This is associated with problems in expressive communication, in understanding other persons' thoughts, and in comprehending the ordinary use of language and the meanings others give by convention to actions and objects. The causal brain fault also affects basic functions of perception, motor coordination, thinking and learning to varying degrees.

One difficulty, over the years, has been the reluctance of psychiatrists and psychologists to believe that a very young child could develop a disorder comparable with the mental disturbances of some adults. Babies were thought not capable of coordinated representational mental activity and undifferentiated in their emotions. On the other hand, autism is different from any psychiatric illness that develops in an adult. It can only be perceived clearly as a disorder that emerges in development of a young brain as it passes through a critical phase in mental growth.

This is not to say that any stage of normal development is autistic, or that a normal child will develop autism if it does not receive an adequately 'constructive' mothering that builds a boundary for the infant's ego or self-awareness. There is, as we have explained, no 'normal autistic phase'. The view of some psychoanalysts that autism is a failure of differentiation of self due to unresponsive, cold and emotionless mothering in early infancy misread the direction of the emotional effects between mother and child. There is a principle motivational fault developing *in the child* which may seriously distress the mother and impair her self-confidence. Nevertheless, there are points in which the confusion of interpersonal relating of an autistic child and the symptoms of isolation and lack of contact in a mentally ill adult may bear important similarities. To understand these we need to have a conception of the emotional system that regulates relationships and contacts at all stages of life (Stern 1985; Schore 1994). Giving support to the ill-defined self-and-other awareness of an autistic child requires special dedication, and appropriate support can significantly improve communication and learning (see Chapter 12).

The diagnostic or descriptive systems that we have reviewed affirm that autistic children have a primary inability to perceive others as people and to conceive what they may communicate. This is easiest to understand in the perspective of normal development, because children normally have such explicit and demanding motivations to communicate with and learn from others. Again, the most informative and reliable diagnostic instruments are those that examine the ways the child uses objects in the context of communication with familiar others. They record both object use and interpersonal behaviours. Recent attempts to identify autism at younger ages have tended to confirm that the abnormalities are usually absent or very subtle and difficult to detect before about nine months. As we shall see, in Chapter 8, nine to twelve months is a stage in development when a baby is normally changing rapidly; in alertness of investigative intelligence and in systematic, purposeful, constructive handling of objects, in memory, and in willingness to share experiences and actions with companions with the help of early language-like behaviour, combining vocalisations and gestures. There are new demands on selective attention, memory and coordination of action, as well as a much greater involvement with other people and their interests and purposes.

Individual autistic children differ in their intelligence, capacity for learning and use of language, but all are abnormal in the ways they relate to other persons. It is significant that their insensitivity to other persons' feelings, purposes and experiences appears before the child is three years old and after an early infancy that was apparently almost normal. That is, the development of the child's mind fails at the time when most children begin to be extremely sensitive to and interested in other people's ideas and actions, and when speech is beginning (see Chapter 8). This is normally a time of the most intense communication and sharing of imaginations and habitual ways of doing things, when children are expected to be insatiably curious and full of fantasy about meanings in their play, and wanting to put these ideas into language.

Autistic children do respond to others' emotions and they are, as was mentioned above, able to form affectionate attachments (Capps, Sigman and Mundy 1994), but they do not show an intense eagerness to share and in play they do not pretend to act like other people, except in a ritual, echolalic kind of way. Autistic children may imitate, but they do so self-centredly or like an echo, without the creativity, humour and companionship that is so remarkable in ordinary toddlers' play, and they often seem not to be aware of what language is for – how one normally negotiates meanings, intentions and beliefs with it.

They do not readily seek adults' attentions and respond badly when efforts are made to force them to attend to others' interests and purposes. Communication with an autistic child often requires great patience.

Close observation of autistic children and many tests of their reactions to stimuli have shown that they have characteristic problems with experience, and that they explore objects differently. They show peculiarities of gaze and listening. In some respects they are hypersensitive and unable to shut out adverse experiences by attending elsewhere, but they also show strangely blunted reactions to stimuli and are likely to not notice things that one would expect to be of great interest or concern to a child. They develop meaningless habits of repeating self-stimulation, and they tend to fear novelty and change, apparently being easily overwhelmed by complex new situations. These features indicate that there are problems with the way their brains admit or select stimuli – the investigative intelligence of autistic children is incoherent or distorted compared to that of unaffected age-mates. Abnormalities of perception, attention and exploration undoubtedly handicap the learning and thinking of autistic children, leading to an accumulation of disability. Those that appear to develop high intelligence usually do so in narrow or specialised areas that seem to be practiced through the child's unusual capacity to become absorbed over and over again in a preferred activity in isolation from other people.

The perceptual, attentional and cognitive difficulties of autistic children, and their tendency to protect themselves by repeating familiar actions and forming odd attachments to objects, are of great significance to parents and teachers who are seeking to make contact and to help the child's learning, but these features cannot be viewed as the heart of the problem, and they may not be the aspects that will respond best to remedial education.

There are clearly also problems with the generation of movements, especially those that a normal child would use efficiently to communicate feelings. Autistic children make strange gestures, hand-flapping, blinking, fiddling with things, repeatedly tapping. They may be hyperactive and often have ritualistic activities that make no sense. Many have some degree of motor weakness and are delayed in motor milestones (Gillberg and Coleman 1992a). They do not use pointing communicatively and may not understand the gestures others use to direct their attention. Like the peculiarities of perception, the abnormal spontaneous movements of autistic children indicate something about abnormal brain processes, but they are not individually peculiar to autism. Many disorders of the young brain are likely to be associated with an excess of repetitive involuntary movements (Lees 1985; Comings 1990).

Autistic children do not lack emotions. They can show strong and disturbing reactions to difficult, frustrating or frightening situations and are inclined to become restless and have sleep problems. On the other hand they often have an empty gaze and tend to smile to themselves and not in reaction to others' greetings. They often appear to lack curiosity and initiative. Affectionate responses are shown to familiar persons and responsive enjoyment can be gained with body or contact play. Autism seems to combine an unbalanced motivation for learning the conventional meanings of objects with defense against complexity and change. The imagination is hemmed in by desire for sameness and obsessional exploratory behaviour.

The fascinating studies of the ways older, 'high functioning' or verbally fluent children fail to understand other persons' beliefs and what others can imagine about what other people think and know seem to be clarifying disorders of later development that may follow from the deeper failing in the younger child, without language or with distorted awareness of language, to relate directly to other people. Clever autistic children who may read exceptionally well do not understand original jokes or metaphors and cannot create new evolving narratives with adjustment of the dialogue to different character's 'voices'. Their occasional very fluent and expressive 'readings' of characters' performances will most often be echolalic reproductions of what they have seen and heard others perform, and they may be often repeated with little variation. The majority of autistic children cannot be examined for verbally mediated 'theories of mind' as they have a level of language expression and/or comprehension insufficient for such material to be administered with them (Fay 1993).

CHAPTER 3

Similar Disorders and Important Distinctions

Correct identification of autism, paying close attention to how it develops, is important for a variety of reasons. Some conditions that are easily mistaken for autism in a young child will develop differently and require different treatment or care, and they have different implications for education. For example, although all autistic children have some problem with language and about 50 per cent never develop functional speech, they are quite different in their interpersonal and social behaviour from the majority of children who have specific disorders of language and communication (Donaldson 1995). They need a different kind of help with communication. Other conditions such as Rett's syndrome and 'childhood disintegrative disorder' show evidence of sharp deterioration in various areas of functioning over time which would not typically be affected in autism.

Autistic-like behaviour is significantly more common in both the visually and hearing impaired populations (Ellis 1986; Hobson 1993a,b); however, such a condition is likely to respond to aids that reduce the child's sensory isolation in a way that typical autism never would. Autism is a condition that affects the child's contact with the world and people in it, even when all the child's senses are responsive, or even when they are hyper-responsive to simple stimuli.

Once a primary sensory handicap has been excluded as a sufficient cause of autistic-like behaviour, several alternative possible causes of behaviour presenting features of autism need to be excluded. The following descriptions identify the chief differences between autism and closely related disorders of brain development and behaviour, or other psychological disorders of childhood which can be confused with autism in some of its manifestations:

Asperger's Syndrome and 'High Functioning' Autistics

Asperger (1944) defined a new condition one year after Kanner's classic description of autism. However, Asperger's syndrome did not receive significant attention until Lorna Wing's clinical analysis of the disorder in 1981. The main diagnostic systems have only recently, with DSM-IV and ICD-10, acknowledged that Asperger's syndrome is a distinct disorder. A variety of diagnostic criteria have been proposed (Ghaziuddin, Tsai and Ghaziuddin 1992). The seven of the most widely used compared in Table II clearly show that Asperger's discrimination of the key features has been upheld.

Table II Diagnostic Criteria for Asperger's Syndrome

	Autistic Social Impairment	*All Absorbing Interests*	*Pedantic Speech*	*Clumsiness*	*Speech Delay*	*Cognitive Delay*
(1) Asperger (1944)	YES	YES	YES	YES	NO	NO
(2) Wing (1981)	YES	YES	YES	YES	Possible	Possible
(3) Gillberg (1989)	YES	YES	YES	YES	Possible	Possible
(4) Szatmari *et al.* (1989)	YES	YES	YES	Clumsy Gestures	Not stated	Not stated
(5) Tantam (1988)	YES	YES	YES	YES	Possible	Possible
(6) ICD-10 (1988)	YES	USUAL	Not stated	USUAL	NO	NO
(7) DSM-IV (APA 1994)	YES	YES	Not stated	Not stated	NO	NO

In summary, the most widely accepted features of persons with Asperger's syndrome, as a population, are:

(1) Autistic social impairment

(2) Clumsiness (usual but not necessarily present)

(3) 'Concrete' or pedantic speech

(4) All absorbing circumscribed interests (usual)

(5) Lack of appreciation for humour (commonly described)

(6) No significant delay in language development

(7) No significant delay in cognitive development.

A critical question at present is whether Asperger's syndrome can be seen in individuals who have been identified as delayed in development of speech or cognitive ability. Both ICD-10 and DSM-IV explicitly state that individuals with Asperger's syndrome do not have delays in language or cognitive development, while three of the leading clinical authorities, Wing (1981), Gillberg (1989) and Tantam (1988), claim Asperger's can be seen in the presence of either form of delay. These different conclusions about how to define the disorder generate widely different estimates of the likely numbers with Asperger's syndrome in populations, as well as to disagreements over diagnosis in individual cases (Ghaziuddin, Tsai and Ghaziuddin 1992; Gillberg and Gillberg 1989).

Debate also continues among developmental psychologists over whether Asperger's syndrome can be differentiated from high-functioning autism

(Bishop 1993; Ozonoff, Rogers and Pennington 1991; Happé 1994). Children with Asperger's syndrome are, unlike those with Kanner's autism, commonly able to perform well on 'Model of Mind' tests (Ozonoff, Rogers and Pennington 1991). They show more subtle socio-linguistic deficits, such as failure to modify pronunciation to express context-specific meaning and, indeed, a generally poor attention to subtleties of the interpersonal context.

While most autistic individuals have below normal intelligence scores, those with Asperger's syndrome usually function in the normal range of intellectual ability (Baron-Cohen and Bolton 1993), and may show evidence of savant skills. Likewise, in Asperger's syndrome early language milestones are not delayed, and speaking may even be precocious. Even so, once language is fluent it is used in a characteristically stilted and stereotyped manner scarcely to be distinguished from that of the high functioning autistic child. In the ICD-10, it is admitted that psychotic episodes may occur in the early adult life of a child with Asperger's syndrome. According to the DSM-IV criteria, Asperger's syndrome, in contrast to autistic disorder, cannot be coded as comorbid with schizophrenia. This is a surprising conclusion in DSM-IV in view of the psychotic symptoms shown in a significant proportion of subjects with Asperger's syndrome described in the early literature (Tantam 1991).

Our view, considering both the developmental nature of the psychological dysfunctions and their probable cause in brain development, is that individuals who fulfill diagnostic criteria for autism and Asperger's syndrome will fall on a continuum of impairment, a concept captured by the term 'autistic spectrum disorder' (Gillberg 1991a). A broadening of the criteria to encompass Kanner's autism and Asperger's syndrome within a multi-dimensional structure of features that express different aspects of motivation for attention to the environment, to persons, and to language is warranted. We believe such an approach to diagnosis, rather than an attempt to divide the affected population into two separate groups, would offer more precise guidance for treatment and teaching.

By all definitions, Asperger's syndrome shares many features with Kanner's autism. The distinctions are matters of degree. Diagnostic systems, we should remember, force categorisation onto named disorders. Thus, DSM-IV and ICD-10 give the impression that autism and Asperger's syndrome are easily differentiable and different entities. In reality they are clearly related conditions that affect interpersonal activity, and they may best be described as different manifestations in a 'spectrum' or continuum of psychological dysfunction along an empathy dimension (Gillberg 1991a). The work of Szatmari and his colleagues (Szatmari, Tuff, Finlayson and Bertolucci 1990) indicates that there is a significantly higher rating of affectionate behaviour in early childhood, enjoyment of others and sharing of interests in individuals with Asperger's syndrome compared with individuals with autism whose IQ is normal, and the former also exhibit fewer abnormalities of language use, stereotypies of behaviour and bizarre obsessions (Table III). The two groups were found to be alike in other areas of functioning, that is in gaze avoidance, reluctance to initiate communication and insistence on routines and rituals.

There are fewer neurological abnormalities in individuals with Asperger's syndrome as a group (Gillberg 1989) when they are compared to autistic children (Table IV). Some individuals in both groups show defects in neural migration, which suggest a similar pathophysiology (Berthier, Starkstein and Leiguarda 1990).

Table III Clinical Differences between Asperger's Syndrome and High-Functioning, Normal IQ, Autism. (Szatmari, Tuff, Finlayson and Bertolucci 1990)

	Children with the feature (%)		
	Asperger's Syndrome	*Normal IQ Autism*	*Maximum p-value of difference between groups*
Social Responsiveness			
Autistic more:			
Lack of social response to parents	25	72	0.001
Complete lack of interest in peers	38	72	0.02
Asperger's more:			
Enjoys other adults	80	34	0.004
Shares interests with parents	68	33	0.03
Affectionate baby	67	33	0.04
No difference:			
Shows gaze avoidance	36	50	0.48
Language and Communication			
Autistic more:			
Babbled less than siblings	24	65	0.009
Echolalia or pronoun reversal	37	75	0.007
Repetitive speech	22	48	0.04
Lack of imaginative play	12	48	0.02
No difference:			
Seldom starts a conversation	59	65	0.88
Range of interests			
Autistic more:			
Bizarre preoccupations	37	86	0.001
Stereotypies	48	86	0.003
Little difference:			
Insistence on routines	30	50	0.23
Rituals	13	25	0.46

A recent paper (Klin *et al.* 1995) provides a fascinating comparison of two groups; 19 high functioning autistics and 21 with Asperger's syndrome, similar in IQ age and sex distribution, diagnosed on ICD-10 criteria. The principal difference between the two groups on cognitive tests showed that the Asperger's group had a pattern of scores consistent with their non-verbal learning disability, which was not the case for the high functioning autistics. This study argues for a clear differentiation between the two syndromes, rather than an empathy continuum. It appears to indicate that Asperger's syndrome has more impact on functions of the right hemisphere.

Table IV Neurologic Findings in 23 Children with Asperger's Syndrome and 23 Children with Infantile Autism. (Gillberg 1989)

	Asperger's (N)	*Infantile Autistics (N)*
Physical Diagnosis		
Epilepsy	1	5
Fragile-X	0	5
Tuberous sclerosis	0	2
Other abnormality	4	3
Other chromosome abnormalities	3	5
Abnormal EEG	6	12
CT Scan Abnormalities	3	5
Left Handedness	4	5
Reduced birth optimality	9	5
No major abnormalities detected	8	16

Other Childhood Psychoses and Mental Handicap

Childhood Schizophrenia

Some children, after the age of six or seven or in the early teens, begin to show bizarre detached behaviour with evidence of hallucinations. These are the early manifestations of schizophrenia. A diagnosis can rarely be made before this age. Nevertheless, there is some evidence of earlier abnormality of psychological function in children who later become schizophrenic from analyses of home video recordings (Walker *et al.* 1993).

Delusions and hallucinations are the main feature of childhood schizophrenia, but they are not common in autism, and they have been explicitly excluded for autism in some diagnostic systems such as DSM-III-R, while co-morbidity is acknowledged as possible in DSM-IV. Current models of psychopathology treat the conditions of autism and schizophrenia as mutually exclusive. Indeed, surveys of family pedigrees and population studies indicate that there is no causal association between the two conditions, but that a child can suffer from the two conditions by chance (Volkmar and Cohen 1991). A family history of schizophrenia is common in childhood schizophrenia but is uncommon in autism. Moreover, with the exception of occasional cases who show sudden loss of early language, autism does not typically show a fluctuating course. Childhood schizophrenia can fluctuate wildly in its presentation. Seizures are a common feature in autism affecting 25–35 per cent of cases, but they are rarely a feature in childhood schizophrenia (Gillberg and Steffenburg 1987; Wing and Gould 1979).

Mental Retardation: Williams and Down Syndromes

Children with cognitive handicap due to the genetic disorders of Williams syndrome (WS), Down syndrome (DS) and Rett's syndrome (RS), also have various impairments and differences in their social reactions, joint attention and communication about objects (Berger 1990; Wang and Bellugi 1993; Franco and Wishart 1994). Less severe disorders of intelligence are classified as deficits in attention, motor control and perception, as recently suggested by Gillberg (1991a).

When retarded autistic children are matched with others for Mental Age by appropriate standardised tests of intelligence, non-autistic children with low scores, such as those with DS, are different in their associated illnesses and in their communication (but see Howlin, Wing and Gould 1995). The cognitive problems of autistic children also show a characteristic pattern, with relatively poor abilities in language and abstract thought. Autistic children, by diagnostic definition, have a special difficulty with interpersonal understanding, and they show characteristic deficits on 'Model of Mind' tests of interpersonal perspective taking. Even those with a relatively high Mental Age on standard intelligence tests show these features (Bartak and Rutter 1976; Hobson 1986a, b; Hobson, Ouston and Lee 1988; Yirmiya, Kasari, Sigman and Mundy 1989; Baron-Cohen 1990; Capps, Yirmiya and Sigman 1992).

Down syndrome, due to trisomy (triplication of chromosome 21), is easily identified at birth by the characteristic appearance of the face and hands. Older DS children are typically defective in ability to represent objects and events in the environment and they have impaired spatial representation. Cognitive abilities remain those of a young child with little progress beyond the second decade. Motor control of hands, tongue, lips and respiration has problems, and vision and audition may be affected. Language development is slow, speech production being most affected, and it usually remains at about the level of a three-year-old, though there is a considerable range. Early vocalisations and 'universal phonemes' develop normally, but both babbling and hand banging are delayed about three months. Learning of reading, by-passing auditory sequencing requirements of speech perception, may assist development of language. Responses to speaking and touching are much more positive than in autism, but vocal activity and vocal turn-taking are slow, and use of referential gaze in communication is retarded, which causes clashes with the mother, who may become too intrusive. Unlike autistic children, DS show similar preferences to normal children of the same level of development for nursery rhymes and for their mother's voice when she is addressing them. However, they are less expressive vocally in strange situation test, and less overtly affective, their emotional reactions being reduced and flat, with less laughter for interpersonal jokes.

Infants with DS develop essentially normal expressions in communication (Franco and Wishart 1994), but there emerge differences in the effectiveness of their signals (Cicchetti and Sroufe 1978), often exacerbated by the emotional responses of parents in face of the child's slow development, especially in language (Berger 1990). Infants with DS are slow to develop a cooperative combination of interest in a partner's communication and use of objects. They show less interest in the object world and, as their attention is easily overtaxed, they fail to switch between the partner's motives and the objects used (Wishart 1991). Thus at 12 months infants with DS have marked difficulty in maintaining joint attention to their caregivers and objects. It is often true that play becomes more difficult for a handicapped child if a parent tries to join in, possibly because of the way the parent enters. A lack of referential eye contact and a poverty in initiatives to play leads mothers to have difficulty interpreting intentions. Many of these features of behaviour resemble those of autistic children, but DS children are more attentive to people and more positive in emotional responses.

Epileptic seizures appear earlier on average in mentally handicapped children. In autistic children fits commonly begin in late childhood or adolescence. The sex distribution is different in the two groups: the male/female ratio is 4:1 in the autistic population and 1:1 in the non-autistic handicapped. However, as intellectual level reduces in the autistic group, so does the markedly increased male preponderance.

The recently discovered Williams syndrome is a condition in which language may be well developed while other aspects of cognition are considerably impaired. Both DS and WS children are delayed in vocabulary acquisition and motor milestones as preschoolers, but adolescents with WS have correct, complex if somewhat echoic grammar, a large vocabulary with uncommon words and they are reported to be strong in discourse abilities such as narrative cohesion and conversational turn-taking (Wang and Bellugi 1993). Prosody has not been systematically studied but appears relatively preserved though possibly 'over-rich' in affect tone. Children with DS, in contrast, have poor, simple grammar, a smaller vocabulary and reduced linguistic affective expression. There are interesting differences in visuomotor ability. Drawings of children with WS are poor and fragmented, retaining local detail but losing the Gestalt; those of children with DS are simple but cohesive, representing the overall shape without detail (Wang and Bellugi 1993). When compared to of brain lesions in adults who were normal before the injury, these would suggest that while children with WS are impaired in parietal cortex of the right hemisphere, those with DS have left hemisphere deficiency. Children with WS are proficient at face recognition, but this could be based on a left hemisphere strategy of feature listing.

Non-verbal interpersonal communication, joint attention with sharing of spatial reference and affective exchange are, as we discuss below, critical in the early development of both language and cognition (Adamson and Bakeman 1985; Bates 1979; Bruner 1983; Dore 1983; Rheingold, Hay and West 1976; Stern 1985; Tomasello and Farrar 1986; Trevarthen and Hubley 1978). Deficiencies in non-verbal communication (Mundy, Kasari and Sigman 1992) distinguish not only empathic disorders such as autism (Mundy, Sigman, Ungerer and Sherman 1986), but also, as described above, varieties of mental handicap (Kasari, Sigman, Mundy and Yirmiya 1990). Reasoned or intentional response to a clinically identified deficit in the non-verbal communication of the child, in other words, an intellectual response to an expert diagnosis, may be the cause of maladaptive or unsupportive communication from the carer that makes the child's problem worse (Berger 1990; Mahoney, Fors and Wood 1990).

As with autistic children, the difficulties of attention and coordination of even profoundly mentally handicapped children can be reduced by communication with a partner who adapts stimulation and response to the child's ability to share feelings and actions (Burford 1992). Conversely, children classified as suffering from emotional or empathic disorders fail in cognitive tests, and this is taken to show they are mentally handicapped in some degree. That is why Kanner's autism was not specifically recognised by the DSM-III-R diagnostic system, which conceived the intersubjective processes of such a 'pervasive developmental disorder' to be consequences of general deficiencies in behavior and cognition (Aitken 1991c).

Rett's Syndrome

This syndrome was first described by Rett in 1966 in a paper describing a link between a consistent constellation of behavioural and physical features and elevated levels of ammonia in the blood. It was seen only in girls. Although the association with blood ammonia has since been shown to be atypical, the physical and behavioural phenotype that Rett and Hagberg described is now accepted (Rett 1966; Hagberg *et al.* 1983; Hagberg 1989, 1993). It is thought to be the commonest cause of severe mental retardation affecting girls.

Rett's syndrome is a rare condition but, with its variants at a prevalence rate of 1 in 10,000, it is second only to Down syndrome as cause of severe mental retardation in girls (Hagberg 1993). The suggestion that Rett's syndrome is an X-chromosome disorder fatal to males in the embryo (Comings 1986) has not, to date, received empirical support.

At around nine months, a baby, who at six months was thought to be norm... shows distracted attention, weak posture, and poor coordination of limb movements (Kerr 1995). The girl may advance through protolanguage and learn a few words but, by 18 months, she will be retarded and deeply disturbed in motivation and emotions. She will show autistic withdrawal and fits of agitation, and will lose voluntary use of her mouth, arms and hands, and make stereotyped licking and tonguing and patting or stroking movements, rubbing the hands together and bringing them, with athetoid twisting, to the mouth. Object prehension will cease, as will all deliberate gestures of communication and speech. By two, the autistic and agitated emotional features pass, leaving a profound and permanent mental handicap. The girls, who utter only undifferentiated cries and laughter, with primitive babbling, seek eye contact and smile or laugh in response to an approaching face accompanied by friendly cheerful speech and encouraging hand contact. There is little evidence of learning, no voluntary hand use, and no comprehension of language. Measures of head circumference are subnormal by six to twelve months, and below the two per cent level of the normal population by two to four years, when brain growth ceases. Available evidence points to a non-Mendelian gene fault expressed in the core of the brain in the mid embryo stage, possibly first in the *substantia nigra* and *locus ceruleus,* whose activity in producing and distributing biogenic amines is essential to the formation of effective cortical networks (Armstrong 1992; Hagberg, Naidu and Percy 1992; Nomura, Segawa and Higurashi 1985; Segawa 1992; Trevarthen and Aitken 1994). Girls with Rett's syndrome have reduced blood circulation in the midbrain and upper brainstem from early in development as well as in the frontal lobes and may have failure of left fronto-temporal function. It has been proposed that the frontal lobe remains immature (Nielsen *et al.* 1990).

Rett's syndrome is usually reported to occur only in females, but some males appear to have the same features (Philippart 1990).

Childhood Disintegrative Disorder: Heller's Syndrome

Heller first described a group of children in 1908 who, after a period of normal development, typically between age three and four, showed changes in mood and character followed quickly by loss of speech and ultimately by extreme regression in development (see Hulse 1954). Heller called this condition 'dementia infantilis'. More recently it has been called either 'disintegrative psychosis' or Heller's syndrome.

Until recently, this group of children was considered to have an atypical form of autism. They show marked deterioration in many areas of psychological functioning after at least the first two years of generally normal development. The timing of onset often leads to a suspicion of brain damage following vaccination. Seizure problems are frequent, there is often loss of functional language, and males are more commonly affected than females (Volkmar and

Cohen 1991b; Volkmar 1994). Heller's syndrome has only recently been defined on the DSM-IV system, and we know little about the members of this group.

Language Disorders

Receptive Developmental Dysphasia (Poor comprehension of speech)

Disorders in the perception and comprehension of language affect boys and girls equally. Autism is the only disorder that impairs receptive language that is significantly more common in males. The prognosis in terms of social adjustment is, at least in the short term studies to date, significantly poorer in the autistic population compared to children diagnosed as receptive dysphasic. Autism leads to a pervasive failure of orientation towards messages of all kinds from other persons. Children with receptive language disorders, though they often fail to understand language properly, usually are attentive and responsive to other persons (Donaldson 1995). After language disability has been taken into account, autistic children as a population also have a broader range of cognitive problems and lower IQ than in children diagnosed as having a 'pure' receptive dysphasia (Bartak, Rutter and Cox 1975).

Semantic-Pragmatic Disorder and Specific Language Impairment (SLI)

Semantic-Pragmatic disorder was first described by Rapin as a distinct clinical entity, differentiated from autism, with unusual language use (Rapin and Allen 1983). In her more recent writing, Rapin has suggested that the distinction between autism and 'semantic-pragmatic disorder' is not as clear as she had originally drawn it. She now believes there to be a high degree of comorbidity, a significant proportion of high-functioning autistic children having semantic and pragmatic disorders in their language (Allen and Rapin 1992).

Whether a semantic-pragmatic disorder is a clinically significant entity has still to be determined, but the term is in widespread use by speech and language therapists. Many children so diagnosed may, in fact, be autistic by accepted criteria. However, while many children who misunderstand the meanings of words or who make grammatical errors may make mistakes like those of autistic children, and these problems may make communication with them difficult, they may not avoid all communication like autistic children do, and they are not likely to have difficulties with non-verbal communication (Bishop 1989; Donaldson 1995; Jordan 1993).

Most children show transitory deficiencies in phonology and grammar at the stage just before fluent speaking, and many with language deficits or delay in preschool, lose their problems in primary school. With Specific Language Impairment (Bishop 1992), or Developmental Language Disorder, these idiosyncratic and undifferentiated elements persist in the absence of mental or physical handicap, hearing loss, emotional disorder or emotional deprivation.

It is not clear that a specific language process is impaired in SLI, and the common auditory processing difficulty may be a consequence of loss in 'speed of processing' that impairs sequential auditory information more than persisting visual patterns. Language-disordered children experience general difficulties with combining skills, as in doing two tasks at once, and they perform below age expectations in a wide range of tests of knowledge, symbolic and non-symbolic activities, and non-verbal skills. The cognitive deficits and 'social immaturity' of children with SLI may be secondary to language losses, or the interpersonal aspects may be more fundamental. SLI children can have difficulty with prosody including stress segmentation rules, and with comprehension of other paralinguistic cues, such as eye movements, and therefore fail to perceive the communicative context of language use. This is more likely in the sub-group with 'semantic-pragmatic disorder', closer to autism.

CHAPTER 4

How Many Autistic Children?

The Prevalence or Rate of Autism in the Population

A number of studies, using varying diagnostic criteria, have attempted to determine how many autistic children there may be, to find the prevalence or 'rate' at which the disorder occurs in a population of given size. Earlier studies, most of which used DSM-III or ICD-9, give estimates of approximately 4.5 to 6 cases per 10,000 population. More recent studies, using DSM-III-R, gave higher rates, in the region of 10 to 14 cases per 10,000 population (Table V).

The increase is not to be taken as evidence for an increase in the real number of autistic children, but rather is it a consequence of a weakening of the definition since 1987 when DSM-III-R was introduced. The DSM-III-R description includes more so-called 'non-nuclear autistic' children; that is, boys and girls with difficulties in language development who do not show the deficits in interpersonal relating that were considered specific to the condition, called 'nuclear autistic', described by Kanner. When it is compared to earlier systems, the DSM-III-R appears to classify approximately twice as many children as autistic. This discrepancy is now being corrected, with a return, in DSM-IV, to stricter criteria, essentially the same as those by which the condition was originally defined.

Over the past thirty years, rates appear, in fact, to have been rather constant. Moreover, there is little evidence for an increase in the numbers of children who fulfil any particular set of diagnostic criteria over time, except where environmental factors, such as epidemics of rubella, are known to have caused geographical and temporal variations in disorders attributable to early brain damage.

The Predicted Incidence of Autism in Given Populations

The incidence of autism in a population of known size is estimated from the prevalence data, assuming the latter identifies all cases fitting the definition of autism, and that few false positive identifications are made. In reality the number of children who are diagnosed to have autism will be somewhat less than the

Table V A Selection of Population Studies

Author	*Place*	*Prevalence Number in 10,000*	*Age Group Studied*	*Population*
Rutter 1966	Scotland	4.4 ('psychotic')		
Lotter 1966, 1967	England	4.5	8–10 y	78,000
Brask 1970	Denmark	4.3		
Wing, Yeates, Brierly & Gould 1976	England	4.8 mild to moderate 2.0 severe	5–14 y	25,000
Wing and Gould 1979	England	4.9		
Hoshino *et al.* 1982	Japan	4.96 2.33	5–11 y 0–18 y	217,000 609,848
Bohman, Bohman, Bjorck and Sjoholm 1983	Sweden	6.1		
Gillberg 1984	Sweden	3.9	4–18 y	128,584
Steffenberg & Gillberg 1986	Sweden	7.5		
Bryson, Clark and Smith 1988	Canada	10.1	6–14 y	20,800
Tanoue, Oda, Asano and Kawashima 1988	Japan	13.8		
Sugiymama & Abe 1989	Japan	13.0		
Ritvo *et al.* 1990	USA	4.0 (estimated)	3–25 y	1,461,037
Cialdella & Mamelle 1989	France	4.5	3–9 y	135,180
Gillberg *et al.* 1991a	Sweden	11.6		

* In this table the numbers, expressed per 10,000 of population, record children classified as having either 'nuclear' (Kanner's) or 'non-nuclear' autism, unless stated otherwise.

Table VI Incidence of Autism and Related Disorders for the UK (Estimates, derived from 1993 Census Data CSO Annual Abstract of Statistics, 1995, which gives the population to the nearest thousand)

	Total Population	*Autism Proper**	*Other Autistic Spectrum**
UK			
All Ages	58,191,000	26,200	151,300
0–4	3,888,000	1800	10,100
5–19	10,847,000	4900	28,200
19+	43,454,000	19,600	113,000
England			
All Ages	48,533,000	21,800	126,200
0–4	3,244,000	1500	8400
5–19	8,950,000	4000	23,300
19+	39,264,000	17,700	102,100
Scotland			
All Ages	5,120,000	2300	13,300
0–4	324,000	c.150	800
5–19	960,000	400	2500
19+	3,836,000	1700	10,000
N. Ireland			
All Ages	1,632,000	700	4200
0–4	130,000	c.60	300
5–19	385,000	c.170	1000
19+	1,117,000	500	2900
Wales			
All Ages	2,906,000	1300	7600
0–4	189,000	c.90	500
5–19	552,000	c.250	1400
19+	2,115,000	1000	5500
		*At 4.5 per 10,000 to nearest 100	*At 26 per 10,000 to nearest 100

incidence figures predict because no cases will be found until the second year or later, and some will escape recognition altogether because they are not presented for medical or psychological attention, or because they have been misdiagnosed as belonging to some other condition (e.g. they are identified as 'language-delayed' because only their language was assessed). Nevertheless, the following figures are sufficiently accurate to serve as a guide for an adequate educational provision that meets the special needs of autistic children.

The estimates of children with autism shown in Tables VI, VII and VIII are based on the more conservative Prevalence Rate of 4.5/10,000 and a sex ratio of four males to one female. Numbers are rounded to the nearest ten. On the most recent Swedish estimates, there will be many more other cases of related 'autism spectrum' disorders, in addition to autism, who also require specialist help and provision. Gillberg and Gillberg (1989) found a prevalence rate of 26/10,000 for Asperger's syndrome, which is by far the most numerous of the autistic spectrum disorders.

Table VII Estimated Affected Individuals in Major UK Cities and Towns

	Total Population	*Autism Proper (At 4.5 per 10,000)*	*Other Autistic Spectrum (at 26 per 10,000)*
London	6,803,000	3060	17,690
Birmingham	994,500	450	2590
Leeds	706,300	320	1840
Glasgow	687,600	310	1790
Sheffield	520,300	230	1350
Liverpool	474,500	210	1230
Bradford	468,700	210	1220
Edinburgh	438,800	200	1140
Manchester	432,600	200	1130
Cardiff	290,000	130	750
Belfast	287,100	130	750
Aberdeen	213,900	100	560

Table VIII International Comparisons for Estimated Incidence of Autism (Cumulative total population data only: Statistical Yearbook (39th Edn), UN, New York (1994))

These figures are based on the unlikely assumption that children with autism and related conditions will have the same life expectancy as the general population. In countries where, for example, medical management is less advanced, the above figures will considerably overestimate the numbers actually surviving with autism.

	Total Population	*Autism Proper (At 4.5 per 10,000; to nearest 100)*	*Other Autistic Spectrum (At 26 per 10,000; to nearest 100)*
Algeria	23,039,000	10,400	59,900
Argentina	32,609,000	14,700	84,800
Australia	15,602,000	7000	40,600
Bangladesh	87,120,000	39,200	226,500
Brazil	121,149,000	54,500	315,000
Canada	25,309,000	11,400	65,800
China	1,160,017,000	522,000	3,016,000
Colombia	27,838,000	12,500	72,400
Egypt	48,254,000	21,700	125,500
Ethiopia	42,169,000	19,000	109,600
France	57,000,000	25,500	147,000
Germany	77,781,000	35,000	202,200
Greece	10,269,000	4600	26,700
India	844,324,000	379,900	2,195,200
Italy	56,557,000	25,500	147,100
Japan	123,611,000	55,600	321,400
Kenya	21,000,000	9600	55,600
Morocco	20,500,000	9200	53,300
Nepal	15,023,000	6800	39,100
New Zealand	3,307,000	1500	8600
Nigeria	88,515,000	39,800	230,100
Pakistan	84,254,000	37,900	219,100
Republic of Ireland	3,541,000	1600	9200
Republic of Korea	40,488,000	18,200	105,300

Table VIII International Comparisons for Estimated Incidence of Autism (continued)

Russian Federation	147,022,000	66,200	382,300
South Africa	23,386,000	10,500	60,800
Spain	37,746,000	17,000	98,100
Sri Lanka	14,847,000	6700	38,600
Sudan	20,594,000	9300	53,500
Sweden	8,360,000	3800	21,700
Switzerland	6,366,000	2900	16,600
Thailand	54,533,000	24,500	141,300
Turkey	50,664,000	22,800	131,700
Ukraine	52,000,000	23,300	134,300
USA	248,710,000	111,900	646,600
Vietnam	64,411,000	29,000	167,500
Zaire	29,917,000	13,500	77,800

Age Distribution of Autism

The total number of children with autism will depend on the age at which the condition can be recognised. As we explained in Chapter 2, it is still unclear how early it is possible to diagnose autism from the behaviour of a child.

Autism probably originates in the genes or from a pathogenic influence that affects brain organisation in early embryo or foetal development long before birth (Chapter 7), but the effects do not appear until the brain has attained a certain level of maturity – until certain psychological functions emerge. This results in different estimates of the beginning of the condition, depending on what behaviours are taken to be the best indicators. For example, it is not possible to identify a language disorder before a normally developing child can be expected to speak and understand words.

Nevertheless, there is agreement that most autistic children show a number of characteristic abnormalities in the second year, and secure diagnosis of Kanner's autism is usually possible before the child is four. Late diagnosis results from a justified professional reluctance to attribute delays in communication and language development to such an incurable condition. It is also the case that a focus on language or intelligence may lead to important and reliable signs of early failure in awareness of persons and their feelings and purposes being overlooked. Psychological rating systems frequently assume that language and intelligence are more measurable and therefore more 'reliable'. This is largely

..ect created by the tests themselves. It is also the case that ..d tests of early mental development require high levels of psycho-.. training in their use and interpretation.

With the greatly improved understanding of the early stages of autism that we now possess, and recognition that motivation and expressive behaviour can be measured with appropriate techniques, it will become possible to identify more autistic children in preschool stages, when they are most receptive to intervention. This will be a key element in an effective educational provision.

Efforts to trace features of the disorder down to the first nine months of infancy are, however, less likely to succeed. No behaviours have been reported in retrospective accounts that could serve to separate reliably an autistic child from the wide variation that is usually seen in the behaviour of infants at this stage (Adrien *et al.* 1993). The limited data we have at present come from retrospective parental accounts, which have uncertain validity, and from analyses of a limited number of home video recordings, are suggestive, but they need systematic, prospective validation. Current research on behaviours of infants in high risk families may identify important marker behaviours leading to more efficient diagnosis in the second and third years (see Chapters 2 and 9).

The brain structures that are believed to be most affected in autism, and most involved in the manifestations of the disorder (Chapter 7), include the prefrontal cortices, which, though they are first laid down in very early foetal stages, only begin to take on their primary functional roles around 12–18 months after birth (Dawson and Fischer 1994).

Sex Differences

As in a wide range of other developmental disorders, there is a preponderance of males in the autistic population, most studies reporting around four males to one female (see Rutter 1985, for review). Higher male/female sex ratios appear for the classical Kanner autism, which describes a population that have comparatively high intelligence. Ratios as high as 13:1 (Gillberg, Steffenburg and Schaumann 1991) and 16:1 (Wing and Gould 1979) have been reported. In autistic individuals with lower IQ, however, the ratio has been reported to be much closer to 1:1. Wing (1980b) found a ratio of 1:1.1 in the lowest IQ range of 0–19, of 1.3:1 for IQ = 20–49 and 14.2:1 for IQ>50. This finding could be confounded by the failure at the time of the study to differentiate Rett's syndrome, a progressive disorder leading to Profound Mental Handicap that affects only girls (Hagberg *et al.* 1983; Hagberg 1989. If the Rett's syndrome girls were removed, the male/female ratios for autistic children with very low IQ would be higher.

Social Class or Level of Education

A once commonly held view was that autism occurs more frequently among the childen of families in higher, more-educated social classes. This impression is probably related to the surprising focusing of intelligence of some autistic children in families with a high level of education where such concentrated interest is valued and encouraged. Furthermore, better educated, well-off parents will be more likely to come forward for professional help. In an extensive research literature, only one study (Lotter 1967 has found evidence for a slight effect in this direction. Other publications (Wing 1980a; Gillberg and Schaumann 1982; Ciadella and Mamelle 1989; Gillberg, Steffenberg and Schaumann 1991) find no effect of social class. This finding remains of interest, however, because developmental disorders in general, like other health problems, occur more frequently in lower social classes. Autism is, therefore, exceptional if there is no bias of this kind. This can be taken as further evidence for a genetic rather than an environmental cause.

Handedness and Autism

Considerable attention has been given to reports that handedness, the preference for using the left or right hand in more skilled actions and for gestures of communication, and therefore cerebral dominance or asymmetry of brain function, may be anomalous in the autistic population. This interest has been fuelled by the predictions of the Geschwind and Galaburda hypothesis (Geschwind and Galaburda 1985), described below, that ascribes variations in asymmetries of brain development, behaviour and cognitive functioning to the influence of the male sex hormone, testosterone.

Several studies (Boucher 1977; Tsai 1982; Fein *et al.* 1985) have failed to demonstrate an increased rate of familial left-handedness in relatives of left-or right-handed autistic individuals, which suggests that any increased rate of anomalous hand dominance has a pathological and not a genetic basis. The currently favoured explanation is expressed by Dorothy Bishop, who describes what is found as follows:

> ...increased non-right handedness in autism arising as a consequence of generally poor motor functioning which results in a failure to learn the types of motor skills for which hand preference is normally shown. (Bishop 1990)

It should be noted, however, that mechanisms of the brain that have been hypothesised to be the sites of primary defects that cause autism, i.e. limbic and midline interneuronal systems, have asymmetric organisation from early in brain development (Chapter 7; Trevarthen 1990b, 1996). Anomalies of handedness, in addition to disorders of motivation affecting social responses, attention and cognitive functioning, could be initiated by abnormal prenatal developments in these systems, and then lead to aberrant postnatal motor learning.

Seasonal Variations

A number of studies have investigated the possibility of seasonal variations in the birth rate of autistic children, and, indeed, all have found that children who develop autism are more likely to have been born at certain times of the year.

The first study reported an excess of March and August births and a relative shortfall in October and November (Bartlik 1981). Data on 179 Canadian DSM-III autistic subjects also showed an excess of spring and summer births (March to August) with a winter shortfall, the effect being evident primarily in non-verbal, developmentally-delayed subjects (Konstantareas, Hauser, Lennox and Homatidis 1986). In 80 Japanese autistic DSM-III children, an increase in spring births was again reported (April to June), with a high level of annual fluctuation correlating with a coefficient of 0.92 with rates of admission for bronchiolitis and pneumonia (Tanoue, Oda, Asano & Kawashima 1988). A series of 100 Swedish children with autistic disorder of uncertain origin showed a significantly higher than expected incidence of March births (Gillberg 1990). The largest study to date is a national UK survey. Data were collected on 1435 autistic individuals by questionnaire along with a clinic sample of 196 cases with 121 sibling controls, and normal population data (Bolton *et al.* 1992). This study has thrown up major inconsistencies between the clinic and survey data, and it failed to replicate the earlier findings on seasonal variation in birth of autistic individuals. Nevertheless, significant deviations from normal expected seasonal birth patterns in certain times of year, but not in March, were identified for the autistic individuals.

One possible explanation for any seasonal birth effect, which is also observed in other anomalies of brain development, is that environmental stress on the mother at a particular stage of pregnancy may contribute to abnormal development of the brain, early foetal stages being more vulnerable. Infants born in spring or summer would be early foetuses in winter when the mother's health may be most likely to suffer from stress or infection. This could increase the effects of a genetic factor that weakens brain development in early stages. Aspects of such a model have been discussed in a series of papers by Geschwind and Galaburda (1985).

CHAPTER 5

What Causes Autism?

Rival Concepts of the Psychology of Autism, and of Biological Causes

There are many ways to an understanding of how our minds work and develop, and there are, inevitably, many ways of explaining how a complex psychological disorder like autism begins. Psychologists, educators, psychiatrists, brain scientists, geneticists have different ways of looking at, describing and explaining human behaviour, and the behaviour of children with autism. Unravelling causes is difficult because autism, like psychological life itself, is a condition that has many and varied manifestations, and these manifestations change with age.

Some will pay more attention to signs of abnormal coordination of movements, or sensations, or thinking, or emotions; some will attempt to measure problem solving activities of the children, using methods that have proved useful in the study of psychological developments; others will be more interested in the children's interpersonal or social responses.

In recent years, new methods for studying brains, their anatomy and chemistry, and their development, have led many to pin their hopes for understanding, and perhaps for improved methods of treating autism, on research into neuronal systems in the brain that are turning out to be consistently different in autistic individuals. Finally, new genetic and molecular-biological theories that seem to explain how inherited factors control normal and abnormal building of the tissues and organs of the brain, offer a much more fundamental explanation of the source of trouble.

Whatever approach is taken, it is always necessary to remember that autism is a condition that develops. Like all developments in brain function, it will be a consequence of interacting factors, some from inside the genetic growth programme that controls steps in the formation of different cell populations and networks in the brain, some coming from the environment that stimulates and transforms the brain as it is growing and its connections are being sorted out, some cell-to-cell contacts being confirmed and many others lost. Most of the arguments about rival concepts revolve around this problem: is autism caused 'genetically' or is it caused by an abnormal environment of the brain, either in the body or coming from stimuli and especially from experience of the social world outside? The answers are important because they will influence how autistic children are perceived and the attempts that are made to help them develop with less handicap.

The Psychiatric Approach and Psychoanalytic Theory[1]

As we have seen, Leo Kanner (1943) first suggested that all symptoms of autism, which he described with such skill, stem from an *innate inability for interpersonal contact*, implying that a disturbance in the growth of brain is responsible. Later he considered that experiential factors combined with innate ones produce the clinical picture of autism (Eisenberg and Kanner 1956). Having first presented autism as a disorder of affective contact, he was persuaded that the emotional characteristics of the mother, with a possible link to high intelligence and upper social class of the parents, could be a cause. This latter idea is not supported by evidence from later population studies, as has been mentioned.

At the time when Kanner was pondering the alternatives, many authors influenced by the psychoanalytic theory that emotional trauma in infancy was a prime cause of psychiatric disorders they were treating in adults, and taking account of evidence for the emotional dependency and need for affection of the young child, proclaimed the *social/emotional environment* to be crucial. Bettelheim (1967), who was deeply impressed by the serious mental illnesses of children who had experienced extreme neglect or maltreatment, concluded that an unsympathetic and neglectful mother could be responsible for the 'empty fortress' state of mind of a child with autism. At one time Kanner, too, was so impressed by the strength of the emotional tie between infants and their parents, and the interpretations of adult psychoses by analysts, that he described the parents of autistic children as 'refrigerators', essentially reversing his earlier theory (Kanner 1949). Autism has thus been taken to be caused by negative interactions with the parents, or by maternal deprivation, or by emotional stress originally suffered by the mother and then transmitted to the child. A more cautious opinion of the early days, when the newly recognized syndrome was being investigated as an important medical condition, was that parental coldness can support the development of autism in a child with a constitutional weakness in brain development (Eisenberg and Kanner 1956), or that a combination of unresponsive child and unresponsive mother exists where autism appears (Anthony 1958).

Hobson (1989, 1990c, 1993a) claims that the observed social impairment in autism is created by a fundamental *inability to respond emotionally* to others. He explains cognitive and language deficits in autistic children as developmental

---

1 See Chapter 12 by Dr Olga Maratos for an account of psychoanalytic interpretations of autism in which she pays particular attention to the French school.

consequences of failures in interpersonal relatedness, and he draws evidence from comparison with the autistic-like behaviour of some children born blind and consequently cut off from contact with other persons' feelings (Hobson 1993b). Tests prove that autistic children do have problems in recognising and interpreting or understanding emotions (Hobson 1986a, 1986b; Capps, Yirmiya and Sigman 1992), and in expressing emotional states (Ricks 1975; Snow, Hertzig and Shapiro 1987; Yirmiya, Kasari, Sigman and Mundy 1989). This disability directly interferes with all their communications with other persons, and it must affect their development in all psychological areas. Hobson's approach is one that recognises that a child develops understanding and skills through 'mediated learning' with the aid of confident and trusting communication with companions of various ages, and he believes that emotional responsiveness and self-awareness in relationships is the bridge that makes such companionship possible.

Now the evidence is overwhelming that a prenatal fault in brain development can cause autism, and that this, and not parental behaviour, is the root cause of the affective and motivational disorder in most cases of infantile autism, as well as the associated motoric, sensory, cognitive, rational and linguistic abnormalities that emerge in early childhood. This fundamental brain disorder can, conceivably, be caused in a variety of ways; such as by a fault in genetic instructions for formation of specific systems in the brain, or an infection or toxic chemical influence that impinges on the same processes, the critical point being that the brain must be disordered at a particular stage of its formation by cell multiplication and migration, to affect the outgrowth of nerve connections. Nevertheless, with respect for the insights of psychodynamic therapists and the attachment theorists who have studied development of the mother–infant bond, we would add that it is important to acknowledge that a child developing autistic behaviour, whatever the prior cause, will be a strain and worry for parents and the rest of the family, and will certainly affect their emotions, and may threaten their emotional health. *Parental anxiety* may then aggravate the child's problem of development, reducing his or her ability to cope.

These issues, which are still highly controversial for theorists of psychological functions and their development, assume great practical importance, as we shall see, when one has to plan intervention to help the autistic child and to advise the parents in their demanding task.

Maternal Sensitivity and Autistic Withdrawal

There is now clear evidence that the quality and consistency of affectionate care an infant receives from the mother or other principal caregiver, and the kind of emotional attachment that the child develops for that person, is important in normal development. The emotional quality of maternal care can affect, or be correlated with, the emotional development and future social responsiveness and self-confidence of the child (Murray 1988, 1992; Main and Goldwyn 1984). However, the psychological disturbances attributable to this disordered or unsupportive kind of experience are not the same, nor as resistant to changes in human relationships, as those seen in autistic children.

Autistic children, unlike, for example, abused children, and in spite of their avoidant or unresponsive behaviours in communication, are emotionally attached to their carers (Sigman 1989; Rogers and Pennington 1991). What they lack is flexibility in interpersonal responsiveness, and they are often unable to learn through communication, or are very limited in what they can learn from other persons' guidance. This is evidence that autism must have a primary cause within the child's systems that regulate interactive learning or companionship, and not in the presumably more primitive systems that maintain emotional attachment to a caregiver (Trevarthen and Aitken 1994).

Even though it may be decided that there is an innate cause of autism in the way the child's brain has grown, we are left by the above diversity of theories with a fundamental question about the psychology of the child. Is autism primarily caused by an affective failure specific for relating to persons, as Kanner's clinical intuition strongly suggested, or is it a more general cognitive deficit, a loss of 'information-processing' capacity? Is it at base an emotional illness, or is it the result of faulty perceptions or reasoning?

The Search for Physiological Signs

Psychiatrists attempting to find an objective or biological cause in abnormalities of brain physiology, studied by measuring signs of electrical activity in nerves, found evidence that *sensory functions and attention* are abnormal in autistic children. Ornitz and Ritvo (1968) postulated that autistic children's inability to maintain constancy of perception stems from a pathologic mechanism with a neurophysiologic basis. They identified the fault in the input pathways from receptors of touch, hearing, vision, etc. Recent evidence indicates that a primary disorder, not in the sensory pathways, but in the functioning of neurones in the core of the brain that distributes and focuses attention and learning, aiming the receptors so they will pick up stimuli in the appropriate direction and with appropriate sensitivity, also leads to faults in brain growth before birth, and in the emotions that serve to regulate learning through communication with other persons in early childhood (Trevarthen 1989b; Rogers and Pennington 1991; Trevarthen and Aitken 1994). The central reticular formation and associated limbic system make up the *core regulator of brain activity* and brain sensitivity; this system is involved in the patterning of selective attention, coordination of perception with action, and in memory. It also determines the levels of activity and efficiency of transmission in sensory pathways.

Innate Behaviour Patterns and Motivations

No amount of information on brain anatomy or basic physiological functions can replace the insight into the nature of psychological functions that can be obtained by careful examination of how behaviour adapts in different circumstances. From the point of view of ethologists, specialists in accurate description of how animals communicate and how they set up their social relationships, *motivation for approach or withdrawal* from social contact with other individuals and for picking up the signals that regulate communication, is critical in parent–child relationships (Tinbergen and Tinbergen 1983). Autism is seen by the Tinbergens as an imbalance of this motivation and emotion leading to a confused state dominated by *anxiety*, and they, with the psychoanalysts and attachment theorists, think the intrusiveness of the human environment toward the child must be a key factor in its cause. Anxiety causes social withdrawal and consequent failure to learn and benefit from social interaction. Holding therapy, described below, has been developed as an application of the Tinbergens' theory, to overcome anxious avoidance (Richer 1983; Zappella *et al.* 1991).

The Search for a Primary Cognitive Disorder, or Fault in Planning Thought

On the assumption that the disorder stems from a *cognitive or intelligence* deficit that interferes with the pick-up of every kind of information, its remembering and recall, Hermelin and O'Connor (1970) claimed that the autistic children's inability to recode all kinds of stimuli meaningfully underlies the apparent social impairment. Tilton and Ottinger (1964) suggested that autistic children's inability to perceive relationships between objects might contribute to their failure to develop social skills, relations between the child and things, or between things and things, being conceived in the same way as relations with persons. Rutter (1983), too, has argued forcefully that a cognitive deficit is the basis of autism, and that the importance of the emotional disorder had been exaggerated, especially by the psychoanalysts. He noted that autism is always accompanied by a measurable loss in intelligence.

Recently, deficits found in autistic children's cognitive '*executive function*', defined as; '...the ability to maintain an appropriate problem-solving set for attainment of a future goal...[which]...includes behaviours such as planning, impulse control, inhibition of prepotent but irrelevant responses, set maintenance, organized search, and flexibility of thought and action' (Ozonoff, Pennington and Rogers 1991, p.1083) have been taken to be fundamental. It has been found that all autistic individuals perform poorly on 'executive function' tasks, and this, taken with neuropsychological evidence (of the effects of abnormal or damaged anatomy or brain chemistry in different brain areas), indicates that all share a loss of function in the prefrontal part of the brain

(Bishop 1993; Dawson and Fischer 1993). This explanation brings in the notion of an active investigative motivation in the brain that directs cognitive functions such as perceiving, knowing, remembering and thinking.

Deficiencies in 'Theory of Mind', and of Symbolic Thinking

Taking symbols to be cognitive representations or codes for concepts, psychologists suggested that the central problem is an impairment of the *comprehension and use, or formation of symbols* (Ricks and Wing 1975; Hammes and Langdell 1981). Studies on the acquisition of language and on the functional and symbolic play in autistic children have been cited to support the idea that a major impairment is in symbol formation (Ungerer and Sigman 1981; Sigman and Ungerer 1984a). However, autism is not simply accounted for as a defect in language or symbolic communication. Indeed, the level of speech function varies from total muteness to a prolific, if abnormal, fluency (Donaldson 1995). Nor is language simply the acquired store of semantic elements and grammatical rules; its development and use involve motivation for sharing interests and feelings with other persons, as we shall describe.

A new kind of cognitive theory has become popular in the last ten years, which identifies the fundamental cause of social deficits in autism with failure in a 'meta-cognitive' mechanism of the mind, one that performs 'thinking about thinking'. This approach has been driven by philosophy of mind and it is, in consequence, both intellectually sophisticated and seductive. Its success has been due to the development of clever narrative tests for determining what children believe about other persons' thoughts as these are represented in a little story. The autistic child is described as lacking a normally developed *theory of mind*, that is, of other persons' minds. The main feature of the disorder is said to be an inability to attribute beliefs to others. The child does not form a mental image of what can go on in other people's heads and this stems from a failure in thinking about his or her own mental states, as well as the mental states of others (Baron-Cohen *et al.* 1985; Leslie and Frith 1988; Baron-Cohen 1989b, 1990).

Experiments on theory of mind tasks use toys or pictures wherein dolls are described performing different roles and experiencing different parts of the story. The child is asked to say what a doll that missed an essential part of the drama will think or know or do. These experiments have proved that autistic children do have a 'theory of mind' deficit; autistic children of five or older make judgements like those of young toddlers who have not yet developed the required imaginative representation. Autistic children have been described as having problems in understanding other persons' 'false beliefs' (Baron-Cohen, Leslie and Frith 1985; Perner, Frith, Leslie and Leekam 1989), 'true beliefs' (Leslie and Frith 1988), and 'desires' (Harris 1989), and, correspondingly, they make aberrant interpretations of event sequences in psychological–intentional terms (Baron-Cohen, Leslie and Frith 1986), of emotion caused by beliefs (Baron-Cohen 1991b) and of deception (Baron-Cohen 1992). They have difficulties in distinguishing mental from physical entities and appearance from reality (Baron-Cohen 1989c).

The normal 'theory of mind' is hypothesised to be an innate cognitive capacity first appearing in the second year of life, which, besides conferring the abilities just described, accounts for the remarkable development of children's *symbolic pretend play* at that age (Baron-Cohen, Leslie and Frith 1985). The same cognitive capacity is also manifested in 'ostensive communication' by which interests and meanings are demonstrated and shared, '...something broader than just pointing and showing: namely, any act in which one person places a stimulus in the environment of another person for purposes of communication and which achieves communication by directing attention' (Leslie and Happé 1989, p.206). This kind of behaviour is a key component of intentional communication (Leslie 1991). It includes gestures, such as pointing to draw someone's attention to an object (Baron-Cohen 1989a) and joint attention (Baron-Cohen 1991a). According to Leslie (1987), infants and toddlers have 'first-order representations' of other persons and objects, and then they form 'second-order representations', imagining that other people have minds like their own. Autistic children are thought to pass through the first stage of this process but to fail in the second step, and that is why they exhibit deficits in symbolic play (Baron-Cohen, Leslie and Frith 1985; Leslie and Frith 1988; Baron-Cohen 1989b).

The theory of meta-cognition is manifestly a rational one that separates the mind from the body and it does not seek evidence on bodily expressions of emotion – vocalisations, facial expressions, gestures and body movements. Such movements are full of information about self–other awareness. This is the principal point of contention between Hobson and the proponents of the 'theory of mind' theory. According to Hobson, who has a psychoanalytic orientation interested in the emotional dynamics and self-regulation of infants and young children, '...children do not develop, nor do they need, a "theory" about the mental life of others. What children acquire is knowledge that other people have minds' (Hobson 1990b, p.199). For the acquisition of this knowledge there is, according to Hobson, a path of three stages that one must follow: first, a person acquires a concept of self; second, the individual establishes relatedness between himself and the others by means of observing others' bodily expressions; and third, he develops a relation based on analogy between his subjective experiences and the others' bodily appearances (Hobson 1990b). Hobson (1990c) does not agree that autistic children are able to form first-order representations for the perception and expression of emotions, and for normal social-affective responsiveness. He suggests that autistic individuals '...from an early age...should be impaired in those primary representations that are relevant for socioemotional and especially affective interpersonal relations.' (Hobson

1990c, p.118). Indeed, evidence on the development of infants that later develop autism does indicate that emotional responses may not be normal from the start of development, long before a normal child will develop a 'theory of mind' (Baron-Cohen 1995). Studies with autistic adults have shown that the difficulty of recognising emotional states remains in adult life (Harris 1989).

Object Concepts or Person Concepts; Evidence from Imitation

The problem of what the consciousness of an autistic child is like has been considered in comparison with supposed stages in the development of *object awareness* (Piaget 1954). It is not clear to what extent a 'general purpose' visual or spatial concept of an object is needed to account for the differentiation between the child's 'self' and another person. Evidence that infants only minutes old can imitate various kinds of expressions of a partner, including the expressions of many emotions, shows that some representation or reflection of the other person who is in front of the infant is normally present from birth. Furthermore, imitations of young infants are manifestly not reflex automatisms – they serve in the purposeful regulation of reciprocal communicative interactions (Kugiumutzakis 1993). The ability to respond communicatively clearly does not wait on the development of rational thinking. In a study formulated in terms of Piagetian cognitive theory, autistic children were not found to be impaired in their ability for self-recognition (Dawson and McKissick 1984) and Hobson (1984) showed they could appreciate others' points of view in a visuo-spatial setting as well as non-autistic children of matching IQ. These studies suggest that autistic children are, in fact, able to differentiate between self and other as separate objects, and that they can imagine themselves to take the position of another subject relative to an object at a given location. Their failure in 'theory of mind' tests must be due to a different component of understanding about the other persons.

Piagetian theory is concerned with the development of logical operations that allow inferences to be made about the consequences of the subject's act on objects and about the interactions that may occur between objects. Durig (1993) has proposed a 'microsociological theory', that is a theory of conversational interactions and social learning of a self-description, that would explain autistic thinking and behaviour as due to a limitation in inductive logic. Where 'deductions' seek specific conclusions from specific premises, keeping fixed in real and certain entities and relationships, and 'abductions' attempt to make, creatively, specific conclusions from general premises, 'inductions' move from specific premises to general conclusions about the likely principles of life and experience. Durig collects evidence that a lack of inductive reasoning makes it impossible for autistic individuals to gain, as normal persons do, from social negotiations with others, and achieve a self-and-other awareness of roles, interpretations, etc. that is readily shared. He explains the pronominal errors, echolalia and other faults in language use by autistic children as due to the breakdown of their understanding of other persons' view of them. They can focus on tasks that yield to deduction and they abduct from memory of personas they have experienced, but cannot project the expectations of others and gauge their own actions accordingly in live transactions. This theory, though it attempts to explain the detailed symptoms of autism, is abstract, like those attributing autistic behaviours to faults in 'metacognition' or 'theory of mind'.

It now seems likely that autistic children's varied impairment in *imitation*, which correlates with the degree of impairment in social relating (Dawson and Adams 1984; Rogers and Pennington 1991; Nadel 1992; Nadel and Fontaine 1989; Nadel and Peze 1993), is part of a fundamental intersubjective deficit, an aspect of an overall impairment in reciprocal communication, and not that both these interpersonal problems result from a deficiency in meta-cognition or any other general aspect of 'thinking'. It seems likely that a fundamental inability to form a responsive internal image of the other who can then be a partner in truly reciprocal interaction, with whom the child can explore how to share orientations to objects, exchange feelings about actions, objects and events and cooperate in performance of tasks, would undermine consciousness of persons and impair all kinds of social learning. The latest theories of the key psychological deficit in autism are considered further in Chapter 9.

CHAPTER 6

Brain Abnormalities in Autism

In nearly every case of autism, when appropriate techniques are available, evidence of an abnormality in the brain can be found (Gillberg 1988a, 1991; Steffenberg 1991). Recent observations on the brains of autistic children, comparisons of the psychological deficits produced in human beings and animals with damage to the emotional (limbic) systems of the cerebral hemispheres, and better understanding of the complexity of the core regulatory systems of brains and their importance in emotional communication, maturation of the cerebral cortex and learning, all support the hypothesis that autism may originate as a defect in the core systems (Aitken 1991a; Schore 1994; Trevarthen and Aitken 1994). Such a defect could cause failure in prenatal development of the neocortex or of sub-cortical sensory and motor systems that are directly involved after birth in information pick-up for awareness and in the making of coordinated behaviour.

A clear distinction between pure or primary autism and other recognised neurological illnesses that result in mental retardation with autistic features may lead to identification of brain systems in which damage by a gene fault or specific noxious agent causes autism when other parts of the brain are intact. Neurologists are familiar with a number of conditions in children that can be attributed to gross malfunction in the neocortex, basal ganglia or other structures. Autism, while it may have manifestations like these conditions, is not associated with such massive neurological abnormalities. But it is not a 'psychological' disorder for which no brain malfunction can be found. The defects that seem to cause autism are increasingly perceived as deep seated, subtle and widespread in the brain. Nevertheless, brain research has recently contributed to considerable advance in awareness of brain activities that could cause the remarkable symptoms of autism.

A functional condition closely similar to autism can evidently be produced in the brain of a young child by socio-emotional stress or deprivation, especially if the defective environment impinges harshly very early in life, possibly even *in utero*. The essential point to be clarified, however, is that evidence now exists that a congenital defect in core systems of the brain with immediate and lasting effects in socio-emotional aspects of behaviour can also bring sensory and motor malfunction due to brain atrophy, and can, therefore, result in characteristic emergent perceptual, cognitive and linguistic defects that are charac-

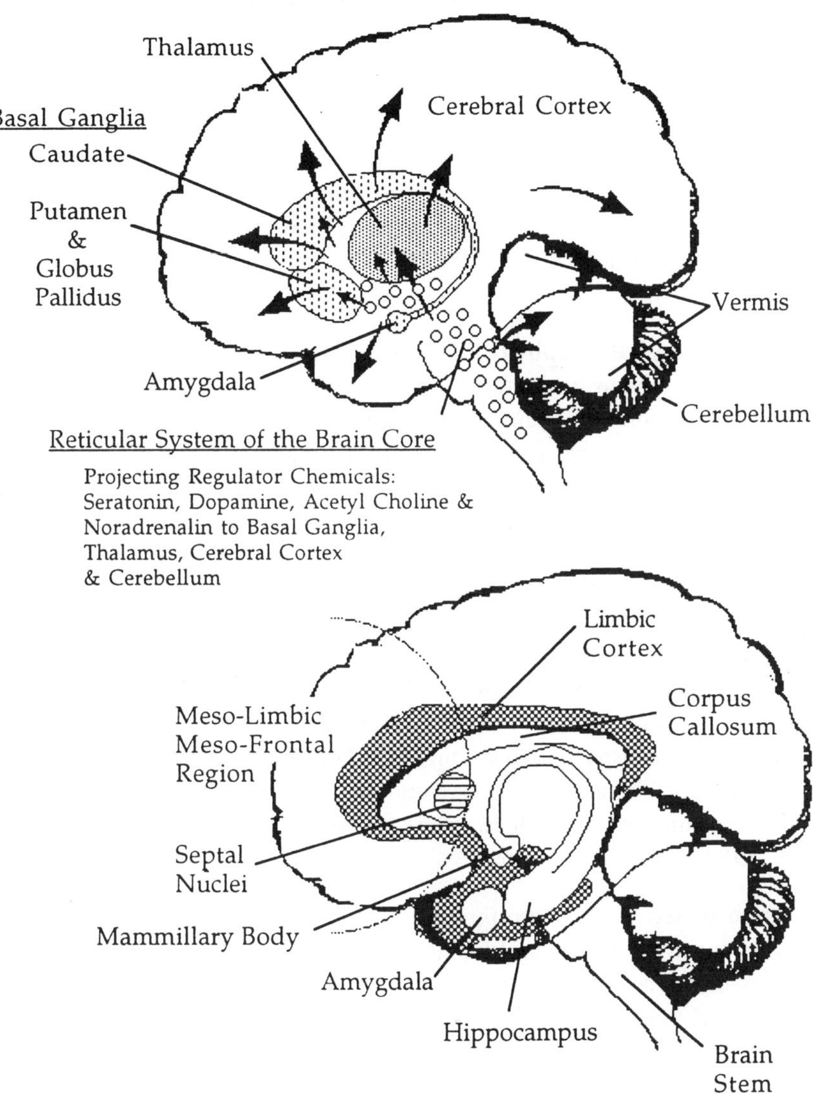

Figure 2: Midline and side views of the human brain. Transparent to show the basal ganglia and limbic structures inside and between the cerebral hemispheres. These are the mechanisms that generate the expressive movements and emotions of human communication

,f the autistic syndrome (Trevarthen and Aitken 1994). In this perspec- .e cognitive and linguistic features of the disorder are not primary.

,vidence from Brain Scans of Autistic Adults

Large scale anatomical abnormalities in the brains of autistic individuals have been sought in images made of the intact brain with the aid of radiography. More recently brain scan techniques have made it possible to visualise regional activity when the subject is performing various psychological tasks. The anatomical and temporal resolution of brain scan techniques is being rapidly improved.

Pneumoencephalography (PEG), in which radio-images are obtained of the cavities of the brain (the ventricles after injection of air into the fluid-filled spaces surrounding the brain), is an invasive and distressing procedure and is no longer in use. It has been superceded by superior non-invasive methods described below. Nevertheless, a considerable body of research had used this method to investigate the brain in autistic individuals. A report in 1975 of left temporal horn dilatation in 13 of 18 cases studied (Hauser, DeLong and Rosman 1975) was the strongest clinical finding, earlier studies having only found evidence of slight and inconsistent patterns of *enlargement in the cavities of the cerebral hemispheres* (Melchior Dyggve and Gylsdorff 1965; Boesen and Aarkrog 1967; Schonfelder 1964). The apparent dilatation on the left side indicates a loss of tissue around the cavity or in the cortex of the left temporal lobe of that hemisphere, which might explain severe deficits in language in some autistic children, though the central features of autism cannot be explained either as a language deficit or as a consequence of left hemisphere atrophy (Fein *et al.* 1984).

Computerised Axial Tomography (CAT). Numerous studies have been carried out using this form of brain scan. CAT scanning is useful for imaging defects in the cerebral cortex, but it has a limited ability for demonstrating structural abnormalities in the midbrain and cerebellar structures that are now seen as likely to be involved in the abnormal motivations characteristic of autistic children.

An early study suggested *atypical patterns of cerebral asymmetry* in 9 of 16 cases (Hier, LeMay and Rosenberger 1979); however, subsequent reports have failed to replicate this finding (Damasio, Maurer, Damasio and Chui 1980; Tsai, Jacoby, Stewart and Beisler 1982). Ventricular dilatation found in 11 of 45 cases (Campbell *et al.* 1982) has also not been replicated (Creasey *et al.* 1986). Some reports from CAT scans claim a wide variety of abnormalities but little consistency across the autistic population (Ballotin *et al.* 1989).

Positron Emission Tomography (PET), see below, and CAT scans have demonstrated a range of non-specific differences between brain structure in autistic and control populations which are neither necessary nor specific to autism. They provide limited aid in diagnosis. The same gross abnormalities of the brain anatomy occur in children who are not autistic.

Magnetic Resonance Imaging (MRI), previously known as Nuclear Magnetic Resonance Imaging (NMR), has yielded the most interesting findings to date on the structure of brains of living autistic individuals. At first controversy arose over their interpretation because they suggest defects in parts of the brain that had not previously been under suspicion. Recent validation of these findings, together with evidence from histopathological studies reviewed below, has advanced our understanding of the brain systems of motivation and learning, and their contribution to psychopathology of thought and communication.

The seminal single-case report appeared in *Archives of Neurology* in 1987, suggesting a previously unknown pattern of *reduced development (hypoplasia) in cerebellar tissue* (Courchesne, Hesselink, Jernigan and Yeung-Courchesne 1987). The paper reported on a high-functioning (IQ 112) 21-year-old right-handed male who showed '...hypoplasia of the declive, folium and tuber of the posterior vermis, but not of anterior vermis.' The medial aspects of both cerebellar hemispheres were also under developed. This individual also showed a reversed structural asymmetry of the cerebral hemispheres and a dilated ventricular system. Subsequent papers from the same group claimed that the findings could be replicated in a series of 18 subjects and was, therefore, not a scan artefact caused by the way the first brain had been positioned (Courchesne *et al.* 1988, Murakami *et al.* 1989). This work has been reviewed by Courchesne (1989).

The cerebellar abnormality is of interest for several reasons:

(1) It appears to provide the first reliable anatomical marker for autism. If validated it would thus establish a 'gold standard' for diagnosis of the disorder, or for recognition of a subgroup.

(2) The tissue reduction hypoplasia reported was unlike any of the other known malformations affecting cerebellar development (cerebellar atrophy; focal cerebellar atrophy; olivo-ponto-cerebellar degeneration; Arnold-Chiari I, Agenesis of the Corpus Callosum or Dandy-Walker). Thus, although cerebellar malformations are relatively common in developmental disorders of the brain, this particular type of fault seems to be associated with autism while the other forms are not.

(3) It could imply a far more complex functional role for the cerebellum in humans than had been previously imagined, implicating it in communication and/or cognition. Such a 'high level' function is also suggested by evidence of strong correlations between metabolic rates

> of cerebellar and frontal cortical areas, indicating that these structures are involved together in thinking and communicating (Junck *et al.* 1988), and by cognitive planning deficits found in patients with 'pure' cerebellar atrophy (Grafman *et al.* 1992).

Since the Courchesne group's studies were published, evidence for cerebellar abnormalities has been found to apply only to autistic individuals with Joubert's and Fragile-X Syndromes who also fulfil diagnostic criteria for autism (Reiss 1988; Reiss *et al.* 1991; Holroyd, Reiss and Bryan 1991).

Piven and colleagues obtained evidence for a different pattern of cerebellar malformations. They demonstrated significantly smaller cerebellar lobules VI and VII and significantly enlarged midsaggital brain areas in 15 autistic adults who were compared to age and parental Socio-Economic-Status matched controls (Piven *et al.* 1990). Controls were not matched for IQ.

There have been negative findings in other investigations. Garber and Ritvo (1992) were unable to demonstrate any significant cerebellar abnormalities in 12 autistic adults with DSM-III defined autism, or in a matched group of 12 normal controls. Kleiman and colleagues also found no differences on a range of cerebellar parameters when 13 autistic children were compared to a nonspecific control group of 28 children (Kleiman, Neff and Rosman 1990). Nowell, Hackney, Muraki and Coleman (1990), who also failed to replicate the Chourchesne group's findings, used a patient group who were shown to be free of Fragile-X chromosome abnormalities. This study appears to identify one group for whom the gross structural cerebellar abnormalities are not seen.

Abnormal Physiology in the Autistic Brain

Positron Emission Tomography (PET) records the relative physiological activity in brain regions, and is increasingly recognised as useful in developmental brain research and in the early identification of developmental brain disorders of all kinds (Chugani and Phelps 1986). However, the few published studies on PET findings in autism lead to varied interpretations. US studies seem to show metabolic differences from controls, with *abnormally high levels of cell activity* overall (Rumsey *et al.* 1985) and lower correlations between metabolism in frontal and parietal areas of the cortex than in controls and between these structures and brainstem nuclei and basal ganglia (thalamus, caudate, lenticular nucleus and insula) (Horowitz, Rumsey, Grady and Rapoport 1988). A UK study (Herold *et al.* 1988) did not replicate these findings in six cases.

Single Photon Emission Computerised Axial Tomography (SPECT) is a simpler technique than PET, requiring less sophisticated apparatus, and it is increasingly used with autistic subjects. The major limitations in comparison with PET are a lower acuity and an inability to provide real-time imaging of task-related brain function.

Zilbovicius and colleagues in France using SPECT found no evidence for abnormal areas of cerebral cortex in 21 children who met DSM-III-R criteria for autistic disorder compared against an age matched group of 14 children with language disorders (Zilbovicius *et al.* 1992). This study was restricted to measurement of cortical blood flow, and did not examine cerebellar or midbrain function. Furthermore, since DSM-III-R criteria were used, many of the children diagnosed as autistic would have slight and mixed symptoms. A second study of four young adult subjects (George *et al.* 1992), again diagnosed by DSM-III-R criteria, demonstrated a significant reduction in total brain perfusion (58–72 per cent of control values), and *reduction in blood flow in frontal and right lateral temporal lobes.*

Research reports using both PET and SPECT have two shortcomings. Appropriate standardised psychological or pharmacological activation procedures have not been used, and the studies compare major diagnostic groups rather than sub-groups with similar symptomatology. Interesting and consistent results are being achieved in adult schizophrenia research when these issues are addressed and patients are grouped by symptomatology not by diagnosis (see Liddle 1992).

In summary, then, there is a wide variation in the abnormalities reported from structural and functional CNS imaging tests. This variation may, in part, reflect current limitations in diagnostic systems and activation procedures, but it seems likely that it is an accurate reflection of differences in underlying pathology that result from differences in causative mechanism. The relationship found between Fragile-X, autism and cerebellar hypoplasia may point the way to more accurate interpretation of the discrepancies. The current status of information about the brains of subjects with primary autism appears as follows: No consistent abnormalities appear in CAT scan (Prior *et al.* 1984), but recent MRI research (Courchesne *et al.* 1987, 1988) confirms histo-anatomic findings (below) that parts of the neocerebellar cortex are underdeveloped.

Pathological Brain Cells and Tissues

There have been few detailed investigations of the tissues of brains from autistic individuals, probably because there was a belief that autism was a subtle psychological disorder unlikely to be associated with visible tissue abnormalities. The most interesting findings have been reported from two groups – Bauman and Kemper in Boston and the UCLA-NSAC study group.

Bauman and Kemper (1985) found abnormal anatomy in many parts of the brain of a 29-year-old autistic man. All were *structures linked with emotional functions* (the hippocampus, subiculum, entorhinal cortex, septal nuclei, mamillary body, central and medial nuclei of the amygdala, and, surprisingly for this time, before the brain scan results discussed above, they also found changes in the *neocerebellar cortex*, the roof nuclei of the cerebellum and the inferior olivary nucleus. Autopsies of 4 autistic/retarded boys 10 to 22 years of age demonstrated reduced numbers of the integrative Purkinje cells in the cerebellum (Ritvo *et al.* 1986). These findings have led to a search for evidence and to the confirmation by several methods that the cerebellum is involved in many functions other than those traditionally ascribed to this structure.

It has been suggested by Ritvo *et al.* (1986) that the Purkinje cell deficits lead to failure of inhibition and the brain becomes flooded with stimuli – hence the withdrawal and self-stimulating behaviours of autistic children. Such an interpretation may be premature until more is known about how patterned inhibition from the cerebellum regulates experience in relation to action. It could be vitally involved, for example, in the timing of communicative engagements, as well as in organisation of exploratory behaviour, and it is certainly important for learning precise motor skills.

There has been remarkable consistency in certain aspects of the neuropathology so far reported in autistic subjects. In particular, the apparent absence of ascending fiber tracts from the olivary nucleus in the midbrain to the Purkinje cell baskets in the cerebellum has been seen across subjects. This finding, if further substantiated, would seem to identify a narrow temporal window in brain development during which that particular abnormality in neural development can take place, and it may reveal the particular form of structural abnormality that makes this temporal window critical. This time window would probably be in the last half of the embryo period, about one or two months after gestation (see Chapter 7).

Hormonal and Neurochemical Abnormalities

Evidence for neurochemical abnormalities comes primarily from studies on the effects of a number of forms of medication on the behaviour and status of affected children.

Raised levels of urinary *serotonin* has been observed consistently in some 30 per cent of autistic cases. This finding has resulted in clinical trials of the drug fenfluramine which tends to normalise serotonin levels. Recent work from two controlled clinical trials in the Netherlands (Buitelaar, Van Engeland, Van Ree, and De Weid 1990; Buitelaar *et al.* 1992) demonstrates clinical improvement in autistic children administered an *adreno-cortico-trophic hormone* (ACTH) analog, suggesting an abnormality in this neurotransmitter system.

The Geschwind and Galaburda Model

A complex descriptive model for a diverse collection of developmental disorders, including possibly autism, has been presented by Geschwind and Galaburda (1985; 1989, a, b, c). They propose that the differences in sex ratio, handedness, epilepsy, immune function and learning problems seen in the autistic population can all be accounted for as consequences of exposure of the foetus to higher levels of the male sex hormone *testosterone*, which is pr both by the mother and by the gonads of the male foetus. This, they argue, results in poor development of the thymus gland and hence immune difficulties, an increase in the rate of growth of the right hemisphere and interference with the normal patterns of nerve cell migration and development, the latter giving rise to structural abnormalities in the cerebral cortex and an increased frequency of both anomalous cerebral dominance and epilepsy.

The major limitation of this model, while it provides a general theory linking hormones with brain development to explain common features in a very broad range of psychological disorders, including dyslexia, mixed dominance and autism, is that it gives no explanation for the characteristic features of autism (Johnson and Morton 1991).

Medical Conditions Identified with Autism: Varieties of Autism

Many medical abnormalities have been reported in the autistic population. There are several excellent and extensive reviews of this area if the reader wants a more detailed coverage (Cohen, Donnellan and Paul 1987; Dawson 1989; Gillberg 1989; Gillberg and Coleman 1992; Schopler and Mesibov 1987). Here we will give an overview of how these are perceived at present.

Recently arguments have been made for subdivision of the diagnosis on the basis of the presence or absence of genetic markers coupled to distinct forms of behaviour, as in the case of Fragile-X (Gillberg 1992), or by discrimination of groups with differing cognitive features (Fein, Waterhouse, Lucci and Snyder 1985) or behaviour (Volkmar 1992). Such sub-classification may give valuable pointers, not only to different ways in which autism can come about, but to differing forms of intervention.

Gene Anomalies – The most commonly reported genetic feature associated with autism is **Fragile-X Syndrome**, an abnormality in the DNA molecules of the sex chromosome. This fault in the gene code, the result of a massive over-replication of a sequence of nucleic acids (a CGG repeat) near the tip of the X chromosome, is apparently a frequent cause of mental retardation (5–7 per cent in males), and approximately 26 per cent of these retarded individuals also fulfill diagnostic criteria for autism. Conversely, analysis of 20 studies of autistic individuals tested for Fragile-X found 8.1 per cent to have this chromosome condition (i.e. they are *'autistic with Fragile-X' or AFRAX*).

Autistic behaviour is now well-documented in Fragile-X children (Gillberg, Persson and Wahlström 1986; Cohen *et al.* 1989). The most obvious correlate of the Fragile-X condition in behaviour is an extreme avoidance on being greeted, by turning head and eyes away (Wolff, Garner, Paccia and Lappen 1989).

A wide range of other genetic abnormalities have been reported in autistic individuals at what are thought to be higher than chance levels. The ways these gene conditions affect brain development are not known. For a detailed review consult Gillberg and Coleman (1992, pp.179–202).

Tuberous Sclerosis (TSC) – Between 17 and 58 per cent of individuals with this condition, in which neurones of the cerebral cortex form amorphous tuber-like clumps indicative of disturbance of the biochemical processes that normally regulate cell migration and formation of cell-surface material, are autistic. They constitute a small but significant proportion of the total autistic group (between 0.4 and 3 per cent). Within the TSC population as a whole the sex ratio is close to one, but those with autism are more likely to be male. Those with autism also have more seizures and are more retarded (Smalley, Tanguay, Smith and Guitierrez 1992). A further interesting finding is that mothers of those TSC cases with autism are significantly more likely to have experienced a depressive episode before the conception of the index child (Smalley, personal communication 1992).

Abnormalities of Melanin – Abnormal skin pigmentation resulting from unusual levels of melanin in discrete areas visible when the skin is examined under ultraviolet (or Wood's light) appear to be common in autistic individuals. This finding may help to unravel the abnormalities of neural migration which give rise to autistic behaviour. In addition to tuberous sclerosis, described above, two conditions in particular, neurofibromatosis (Gaffney, Kuperman, Tsai and Minchin 1989) and hypomelanosis of Ito (Akefeldt and Gillberg 1991; Zappella 1992) have been well-documented, each of which account for between three and five per cent of autistic cases.

Phenylketonuria (PKU) – An abnormal accumulation of the chemicals phenylalanine and phenylpyruvic acid in the urine, is associated with extreme mental defect. Untreated PKU is a well-documented cause of autism (see Friedman 1969 for a review); however, with routine neonatal screening for PKU throughout the UK, this is now a rare factor here. Autism consequent on PKU is still reported in countries where such early detection is less common.

Purine Autism – Abnormalities of purine metabolism resulting in autistic behaviour are well-documented in the literature (see Gillberg and Coleman 1992 for review) and are important in that they are, in many instances, potentially treatable. As severe self-mutilation is a common concomitant of purine abnormalities (Lesch and Nyhan 1969) this is to be noted as an important though rare cause of autism.

Measles in Pregnancy – Stella Chess's study of the New York Rubella epidemic of 1964 (Chess, Korn and Fernandez 1971; Chess 1977) showed that if a mother contracted measles during pregnancy this will increase the chances of her child developing autism. Seventeen of the eighteen children described as autistic also had significant sensory impairments which may have contributed to their autistic symptoms. As with PKU, greater awareness of the disorder together with widespread innoculation have virtually eradicated Rubella as a significant cause of autism.

Epilepsy – Some 20 to 35 per cent of autistic individuals develop epilepsy. Reports vary as to the most likely age of onset. A recent study of 192 autistic individuals (Volkmar and Nelson 1990) found 21 per cent to have developed a seizure disorder. The likelihood increased with lower IQ and risk of seizure onset was highest during early childhood with a second less pronounced peak in early adolescence. Overall this represented an increase of between 3- and 22-fold over normal population rates. It is possible that the concurrence of autism and epilepsy is the result of a common causal mechanism interfering with neural migration, migration abnormalities being significantly more common in the epileptic population in general (Brodtkorb, Nilsen, Smevik and Rinck 1992).

Conclusion: Autism is a Brain Growth Disorder Sensitive to Human Care

All of the evidence now available from studies of the brains of autistic people supports the conclusion that Kanner's autism is caused by abnormal brain development that begins before birth but shows its effects in behaviour only at the end of infancy, when the child should be beginning to develop language. This indicates that whatever goes wrong in brain formation is related to the functions which emerge at that stage of childhood, a stage when the cortex of the brain is growing very rapidly and the brain as a whole is motivating the individual to seek stimulation from the environment to support that growth.

As we shall see in Chapter 8, observations of the normal course of psychological maturation and learning in the last year of infancy and through preschool years confirms that this is a time when emotionally-regulated human communication is vitally important for cognitive growth. Thus it is not surprising that the parts that appear to show abnormality in the brains of autistic people are motivating ones that are involved in patterning of emotions and their communication, as well as in the control of attention and perceptual guidance of action. There is a great deal of supportive evidence from brain science for this view of the disorder (Trevarthen and Aitken 1994).

CHAPTER 7

Brain Embryology and Autism

Here we present a simplified overview of brain development in an attempt to explain how development may become deviant in autism. (For more information see Dawson and Fischer 1994; O'Rahilly and Müller 1994; Schore 1994; Trevarthen 1987b, 1996; Trevarthen and Aitken 1994.)

Basic Brain Design

Brains are organised systems of interconnected nerve cells, each system performing a particular job in the initiating, directing, guiding and elaboration of behaviour. All the brain parts are linked by nerve fibre connections that can synchronise activity in cell groups that are far apart in the body. The activity in nerve circuits is responsive to stimuli, but not wholly dependent on it. There is much spontaneously generated activity in all brains, and an individual's intelligence depends on internal motives as well as information from outside the brain. Autistic people have intelligent brains, but they have more or less serious problems with awareness, learning and investigative acting. As we have seen, they are most handicapped in their perception and responsiveness to what is going on inside other people – how other people feel, what they are conscious of and how they wish to act.

Intelligent behaviour requires 'prospective awareness', a consciousness of what can be done in the world, both in the immediate present and in preparation for future events. Such consciousness is enriched by learning, taking in from motivated experience ideas and skills that can make understanding more comprehensive and more efficient, linking effects inside the mind, its emotions and feelings of confidence or fear to the real possibilities. The human brain in a person has a unique power to do all these things in sympathetic communication with the bodies and minds of other individuals, picking up the patterns and rhythms in their brains. Motor systems of the central nervous system (CNS) generate patterned output to muscles, moving the body and sense-organs and modulating spontaneous activity of the visceral muscles of the gut, heart, glands etc. Sensory mechanisms receive and process input from the receptors of all kinds, including those inside the limbs and trunk of the body and in the internal organs, not just those that pick up visual, auditory, tactile or chemical information about the world outside the body. Intermediate neuronal systems perform a wide range of coordinative and motivating functions, from local adjustment between reflexes to the genesis of coordinated motivations for the whole subject, and they lay down memory traces, producing predictive cognitive representations that guide the choices and adjustments of goal-directed behaviours.

Cells that perform functions at a low level are concentrated in organised groups or nuclei. Nerve fibre bundles may be compacted into distinct tracts. Between the nuclei forming the core of the CNS and the tracts that tend to accumulate near its surface is a network of less compact populations of cells and intermingled axons that serve in regulation of the balance of activity in the whole nervous system, and the changes of physiological and psychological states. The motor mechanisms, including a hierarchical system in which instinctive behaviour patterns are represented, lie within the ventral or basal half of the central nervous system. In the sensory mechanisms of the dorsal half of the CNS very large populations of cells are arranged in layered sheets or cortices that may be greatly expanded for specialised perceptual and cognitive functions and therefore bulging or folded. Mechanisms that control autonomic and visceral functions, including basic appetites and aversions for biological regulation of the whole individual, are concentrated around the cavities of the CNS. The coordinated functions of intelligence and learning are mediated in the anterior enlarged brain stem, and the highest cognitive and learning systems are developed in two vast additions in which all lower functions are re-represented many times – the cerebral cortex and the cerebellar cortex. At all levels, from the spinal cord to the cerebral cortex, the brain centres and the connecting tracts between them are ordered in maps that are linked to the parts of the body in anatomical order, though with distortions depending on the relative density with which different parts require neural representation.

The cerebral cortex and cerebellum of the human brain are exceptionally large, and they are reciprocally interconnected with each other by very large fibre systems as well as with sub-cortical systems of the brain stem and spinal cord. In spite of its very conspicuous additions, which are essential to the resolving power and versatility of our consciousness, the human brain stem still contains the more automatic regulators of the whole subject, including the sensory-motor mechanisms for selectively orienting to locations in the environment, for patterning adaptive behaviour routines and for controlling the relationship between brain-directed behaviour in engagement with the external environment and the changing internal physiological requirements of the whole body.

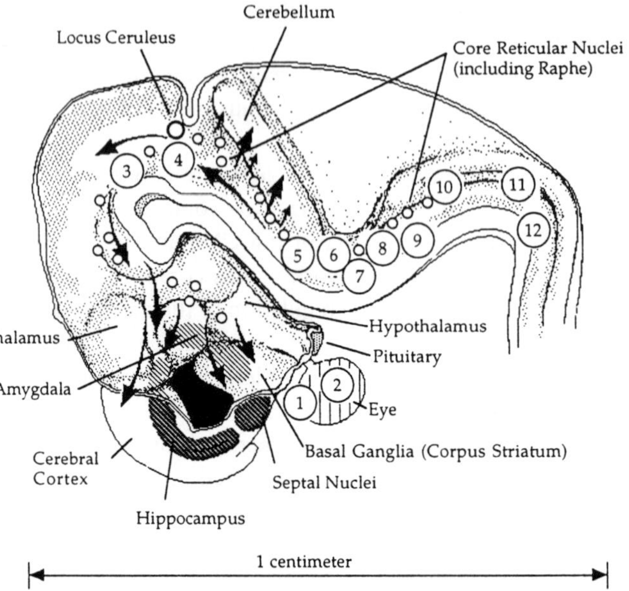

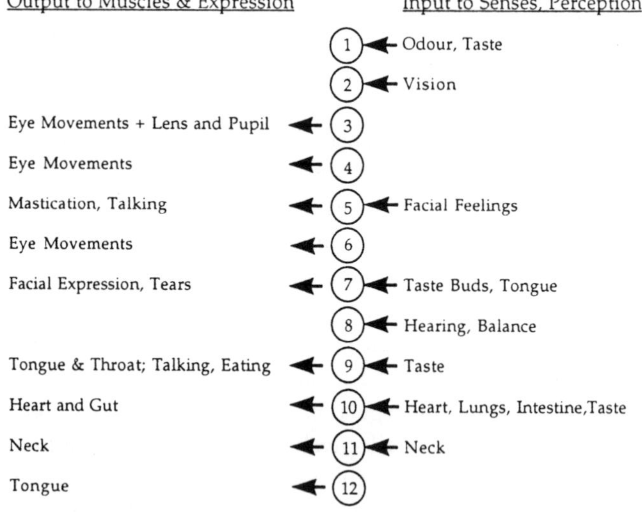

The core regulatory systems assist in the formation of the cerebral hemispheres and cerebellum in the early foetal stage. Our hypothesis to explain autism is that a fault in gene expression in the core regulators of the embryo leads to the known errors in anatomy of cerebral cortex and cerebellum, and thus to psychological problems that appear some months after birth. The nuclei of the peripheral nerves of the head (cranial nerves), indicated by numbered circles, also differentiate in the embryo period. They take part in the perception and production of expressions of communication, coordinated by other brain systems, including the reticular formation in the brainstem

Figure 3: The embryo human brain with its core regulatory systems that later become the organisers of motivation and emotion

Chemistry of Motivation: Inter-Cellular Regulators of Development and Learning

The changes of brain activity that move us to do particular things, with certain intensities and in particular directions, that cause us to seek for particular goals or pleasures, are determined in the core of the brainstem by an intricate set of counteracting neuro-chemical systems. Motives arise among a population of specialised nerve cells in the 'reticular formation' inside the stem of the brain. These cells convey their excitatory or inhibitory molecules down to spinal circuits and up to the cerebral cortex. The key reticular neurons are a few per cent of the population in the whole brain, but their fibres reach to contact cell bodies and their branches throughout the brain. Projections of differing chemical type act collaboratively and are complemented by local circuit neurons that may focus their effects. The chemicals they release at the surfaces of the target cells (neuropeptides (NP) and the classical monoamine transmitters, serotonin (5-HT), dopamine (DA), norepinephrine (NE) and epinephrine), have the capacity to change the excitatory or inhibitory effects of junctions between nerve cells and thus to change the integrative functions of nerve pathways. Hormones circulating in the blood also affect nerve cell activity, and hormone production by glands outside the brain is regulated by the brain, principally from the cluster of nuclei that serves as the 'head ganglion of the visceral system', the hypothalamus.

Reticular neurons, through release of their chemical products to appropriately responsive receptors on the surfaces of other nerve cells, perform or influence a great variety of essential functions: suppressing responses to touch or pain stimuli; organising rhythmic oculomotor (eye muscle) control and visual tracking, and performing analogous functions for hearing, tasting and the sense of smell; sharpening resolution of sensory cortex responses in moments of attention; setting the gain in all senses; activating and directing alertness and learning; regulating cortical habituation and conditioning; activating or suppressing instinctual motor patterns.

The NE system projects from the locus coeruleus and other hindbrain reticular cell groups throughout the brainstem, down into the hindbrain and spinal cord and widely to the cerebral and cerebellar cortices. It is primarily concerned with alertness, defense and attack. In animals it patterns fear and rage and threat-aggression, and possibly submission. A small ensemble of cells in the substantia nigra and parts of the midbrain floor with very widespread effects are the source of the DA rich nigrostriatal pathway, projecting up to limbic cortex and neocortex via the median forbrain bundle. They control the strength of elicited motor activity and involuntary motor patterns. Serotonin-rich cells are found in the hindbrain and through the midbrain in and about the midline. They project from the hind portion of midbrain to the limbic forebrain, neocortex and hypothalamus, stimulating calmness and sleep. The neuropeptides, including the opioid peptides (endorphines and enkephalins), are the largest group of central transmitters. They are found in the dorsal half of the spinal cord and hindbrain visceral region, the gray matter round the cavity of the midbrain, some nuclei in the hypothalamus, and in the central amygdala nuclei. Some are found in in cortical interneurons. NP secretions act as neuromodulators, with the monoamines, in pleasure versus pain sensations, and in the regulation of body temperature, drinking, sexual behaviour and locomotion.

In sum, the aminergic systems contribute state-control-modulation of sensory-motor mechanisms and establish patterns of motivation and affect. Their connections to brainstem nuclei mediate balance and hearing and visual scanning, maintaining meaningful contacts of the organism with the environment while gating and selecting inputs to the cerebral cortex. The hypothalamus and reticular systems are reciprocally linked to the prefrontal cortex and the cortex of the tip of the temporal lobe, both of which are very much enlarged in the human brain. As we have seen, all these mechanisms are thought to have a crucial role in the production of the characteristic abnormalities of behaviour and mental activity in autistic persons.

A new form of intelligence has evolved in humans and this has required the inheritance of changes in the brain at all levels, not just the addition of a large new cognitive and learning capacity in the cerebral cortex. The internal motives for being intelligent have also been transformed. Traces of this massive evolutionary creation can be found very early in the formation of a human brain, many months before birth, and even before the cells of the cortex exist.

Human Brain Development Before and After Birth

A fertilised human egg has a structured interior and surface and it is situated in a patterned cellular and molecular environment. It is possible that the future polarity and mapping of tissues and organs of the body have already been determined, invisibly, before there are any divisions of this cell. However, organisation of the body and its nervous system becomes definite only after two weeks when the embryo is about one millimetre long. Then the presumptive brain (neural plate) can be located in the upper surface of the embryo. Forebrain, midbrain and hindbrain can then be distinguished, but the brain is still just a sheet of quite undifferentiated cells.

In week four the central nervous system rolls into a tube and cells multiplying in the 'germinal layer' around the central cavity migrate outwards in the wall to form rudimentary neural masses in the 'mantle layer' of the ventral spinal cord, hindbrain and midbrain. Nerve fibres will spread through the outer 'marginal layer'. Motor nerves grow from the spinal cord at the same time as the limb buds and primordia of the special senses (eyes, vestibular organs and cochlear, olfactory and gustatory organs) and the first afferent tracts appear. Rudimentary nuclear masses form in the basal (motor) plate of the brain, extending from the ventral horns of the spinal cord through the ventral hindbrain, midbrain tegmentum, ventral thalamus and subthalamus in the diencephalon, to the lamina terminalis and commissural plate in the forebrain. The dorsal alar (sensory) plate is less developed. In the hindbrain the locus ceruleus appears.

In the second half of the embryo period, weeks five to eight, all the main components of the brain are formed and the body takes on the appearance of a miniature human with a disproportionately large head. The special sense organs, eyes, vistibular canals and cochlear, hands, nose and mouth, are rapidly differentiating their dedicated forms. And yet at this stage the nervous system is inactive and it generates no behaviour. The cerebral hemispheres and cerebellum are in very rudimentary condition, but the brainstem regulatory and motivating structures are remarkably well-formed. In week five the brain almost doubles in size and the first monoamine transmission pathways grow from the brainstem into the cerebral hemispheres in which cells are completely undeveloped. The nuclei in the base of the forebrain, called basal ganglia, are relatively large. They will be important in patterning unconscious movements, including expressive gestures. An important link between the emotional mechanisms and the future cerebral cortex, the amygdala, begins to differentiate from the basal ganglia, and integrating tracts appear in the midbrain and hypothalamus.

The reticular formation and the pituitary gland under the hypothalamus develop conspicuously in the sixth week, as does the cerebellar ridge, which receives its first input fibres. Cells in the basal ganglia multiply producing bulges into the cavity of the hemispheres, the cortical and anterior nuclei of the amygdala develop and the hippocampus, insula, red nucleus, subthalamic nucleus and mamillary body appear. All these structures will be important in motivation and learning in the brain later. Tracts continue to develop throughout the brainstem, for example, connecting the hypothalamus and thalamus. The median forebrain bundle carries descending fibres from the amygdala and ascending fibres from the locus ceruleus. The hormonal functions of the hypothalamus plus pituitary appear to begin at this time as well.

In the cerebral hemispheres the first synapses or intercellular connections are seen about six weeks, and then the first radially migrating neurons appear, starting the formation of the elaborately layered cortex. The characteristic cell columns of the neocortex arise from precursor stem cells in the proliferative zone next to the cavity of the hemispheres. All cells in a column come from one germinal cell. The size of each functional cortical area depends on the number of proliferative units, which form a 'proto-map' of the whole cortex in the zone round the hemisphere cavity. The total number of columns is about 200 million, with large individual variation. The neocortex seems to have expanded in evolution by adding proliferative units. Pathological brain organisation appears to come about in the same way under deviant genetic instructions. Neuron cell type in the cortex is determined before cells reach their final position in the cortex. Nerve fibres growing up to the cortex from sensory systems are guided by position specific molecules which are in place on the surfaces of cerebral cells before they arrive. Clearly regulatory inputs from the brainstem reticular formation can impose their influence right from beginning of the development of the cognitive mechanisms of the forebrain.

In weeks seven and eight neurogenesis (nerve cell multiplication) in the cerebral cortex procedes apace, and it continues until week 18. Cells produced in the generative zone migrate radially into the columns along glial strands and come to lie in a layer in which most recently arrived cells move to the outer surface, through those already present. This inside-out migration is thought to enable communication between cells of instructions for differentiation. Differentiation of the migrating cortical cells is also influenced by their passage, before they reach the plate, through a dense cellular lattice and 'sub-plate' of early neurons, axons, dendrites and glia fibres (projections from non-neural cells which are abundant in the CNS). The sub-plate is larger in humans than in other primates and contains waiting afferents generated ahead of their neuronal targets in sequence from brainstem, basal forebrain, thalamus and ipse- and contra-lateral cortex. This structure can be regarded as a mechanism for establishing integrative regulation over the initial steps in morphogenesis of the presumptive cognitive machinery of the hemispheres. Influences from subcortical regions having effect at this time will decide the distribution and laminar structure of the neocortex, including asymmetries of function in left and right hemispheres.

Genes new to humans may decide the formation of additional cortex that makes possible important aspects of culture-related learning of the adult human brain, including the learning of language. These territories are particularly rich in connections with other cortical areas, and they are in close reciprocal relation with limbic or emotional and motivational cortex. Two major motivating mechanisms, the amygdala and hippocampus begin rapid differentiation in the seventh week, with fibre connections through the lateral forebrain bundle, and the septum develops acetyl choline producing nuclei that become of fundamental importance in the regulation of behavioural and cognitive functions. The basal ganglia, substantia nigra and globus pallidus appear, establishing the basic mechanisms for instinctive motor functions. The eye-movement nucleus also shows important differentiations. The cerebellum, which begins complex new developments, and the cochlear (hearing) nucleus grow as the sensory nuclei of the hindbrain develop.

The eighth week marks the end of the embryo and the beginning of the foetus. The first fibres grow down from neocortical cells en route to lower regions, and the hippocampus enlarges. The roof of the midbrain swells, indicating a significant advance in primative visual and auditory centers. Tracts linking the cerebral cortex and the cerebellum appear. The cortical plate has three to five layers (laminae) of cells. Integration of functions within the cortex is achieved by means of a vast number of cortico-cortical connections, which are also important in moulding the folds of the cortex. Long axons grow within and between the hemispheres from about the tenth week.

Cortical nerve cells stop appearing almost half-way through gestation, in the eighteenth week, and cell death starts. Cell numbers are essentially stable from the twentieth week, but there is some further cell loss later in development. Rapid growth in the cerebral wall and buckling of the cortical mantle is due to neuron enlargement and separation, with branching of dendrites. Anatomical asymmetries in the neocortex are evident at this stage, notably on the size of the dorsal surface of the temporal lobe and in the shape of the Sylvian sulcus. Experiments with monkeys prove that while differentiation of cortical areas is self-regulated, relative size of areas depends on input from subcortical centers before there is any environmental stimulation. Basic structures and biochemical characteristics of the cortex develop with no sensory input.

Brain development is linked with differentiation of the gonads and the appearance of secondary sexual features of the body in the late embryo, and male/female differences in both brain anatomy and in the gonads appear to stem from differences in the organisation of neuro-hormonal systems of the brain stem. Hormonal control of sexual differentiation in behavior is related to the biochemical mechanism by which gene expression is controlled in the central nervous system itself. There is a feedback loop between neurones of the hypothalamus and medioventral reticular formation and the endocrine system of gonads and adrenals that regulate reproductive activities and development of the body and its secondary sexual features. This connection, which is of importance in the postnatal growth of the mental abilities in children, is first evident in the early foetal stages (MacKinnon and Greenstein 1985).

Cortical cell layers are well-delimited in the newborn human brain, but this is just the beginning of a great development of new functional connections that continues through early childhood. There is a vast post-natal production of synapses (nerve cell contacts) in excess, then a process of selective elimination or stabilisation that responds to environmental influences. Functional systems are formed by a sorting process involving loss of many components. Cell death is important in embryo brains, and then axons, dendrites, dendritic spines, and synapses show competitive selective elimination through to postnatal stages. The initial cell proliferation, neural migration, outgrowth of axons and distribution of receptors generates patterned arrays without nerve impulses. Then elimination of neurons, axons and synapses and shaping of final circuits of topographical maps is regulated by electrical activity via effects on neurotransmitters, hormones and gene expression.

Connections within the cerebral cortex develop throughout life and relative rates of development can be charted. Late maturing axons include both the long association fibers inside each hemisphere and the inter-hemispheric fibers of the corpus callosum. Short associative links in the nonspecific 'association' cortices (intracortical neuropil) myelinate slowest of all the neocortical systems. Axons of the reticular formation of the human brain core also mature for decades. Developments charted from birth to adolescence show asymmetries in the maturation of the cortex, left and right hemispheres showing 'growth spurts' at different times. For example, there is a significant growth spurt in connections of the left hemisphere between two and four years of age that co-occurs with development of speech and the expansion of vocabulary. Regional differences in cortical development relate to gender, handedness, educational level, deafness, or blindness, and other differences between individuals, including the acquisition of different forms of language. Intrinsic regulations of postnatal brain growth, and of hemispheric plasticity of function, have relationship to the education of children in socially desired skills in which motivation for social engagement and learning mediated by communication has a key part.

Maturation of Neurochemical Regulation in the Brain

The widespread axons of the first reticular nucleus to appear, the locus coeruleus, develop in the mid embryo period at the end of the fourth week of gestation. This centre in the hindbrain reticular formation will have a key role in early brain development, as well as in the coordination of emotions postnatally.

The precocious appearance of monoamine neuron systems in the cortex before development of the network of dendrites and establishment of normal cell-to-cell contacts suggests that cortical cells may be responding to the neurotransmitters flowing into the watery medium between cells before they are connected. However, selective growth into nuclei and cortices by transmitter-secreting axons that do make close contacts with them has the greatest potential for selective control of nerve net development and function.

Cortical neurone assemblies are built up cooperatively, by effects transmitted from different active nerve fibre endings to postsynaptic cells, according to how action potentials and secreted transmitter chemicals become distributed in space and time within the nerve network and interact (Hebb 1949; von der Malsburg and Singer 1988). In the epigenetics of the developing nervous system, components of all kinds are produced in excess and more refined functional cell groups and cell-to-cell transmission lines are selected by eliminating the great majority of elements, or closing off contacts (Changeux 1985). Quantitative matching of cell systems is achieved by death of cells that fail to gain access to growth substances (Oppenheim 1984). The selection processes driven by impulse activity of the cells and exchange of messenger substances begins *in utero*, without excitation from stimuli of environmental origin. After birth environmental stimuli enter an already active and highly structured nervous system in which the values of experience can be specified in advance.

Learning in the cortex requires change in interneuronal circuits, and this process is regulated by biogenic amines projected from the brainstem. The brainstem reticular formation 'gates' the responses of cortical neurones both by these chemical effects and by aiming receptors, the eyes, ears, hands, in relation to objects round the body. The process is driven, not only by stimuli, but also by the coordinated, internally generated, interest and attention of the subject, and these investigative activities can be seen in a newborn baby immediately after birth, though they are still rudimentary at this stage. Later the same core regulations selectively enhance, and retain discriminatory or 'semantic' memories in category-defining cell assemblies. The internally generated 'interest', with affective evaluations transmitted in communication with other members of the social group, effectively 'rewards' or 'punishes' the receptive networks.

In infants, very important developments occur in the frontal cortices of the cerebral hemispheres and in the temporal lobes, in both of which limbic or emotional activity joins with cognitive information distributed from the rest of the neocortex (Goldman-Rakic 1987; Schore 1994). Recognition and recall memory for recognition of a caretaking individual (a cortical-limbic-brainstem system) and species specific habits (a cortical-basal ganglia system) are both involved in attachment (Goldman-Rakic 1987; Mishkin and Appenzeller 1987; Squire 1986). Affectionate contact between an infant and a mother involves activity in limbic and mesofrontal regions which undergo developmental changes for years after birth (Schore 1994).

Nerve fibres from monoamine systems are intensely active in the early postnatal period, when there is most rapid selection of cortical circuits. This is certainly related to the regulation of early brain development with the aid of affective support from a caretaker (Kraemer 1992). The DA (dopamine) system, associated with tuning of attention and response to stressors, reinforcement, circadian rhythms and neuronal plasticity, which develops postnatally, is especially sensitive to breakdown of attachment. In normally developing babies NE (seratonin), DA and 5-HT output is stable and correlated, but this balance is disturbed in social isolation, which also produces reductions in cortical and cerebellar dendritic branching as well as altered limbic and cerebellar activity, as for a neural lesion. This is believed to give rise to denervation supersensitivity (Kraemer 1992), such as occurs in certain developmental disorders like autism that interfere with emotions and communication. Social deprivation seems to produce depression followed by 'supersensitivity' to both biogenic amines and novel situations.

Genetics of Brain Development and its Disorders

A range of genetic mechanisms are emerging as crucial to the integrated development of the embryo and foetus. These factors determine a coherent individual with body-form, internal organs and central nervous system adapted to maintain and direct an active life and intelligent behaviour (Gardner and Stern 1993). Presumably they establish first steps in the embryology of motive systems in the brain. Of particular interest are the so-called 'Hedgehog' and 'Homeobox' gene sequences, both of which show a high degree of conservation across animal phyla, from insects to mammals (Duboule 1994). Hedgehog gene products (morphogens) can be detected in very early stages of the embryo and appear to be crucial to the regulation of whole CNS polarity, with effects on cell division and axon growth at subsequent stages (Echelard *et al.* 1993). Homeobox genes expressed in the CNS are important in imposing a segmental organisation on the nervous system. Integrated activity of the nervous system depends upon the establishment of somatotopic arrays of cells in which body axes are represented and that have matching connective affinities (Sperry 1963). Apparently hedgehog and homeobox genes control the induction and polarisation of these maps in the early embryo brain.

It is likely that anomalies of development in the motivating and emotional systems that originate in the embryo brain are mainly of genetic origin (Lyon and Gadisseux 1991). The neuro-developmental effects of certain gene abnormalities are beginning to be elucidated. For example, examination of FMR-1 (the gene locus for the CGG repeat sequence responsible for Fragile-X Syndrome) in the human foetus shows FMR-1 messenger RNA to be expressed in proliferating and migrating neuroblasts at least by 8–9 weeks post-conception and to be in most of the differentiated CNS structures by 25 weeks (Abvitbol *et al.* 1993).

There is now evidence for genetic bases to many disorders which have core affective components, and this includes the autistic spectrum disorders (Gillberg and Coleman 1992), schizophrenia (Fish *et al.* 1992; Weinberger 1987), Gerstmann syndrome (Grigsby, Kemper, and Hagerman 1987) and Fragile-X (FraX) syndrome (Hagerman and McKenzie 1992). Autism frequently occurs in populations with FraX (Brown *et al.* 1986; Blomquist *et al.* 1985; Fisch *et al.* 1986; Rutter 1991). While it is variable in its manifestations autism has associations with genetic disorders that are known to affect brain development or with nerve cell pathologies. FraX cases exhibit different neuropsychological signs in males and females, and autism, Tourette syndrome and dyslexia are more common in males. Tuberous sclerosis (TSC) and Fragile-X are genetic conditions linked with autism, as described in Chapter 6.

Conclusion

The brains of persons who become autistic in their early childhood undoubtedly had abnormal developments early in intra-uterine life, probably first expressed among cells of the early embryo, in the first month. It is likely that the differences between autism and related pervasive disorders of mental development, and between these and mental handicap on the one hand or disorders of higher cognitive processes such as specific langiage impairment or dyslexia on the other, depend on the time in the developmental program when gene faults become expressed. If the core regulators of the CNS in the reticular system of the brainstem are, as we have suggested, the Intrinsic Motive Formation through which regulator genes act in shaping the cognitive systems of the cerebral hemispheres and cerebellum (see Trevarthen and Aitken 1994), then the first error may be in the generation of particular species of reticular cell, leading to an imbalance in neurochemistry of the embryo brain before there are any cortical neurons. Another possibility is that the time at which an error of this kind is transmitted to the intra-cortical regulatory mechanism, altering the multiplication and/or migration of neurons or their selective reduction in number, in systems that will become the cognitive machinery of the child after birth, may be critical. Different cortical sectors mature and become functional at different ages. The earlier they are disorganised the deeper the abnormality, Rett syndrome being an example of a genetic disorder in which the development of the whole cerebral cortex appears to be compromised, leading to atrophy. In autism it appears that the prefrontal and temporal regions with important limbic connections may be critical, along with parts of the cerebellum that also mature after birth. In dyslexia a restricted part of the cortical machinery in the junction of temporal and parietal lobes, which is important in the seeing and recognition of written words, appears to show abnormalities due to disturbed neural migration at a late stage of cortical neurogenesis.

CHAPTER 8

Where Development of the Communicating Mind Goes Astray

Conversations in Early Infancy, and the Emotions that Regulate Them

Recent studies, using microanalysis of film and television, show that infants are born able to communicate with the feelings, interests and purposes of other persons, and that it is by development of these innate abilities to communicate that they become capable of cooperation in ideas and use of symbols (Bullowa 1979; Stern 1985; Trevarthen 1979, 1980, 1987a, 1992; Trevarthen and Hubley 1978; Trevarthen and Logotheti 1987). Many experimental studies proved infants to be capable of remarkable discriminations among the signals from people (Field and Fox 1985; Mehler and Fox 1985; Stern 1985; Trevarthen 1985, 1993a).

A newborn may show complex responses when greeted by a person, picking up information on their feelings through many senses and showing emotions by expressions of face, voice and hands. They can imitate expressions of face voice or hands in a communicative way (Meltzoff 1985; Kugiumutzakis 1993) or enter into a 'proto-conversational' exchange. Some of the infant's signals, such as crying and smiles, serve to solicit human aid, for protection or comfort and for feeding. These, obviously, are important for the infant's physiological well-being and survival. But information from people about their emotions when they offer face-to-face play has a special extra interest for the infant. From very early in life infants reveal their ability to recognise the special nature of a person in the way they move their hands. And even newborns move their own hands in more complex patterns when they see a person, differently from the way they reach out or point at an object that is not alive and not capable of communicating (Rönnqvist and von Hofsten 1992).

A baby learns quickly to identify who is his or her most constant caretaker. A mother's voice can be learned by the foetus *in utero* (DeCasper and Fifer 1980). Very soon after birth her individual odour may be preferred, and there is rapid learning of her face.

By analysing the timing of the infant's sounds in their interactions with the vocalisations of the mother (Beebe *et al.* 1985; Stern and Gibbon 1980), as well as by describing the special kind of affectionate speech of a person who is trying to get a response from the baby (a special kind of speaking called 'intuitive motherese'), it has been possible to show that infant and mother share the same feelings about expressions (Fernald 1985; Papousek, Papousek and Bornstein 1985; Stern, Spieker and Mackain 1982; Trevarthen and Marwick 1986). Thus they can share in a mutual regulation of feelings. Motherese has unconsciously regulated features of pitch-variation, duration and spacing of utterances, and these features appear to be the same in all languages (Grieser and Kuhl 1988). Not surprisingly, the universal, intuitive features of motherese, transcending differences between languages, are found to be the features that the infants prefer to hear. They are part of the baby's inborn 'sketch' of the 'ideal mother' (Trevarthen 1993b).

Six weeks after birth a baby has more sharply focused sight of a familiar person's eyes and mouth and a greater readiness to greet a friendly face and voice with a smile and a coo. Cyclic 'proto-conversations' now develop, in which the baby replies to evenly spaced invitations of motherese with a pattern that links focused attention, smiling, cooing, 'prespeech' movements of lips and tongue and gestures of the hands (Trevarthen 1979, 1993a,b; Trevarthen and Marwick 1986).

The complex emotions that regulate these exchanges is further revealed when the infant's conversational partner does not fulfil optimal requirements. In experimental studies, various awkward situations are contrived; either a stranger attempts communication with the two-month-old, or the mother behaves with inappropriate timing or withholds her normal responses. Artificial interference of this kind causes infants to make signals of distress mixed with withdrawal or protest (Tronick *et al.* 1978; Murray and Trevarthen 1985). Evidently the infant's pleasure in normal chat with a loved caretaker needs the response of the affectionate, joyful and 'considerate' partner, supported by recognition of a familiar face and voice.

Double Television Intercom recordings made at Edinburgh for this research also prove that proto-conversations can be well-sustained between baby and mother by two-dimensional TV images with accompanying voice from a loud speaker, i.e. by sight and sound alone (Murray and Trevarthen 1985; Trevarthen 1985, 1993a,b). The two-month-old can communicate with a mother who is out of range of touch or body contact. Touch and odour may be more effective ways for the infant to perceive the mother immediately after birth, but they are soon superseded by sight and sound, channels of human contact that have vast potential for carrying specific information, both about mercurial states of mind and, with the aid of pointing and looking, and especially with the addition of language, about an infinity of significant elements of the shared world.

In our attempt to understand autism, it is important to note that when the contact of a two-month-old with the mother has been cut off by her assuming a still face, the baby's signs of distress may show 'autistic' features, such as avoidance of eye-to-eye contact, compulsive fingering of clothes, cessation of smiling and a complaining kind of vocalisation (Murray and Trevarthen 1985;

Wienberg and Tronick 1994). An avoidant or unresponsive state of this kind may persist for a minute or two after the mother resumes normal behaviour and tries to get the infant to communicate warmly with her again. This is not to say that it is autism that is caused by a mother's lack of response, but that the older autistic child's brain cannot use the efforts of other people to be friendly and intimate at a distance. The child effectively suffers from being cut-off from the other person's feelings for communication, like the infant is in the still-face situation, and comparable expressive movements of a disordered, distressed, detached or avoidant kind are released as a result. There may be important implications for the facilitation of one-to-one teaching approaches to help autistic children who may have to be supported or encouraged somewhat like an avoidant infant, with measured, responsive and unintrusive approaches.

The elaborate dependence of the two-month-old on a particular patterning and emotional quality of sensitive and instantaneously-reactive face-to-face communication with the mother, capable of generating a specific mutuality of active emotion, changes within a few weeks. Perturbation experiments with infants over three months of age give different results. When the mother withholds her responses, the older baby's attention usually becomes side-tracked into an exploration of the environment, interrupted by periodic glances at the unresponsive mother and by calls for her attention. The baby has less distress than at two months, along with an increased curiosity and autonomy.

With a stranger, a three- to four-month-old may exhibit a rapidly changing array of reactions, varying between timid withdrawal and an expression of fear or crying, coquettish or bold smiles of short duration, and self-conscious avoidance with self-touching, exploration of clothes, or studious examination of hands or nearby objects (Trevarthen 1984, 1986). The intricate, sometimes conflicting, relationship between the motives for attention to and exploration of the environment, and those for getting into communication with people who are familiar and whose affections can be counted on, is already clear.

Growing Awareness of Objects, and a New Playfulness with People

From birth, infants can certainly pay attention to and begin to explore the evidence they get from their senses about the existence and nature of objects and events in the physical, impersonal world. They orient to auditory and visual stimuli, and they even make 'prereaching' attempts, as yet unsuccessfully, to get hold of nearby objects. They learn to recognise familiar things and to forget those things that turn out to have no special interest or usefulness. Such attentions, explorations and learning are, however, relatively weak and undeveloped compared to the behaviours of communication described above.

Infants have few effective object-related behaviours before three months, at which age a baby begins rapid development of a strong body capable of lifting itself against gravitation to give the head stable and mobile support and to stretch out the arms and hold the hands close to nearby objects so that they can be explored by the fingers or grasped and picked up. This development of body-action and orientation to surroundings is associated with a fall in readiness to engage in face-to-face proto-conversation (Trevarthen and Marwick 1986). Curiosity about the environment of things to be watched, grasped, sucked, rattled, etc. evidently competes with, or takes motivation away from, the desire for direct engagement with a person at this age.

At the same age, however, communication, too, advances to a new level. The infant gains in speed and elaborateness of moves with another person in body play, becoming humorously combative and laughing when teased (Reddy 1991; Trevarthen 1986, 1990a). Play with people is not abandoned while cognitive mastery of objects is sought. A familiar partner, who is affectionately attached to the baby reacts to this change towards playfulness and a more complex attentiveness to the world by presenting more animated and complex patterns of communication, which may take the form of a culture-specific repertoire of ritual nursery songs or action games (Trevarthen 1987a). In many of these games, objects are presented in a way that amuses the baby.

Baby songs, rhyming chants and action games that are played with infants about the middle of the first year have recently been found to be similar in different languages and cultures. They have predictable features of beat, rhythm, melody and use of rhyme that suggest innate foundations in brain activity for what turn out to be universals in the timing and prosody of music and poetry. By six months, a normal infant in a happy family will most likely have learned several favourite routines of play with familiar people, adults or older children, at the same time as he or she has been gaining efficiency in tracking, recognising, grasping and manipulating objects. At this age, the vocalisations of infants may imitate musical forms (Papousek and Papousek 1981).

After three months, infants characteristically begin to show systematic 'problem solving' behaviours, and thus they become good cooperative subjects of experimental psychologists' tests of their powers of perception, object awareness and instrumental activity. Some 20 years ago Papousek made the important observation, in an experiment in which he also made films of his subjects' faces, that such problem-solving behaviour was normally accompanied not only by a studious, serious concentration or tracking on the patterns of test stimuli, which were made contingent on the baby's movements, but by smiles and coos of pleasure when a right choice was made, or a pout of disappointment at being wrong (Papousek 1967). He called this a 'human kind of response' to consequences of attempts at cognitive mastery and prediction of events. The baby's expressions are obviously useful for communication. We see that developments in curiosity and affectivity, taken together, show how cognitive processes and active exploration of objects grow in close, partially competitive, relation with the precociously manifested special abilities for communication. It appears, moreover, that rational or object-directed practical abilities may be given motivation to develop by the expressions of feeling, interest and purpose of other people, through communication.

In the middle six months of the first year, an infant's intelligence (awareness, memory, prediction of events, adaptive guidance of movements) clearly advances greatly. With the growing skill of manipulation, occasions for discrimination and exploration of objects automatically increase in frequency and variety, because the baby has better controlled movements and stronger exploratory awareness. Six-month-olds are curious and alert observers of and 'tinkerers' with the nearby world. This is the time in which the 'clinical' tests of Piaget, and the more elaborately systematic experiments of contemporary cognitive psychologists, have revealed the baby to be developing the 'object concept' – that is, the concept that a thing in the present and nearby space may persist in various properties beyond its instantaneous perceptual presence; that it may survive occlusion or concealment by something else; that it has a collection of features that distinguish it as different from other things (Wishart and Bower 1984). Younger infants follow and identify things with eyes and ears, keeping track of what they are (Spelke 1985). Manipulative 'tests' are used by the older baby to uncover new properties or 'affordances' of objects. The curiosity that infants demonstrate from soon after birth for novel experiences; their declining interest in often repeated events (habituation; their appreciation of 'interesting' transformations that violate expected natural manifestations or motions of objects, especially those that may indicate an animate object), allow for experimental demonstrations that they can perceive critical differences and similarities between events in the space around their bodies, demonstrations that increase in variety as the infants gain in acuity of perception and versatility and power of motor action.

The engrossing exploration by psychologists of what infants can perceive, what problems of information pick-up they will try to solve, has led a majority to place cognitive developments first – to see a rational process as the necessary basis for every advance in behaviour. But this approach should not be permitted to explain away person awareness, that selective precocity which infants show for getting into active and effective relation as a person with another person, and with their emotions, their changing interests and their constantly redirected purposes. The one-sided analysis of object awareness has helped to make autism incomprehensible.

'Self-Awareness'

The personality of an infant, it is true, develops markedly after six months (Stern 1985; Trevarthen 1984, 1986, 1993b). The often noted increase in 'self-awareness' at this age is a change in the infant's people-sensitive responses and actions. The self-awareness, not entirely a new faculty, is a manifestation of a development in sensitivity to the way others attend to the infant's person, and it has important feedback effects on this attention from others, changing the way adults communicate to the child, and it makes the child imitate in new ways.

With strangers, the infant becomes less trusting and playful and more watchful or fearful, and may cry. Absence of the mother leads more quickly to distress and efforts to find her, and this is taken as evidence that 'attachment' to her is developing a new intensity. In play, the baby starts to act with well-marked orientation and timing in relation to the awareness and behaviour of familiar partners: 'showing off' to amuse; seeking applause; trying to attract them into play; or, if they are oriented elsewhere, calling to get help with objects or protection from threats. Confronted with a mirror, the baby, who, before five months, would have been disinterested or avoidant, is now observant, coy or demonstrative, and can be seen to be aware of the communication-limiting tension that exists between his or her expressive and demonstrative self and the instantaneously imitative image.

The infant is also now ready to imitate simple actions of other people on objects, as well as their expressions and gestures. Indeed, about one month before starting to experiment with his or her own syllabic babbling at six months, the baby may imitate well the pitch and prosody of other persons' vocalisations, and may also copy hand movements that resemble gestures of communication (Trevarthen 1986). The six-month-old is beginning to be aware of other persons' line of sight and hand gestures, and tries to understand what they mean when they point to things (Scaife and Bruner 1975; Butterworth and Grover 1988; Bruner 1983, 1990; Butterworth 1991). Indeed, before mastering efficient picking up and manipulation of objects, a baby of three to four months can be interested in what a mother is doing with her hands when she presents a toy (Trevarthen and Marwick 1986). 'Other awareness', and even a capacity for 'observational learning', may be present from the earliest stage of these developments.

After a baby has become six months old, people like to present objects in games and to accompany their actions, or the actions of the infant, with synchronised vocalisations and expressive gestures, giving emotional gloss or 'attunement' to the engagement (Stern 1985). They are excited to do this by the eager way the baby responds. The forms of these emotional and dramatic expressions in play give further evidence that the baby is adapted for, and responsive to, particular patterns of signalling from others, and is becoming more critical of the patterning, more aware of its finer points. Mother and baby join in elaborate displays that extend the principles of 'intersubjective' two-mind control which was seen operating in a simpler, more restrained way in proto-conversations at two months.

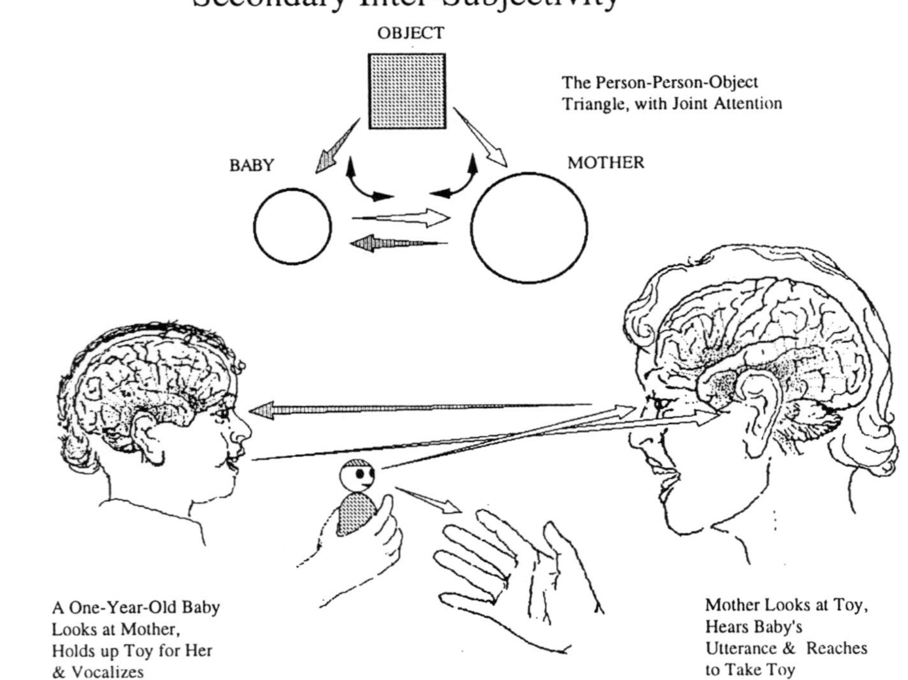

Figure 4: A critical stage in the normal development of human communication that leads to the learning of social and cultural conventions, and to language. At the end of the first year an infant still cannot speak, but does seek to exchange experiences with companions, and cooperates in investigating and acting on the shared world. This involves frequent shifting of the focus of interest and intention from objects to people, and back again.

The rationalist/cognitivist school of psychology explains all such changes in temperament as consequences of changes in awareness, memory or thinking of the baby individual: because tests of orientation to and manipulation of objects with infant subjects show them to have gained new cognitive capacities for all kinds of experiences of 'objects' of interest and goals for action, people, too, are treated in a new way. The baby, they say, *consequently* recognizes strangers as different, knows the mother is temporarily absent and can be expected to return, differentiates effects of self-action from the actions of others (Kagan 1982). Recently, meta-cognitivists attribute such changes in self-awareness to emergence of a 'theory of mind' – the baby starts to act as if attributing consciousness, i.e. awareness and thinking, to others (Baron-Cohen 1987; Leslie 1987). But the facts of the early communication, at a stage when exploration and manipulation of objects has not developed, indicate that emotional or motivational reactions to others, and reciprocal engagement with them and with the direction of their interests, do not require the postulated cognitive development; or, that the cognitive development must be occurring very much earlier than the cognitivist–constructivist theory claims is possible, and without the help of thought in words. A more parsimonious explanation, more in line with the facts of development from birth, is that the self-presenting and self-expressing, and imitative, behaviours of the six- to nine-month-old represent a new state of communication – a transformation of motivations present at birth that are specially adapted to regulate contacts with other people and to engage with their purposes and feelings.

Emergence of Protolanguage, Joint Perspective Taking and Cooperative, Meaningful Use of Objects

At six to nine months infants often concentrate self-centredly on exploration of objects, and on developing their own manipulative activity. They tend to become 'absorbed' in the task; that is, they are for a time mentally isolated and resistant to any overtures from another person to share the object or task.

After nine months there is a crucial transformation in this balance between, on the one hand, exploratory and performatory motives involved in mastery of impersonal objects and, on the other, the motives for contact and communication with people (Bakeman and Adamson 1984; Bretherton and Bates 1979; Bruner 1983 1990; Hubley and Trevarthen 1979; Trevarthen and Hubley 1978). The change is manifested in many new kinds of behaviour that open the child's mind to learning about how other people view the world and how they use the objects in it.

First, the child orients to and follows expressions and actions, for example pointing, by which others present objects for sharing and use them in ways that invite cooperation (Scaife and Bruner 1975; Butterworth and Grover 1988). Conversely, when trying to deal with a task in the presence of the other and encountering a difficulty or a surprising change, the baby tends now to turn to the other for support or help, preferring the mother over the stranger in this, as in all social transactions. When offered instructions, approval or help, the child waits to observe the 'intrusive' gesture or utterance, and then attempts to react to it in a complementary, cooperational way. When attempting to 'perform'; when 'deliberately' teasing or being 'naughty' or 'funny'; when repeating a 'joke' or a forbidden action, such as is usually received with praise or laughter even when the parent is somewhat annoyed – the child observes the partner to see the effect (Reddy 1991).

In short, the expressivity of the child is contrived to make well-timed and well-oriented 'acts of meaning' (Halliday 1975), acts that refer to some event or object in a shared consciousness and that allow for infusion of a shareable emotional appraisal of reality.

In proto-language, vocalisations are combined with gestures to make declarations, indications, observations, orientations, etc., sharing interest in events and combining them with signs of where and when the events are occurring (Bretherton and Bates 1979). This is what is meant by 'protodeclarative pointing', absence of which is one indicator of autism in a one-year-old. Clear invitations, questions, refusals and denials are made by the nine- to twelve-month-old, with appropriately different intonation and gestural form. The combined effect of these behaviours is that the infant becomes a partner in a new level of communication and negotiation of purposes that has been called 'secondary intersubjectivity' (person–person–object interaction (Trevarthen and Hubley 1978)) or 'protolanguage' (Halliday 1975). Its essential feature is the elevation of the shared topic to meaningfulness in joint awareness (Bruner 1975, 1990).

When the development of this remarkable and very human level of communication, which has language-like aspects but which precedes language by several months, is traced in detail, it becomes clear that it is caused by changes in the motivations and awareness of the child. True, it requires support by complementary behaviours of adult partners – they must provide the occasions for a shared perspective on the world and transfusion of knowledge and skill into the infant. But, in an important sense, the initiative is with the child. The older partner enters into a role that has been made active, attractive and satisfying for him or her by the child's new feelings and expressions, alertness and vitality. The mother's emotions are used by the child increasingly to evaluate experiences of the world. The attention an infant gives to how a mother feels about some happening in their common world is called 'emotional referencing' (Klinnert *et al.* 1983; Stern, Hofer, Haft and Dore 1985); and it plays a central role in the child's learning from then on. The partner generously uses praise, shared enthusiasm and 'naming with approval' to expand the infant's interest in reality.

By treating objects and events as having more properties than can be tested by his or her own efforts alone, the child opens the way to conventional and symbolic awareness of a social or cultural reality – one that has been built up by people comparing feelings, interests and actions in relation to their different experiences (Tomasello, Kruger and Ratner 1993). Thus the one-year-old embarks on a uniquely human quest with its own psychological motives – a quest for knowledge or meaning of a kind that is essentially shareable. This is the first step in what becomes a rapid development towards symbolic and cultural life and towards both the need for, and mastery of, language (Halliday 1975; Trevarthen 1987a; Trevarthen and Logotheti 1987; Trevarthen 1992). It is at about this time that a child developing autism becomes noticeably 'different', both less aware and less cooperative.

It is important to emphasise that the motivation for acquiring symbolic means of expression is not confined to a speech and hearing system. Understanding of symbols is organised at a deeper level and can be attached to different senses and expressed by different parts of the body. For example, besides permitting the dawning of recognition of the conventional nature of simple artifacts, rituals, manners, and roles by which people share cultural awareness, it gives the child a capacity to acquire the beginnings of languages that are independent of speech; languages that are felt and seen, instead of heard. In a deaf family that uses hand sign language for daily communication, a deaf or hearing baby can begin to pick up and use signs before one year of age (Bellugi, van Hoek, Lillo-Martin and O'Grady 1988; Newport and Meier 1985; Volterra 1981). Given appropriate affectionate encouragement through use of written words in cooperative games, a one-year-old can begin to read whole words. There is even evidence that instruction of a deaf toddler in reading can enable the child to acquire fluent reading before the age of entry to primary school, and thus keep up with the reading ability of hearing-speaking peers (Söderbergh 1986).

These variants of normal education for language prove that the foundations for learning symbols are not confined to the cognitive system that processes sounds of speech or that coordinates the oral motor apparatus to produce speech. Further support for this conclusion is to be found in the gestures that all people make unconsciously when they speak (McNeill 1992). These hand movements may not be conventionalised in a language, but they do convey thoughts being put into speech, and they do so at the same time, or even a moment before, the utterance of words. They take over and strive to convey clarity when speaking becomes difficult.

An interesting manifestation of the brain's organisation for communication by symbols lies in the fact that both spontaneous gestures and the signs of hand-sign languages are typically asymmetric. The majority of people, of all ages, make more explicit other-directed moves of their hand with their right hands. Most infants, too, start to exhibit a consistent handedness for skilled actions, usually preferring the right hand at the same time as they acquire proficiency in language, in the second and third year (Trevarthen 1986). They show this hand preference for imitated gestures, for pointing, greeting and many other acts of meaning, and for meaningful manipulation of such cultural objects, or tools, as feeding utensils, pencils, brushes, combs, etc. A majority appear to be right-handed, and left-brained, for all such 'other-directed' meaningful behaviours. A minority are firmly left-handed. Others are slower to show consistent handedness and may remain 'mixed' in hand preferences. As we have seen, autistic children have been thought to have less clear handedness.

Toddlers' Role Play: Imitating to Communicate and Pretending to Know

By the middle of the second year a toddler is starting to pick up many conventional, meaningful ways of behaving and ways of using artifacts. Learning by observing others and imitating fuels the development of creative play in socially recognised roles, and leads to acting out of performances such as having a cup of tea, talking on the 'phone, preparing a meal, driving a car, vacuuming, pretending conversations and attitudes in encounters or purposeful actions with puppets or dolls, and so on. Such meaningful tasks or roles are often closely observed and performed with accurate imitation in the second year, before the child has any clearly recognisable words. Thus, some skills of culture start to be picked up, at least as ways of acting, before language, or while language is in its most rudimentary 'protolanguage' phase. The conventional meanings of actions and tools or instruments can be assimilated by observing others before the words used as labels for these things are understood.

Of course, cognitive powers are needed to perceive what the meaningful objects are like, to apprehend their spatio-temporal coordinates, to identify and compare them, to solve practical or physical problems of how they may be combined and transformed. The child has also to be able to discriminate the communicative signs of other people and to perceive how they are combined. But the crucial factor that makes reality meaningful for a toddler is the special orientation the child takes towards other people and their way of intruding on and evaluating reality. A child with severe sensory or motor deficit can master communication well, if it is given a way to meet other people's ideas and respond to their expressions. An autistic child with no defect of senses or movements fails to communicate.

The first two years of life are a period of observation, instruction and practice in detecting and negotiating with the wills and emotions of other persons, an apprenticeship supported in a relationship of trust through affectionate individualised attachments (Rogoff 1990). However, the intimacy and mutual confidence of a good relationship largely conceals these motivations and how they are realised. They can be brought out by comparison with the behaviour of the same child with strangers or with peers, neither of whom can support the toddler in as high a level of imaginative and cooperative play as can the mother.

Peers stimulate a child below two to convergent and imitative patterns of action, in which pursuit of meaning tends to repetition with little progress. Thus two-year-olds find it difficult to cooperate with one another in a creative task, but they may greatly enjoy creating symmetry of play that involves much mimicry, and that may generate conflict if the interest of two children focuses on one goal (Nadel 1986; Nadel-Brulfert and Baudonnière 1982. What they can achieve depends on how well they know and like each other. Non-friends do not play with as much mutual interest and pleasure. Simple acts of giving and taking can go on between friends, they can even express feelings about the rightness or wrongness of actions, but the performance of 'tasks' is limited, in comparison with the asymmetrical play of the same child in the presence of a trusted adult. The adult playmate will automatically supply props in an appropriately considerate and cooperative way, or at least will assure the potential availability of such a supply, and will make approving noises, joining with appreciative comments into the child's efforts at meaningful action (Rogoff 1990). The behaviours of normal two-year-olds show they are passing through a major change in their ability to imagine meaning and to share in social conventions. This development goes beyond the acquisition of language, and beyond cognitive functions that might be called 'self-awareness'.

Most children speak clear words in short telegraphic sentences by two, and this is the beginning of a phase of accelerating vocabulary learning. By 30 months a child and mother playing together may make almost equal verbal contributions (Stewart-Clarke and Hevey 1981). Toddlers chatter about what they are doing and discuss their experiences and plans, demonstrating a considerable repertoire of socially and culturally defined ideas and skills.

Studies of the way children play with meaningful objects and with dolls reveal that after one year they gain rapidly in representational or symbolic awareness. They are also more and more interested in how their ideas are perceived by others. By 18 months, mere 'sensory-motor' play, taking objects for their obvious 'physical' appearances and uses, has become a minor component, the child preferring to take up things as objects that have a defined use in the culture; seeing spoons, cups, brushes, telephones, baskets, pots, knives, cars and so on as attractive because they can be used 'properly' in 'routine representational schemas' (Rosenblatt 1977). When dolls are available play becomes, after 18 months, increasingly doll-directed. This seems to be another manifestation of a spontaneous opening out of self-related imitative consciousness towards more cooperative other-directed understanding.

By the end of the second year pretend play exhibits more complex ideas, requiring more elaborate combinations of objects and sequences of action (Lowe 1975; Nicholich 1977). The child is beginning to make substitutions of meaning or 'metaphorical' uses of objects, taking the act of communication and meaning-creation to transform an object and to have it be named as something else (Lowe 1975; Matthews 1977). At the same time, the two- to three-year-old is taking up socially approved and cooperatively motivated roles, boys and girls beginning to choose different play themes (Fein 1981).

With the use of language that most children have gained by three years, absent things become topics for conversation. This allows anyone who speaks the same 'mother tongue' to meet and satisfy the child's growing imagination and curiosity about the shared world and its meanings and roles, whether the ideas are about things that are actually present in the 'here and now' or not. Sharing stories about people and places – real or imaginary; past, present or yet to come – becomes a favourite game.

Three-year-olds with strong friendships may exhibit clear discriminations about the age and sex of other children, knowing well who is a 'big' child, and who is 'little'. Especially among friends, pretend play is increasingly absorbed in elaborated socio-dramatic themes with the children taking complementary, rather than imitative, roles and often demonstrating elaborate knowledge of real family and social life. This play is sustained and rapidly extended by the increasing fluency in language.

The evidence we have from studies of toddlers and nursery school children, briefly sketched here, shows clearly that growing cultural understanding is in good strong life before formal schooling begins. The reasoning of the preschool child takes place in awareness of everyday things that are shared and evaluated with friends. Adjustments are made to the age and familiarity of companions which reflect the confidence and ability the children have with symbolic awareness. The child learns with what Margaret Donaldson (1978) calls 'human sense'.

This learning by cooperating is seen in all cultures, whatever their forms of language or technology. Studies of cultures that differ widely in family and social organisation, in manners, beliefs and technology support the idea that young children everywhere, in spite of being viewed by adults in different ways, are making the same kind of active entry into their society and its culture well before the age of five (Rogoff 1990; Trevarthen 1992). In this learning they receive support from elders that is matched to the child's interests and abilities. In some cultures, three-year-olds can perform useful 'work', this being but slightly different from the preferred play of children of other cultures who are not given responsibility so young.

Developmental Psychologists' Models of Autism and its Development

Recent attempts to explain autism have been influenced by theories about mental processes derived from cognitive science and computer logic, by the findings of more naturalistic observations of the psychological development of

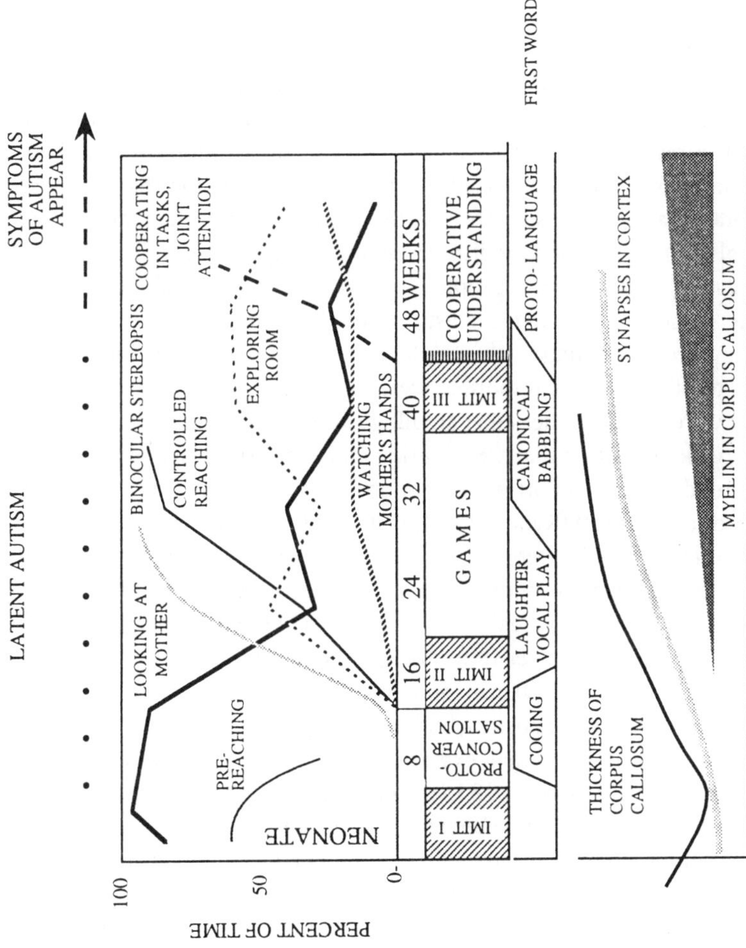

Figure 5: Developments in behaviour during the first year of infancy and some changes in brain anatomy

children and by new discoveries about brain development and about abnormalities in the brains of autistic individuals. There is a greater willingness in recent reviews of the now very large literature on autistic children to take all kinds of evidence into account.

In an effort to establish a scientific, objective and well-measured set of procedures for assessing cognitive or linguistic attainments of autistic children and for administering treatment, Schopler and Rutter, two highly influential authorities, were led to reject ideas that the condition involves a basic abnormality of emotion, or of emotional communication (Rutter 1968, 1978, 1983, 1985; Rutter, Bartak and Newman 1971; Rutter and Schopler 1978; Schopler, Reichler and Lancing 1980). Dismissing the psychoanalytic assumption that such a pattern of emotional stiffness or coldness and unapproachability could only be the result of an environmental stress or deprivation (Mahler 1952; Bettelheim 1967), they overlooked the simpler interpretation that an autistic child's brain has an intrinsic defect in the generation of communicative and emotional responses because of disorganisation in a system specifically adapted for regulating contact with people. In consequence, careful observations, including those by the psychoanalysts, on the behaviours of autistic children when they are interacting with people, with accurate information on their reactions to other persons' responses, were for a time neglected. It was claimed that they were based on ideas that are illogical or too intuitive.

Observations confirm that the orienting and expressive responses of autistic children tend to cut them off from emotional and communicative transactions with those around them (Kanner 1943; Hutt and Ounsted 1966; Richer 1978, 1983; Tinbergen and Tinbergen 1983; Hobson 1983, 1987). This evidently is related to (and may produce, rather than reflect) mis-timing of expressive behaviours of autistic individuals and break-down of the patterns that normally sustain efficient reciprocity or turn-taking in communication (Condon 1975; Feldstein, Konstantareas, Oxman and Webster 1982; Beebe *et al.* 1985). Experiments show that autistic children have difficulty in perceiving the differences between emotional expressions and in judging other personal attributes of people (Hobson 1983, 1986a, b; Hobson *et al.* 1988a, b). At the same time, the affected child is abnormally sensitive and distorted in awareness of and attention to many sorts of environmental stimuli, unable to solve cognitive problems that should be simple for a child of that age and, when not mute, bizarre in social use of speech. But these features of the disorder in no way contradict the view that a specific deficit in person-perception and in motivation toward persons is the root of the problem. Indeed, it is the rule for attentional and cognitive processes to be close-coupled to motivation for communication. Attention, cognition and memory are typically defective or abnormal in emotional illness.

The course of normal development, outlined above, demonstrates that children are dependent on learning by way of sensitive identification and cooperation with people and that they are naturally interested in what other people experience, feel and intend. Autistic children are severely deficient in these vital responses (Sigman 1989).

Mundy and Sigman (1989) review evidence on the social responses of autistic children and conclude that they show impairment first in affective responses and non-verbal communication. Hobson presents a theoretical interpretation of data on interpersonal relations and communications, which he summarises as follows:

> Autistic children have a biologically based impairment of affective-conative relatedness with the environment, which has especially far reaching implications for their social relations. The defining characteristic of autism is a uniquely severe disruption in the children's personal relatedness with others. (Hobson 1989)

In a recent review of the psychological characteristics of autistic children and a discussion of rival models of the disorder and its causes in development, Rogers and Pennington (1991) conclude that autistic children retain affectionate reactions to persons they know well because this kind of learning emerges early in development, in the first nine months. As we have mentioned, affectionate attachment to the mother may, in fact, begin before birth by auditory learning, and preferences in relationships are clear from early infancy. On the other hand, as Rogers and Pennington point out, reciprocal imitation and joint perspective taking, at a level where they contribute crucially to cultural learning, are selectively impaired in autism (Tomasello, Kruger and Ratner 1993). These are behaviours that develop after nine months and that become elaborated in the second and third years.

The philosophical 'Theory of Mind' theory of Leslie, Baron-Cohen and Frith (Baron-Cohen, Leslie and Frith 1985; Leslie 1987), which emphasises developments in general cognition that are hypothesised to generate awareness of awareness, and also pretence in the form of imagination about what might be, and to permit emergence of awareness of other persons' knowledge and beliefs, is set aside by Rogers and Pennington. They also give qualified acceptance to Hobson's theory that the main defect is in emotional relating to other persons in favour of a model based on Stern (1985), who describes stages by which the infant constructs a 'self' in interpersonal relations and through communication. They concur with Sigman (1989) that examination of the deficits of autism within the framework of normal development has both theoretical importance and pragmatic utility.

In Chapter 7 we summarised the evidence that autism is caused by a fault in brain development. There would seem to be very secure anatomico-functional grounds for regarding autism as primarily developmental disorders in the *regulation* of cognitive and learning systems, with a central disturbance of the socio-emotional processes that are essential to communication and the transmission of learning by human instruction (cf Fein *et al.* 1986). This kind of learning is the key process by which a child learns to understand the world like the older members of his or her community. Thus it now seems likely, for example, that slowly maturing cortical systems that result in different cognitive activities in the two cerebral hemispheres, or in development of different sections of the cognitive mechanism in the brain such as may be tapped by different kinds of intelligence test, owe their initial differentiation to the projection into them of different influences from the brain stem during prenatal hemispheric growth (Trevarthen 1987b, 1989b, 1990b).

Increasing evidence that growth and differentiation of the cerebral cortex may be directed by reticular and limbic influences, i.e. by chemicals transmitted from cells in the brain stem and more ancient and earlier developing parts of the hemispheres, cells that can become organised in some independence of input to the special senses both before and after birth, gives new perspectives for theories of learning. It also opens the way for a theory that would give emotional states, which are sustained by patterns of activity in the same reticular and limbic systems, a role in regulation of brain development (Trevarthen 1987b, 1989b). These new ideas tend to reverse the traditional concept that emotions are by-products of rational processes, and they are compatible with the theory that autism is a disorder in the regulation of brain growth that has its effect at a particular stage of development, beginning about the end of the first year of infancy (Trevarthen 1989a). Recent studies of human psychological development compared with developments in the behaviours of monkeys that relate to known steps in the development of the monkey's brain give support to the idea that the symptoms of autism appear when parts of the frontal lobes of the human brain are rapidly developing. The evidence for this 'frontal hypothesis' is reviewed by Rogers and Pennington (1991).

Neuropathological and neurophysiological findings summarised in Chapter 7 support the idea that autism is a disorder of the same regulatory core system of the brain that is found to control the patterning of normal brain maturation and to motivate learning in the adult. If this is so, cognitive and linguistic disabilities that autistic children commonly come to have are probably consequences of abnormal neocortical development *produced by* the core systems, rather than causes of the disease in its emotional facets. It seems justified to conclude that emotional abnormality and consequent deficits in social communication are expressions of an essential starting feature of the abnormal path of brain maturation; not a byproduct of general information-handling cognitive or learning deficits.

A different approach to understanding autism, as well as related developmental diseases of the brain that reduce intelligence, such as Rett's syndrome, promises to assist our comprehension of genetic regulation of growth and differentiation of neural systems in the brain. It may also lead to improved methods for mitigating the effects of autism and related diseases, by helping us understand how best to manage the abnormal child's emotions in communication, and so to assist improved motivation for engagement with the environment, especially the 'human environment', and more efficient retention of experiences that favour positive mental growth.

Arguing from a thorough comparison of symptoms in autism with the effects of neurological disorder in different parts of the brain in adults (see Damasio and Van Hoesen 1983), Damasio and Maurer (1978) proposed that the behavioural and motor disturbances of autism result from dysfunction in mesolimbic cortex, the neostriatum and anterior and medial thalamic nuclei. This region, they point out, forms the entire target area of dopaminergic neurones of the midbrain tegmentum. It is not clear how the more recently discovered cerebellar defects would fit with deficiency in the above system. Ornitz (1983) presents evidence that the disturbances of sensory modulation of autistic children may result from malfunction of the reticular core of the diencephalon and brainstem. There is evidence that autism is associated with the kind of disturbances in attention and perception that would be expected to follow from disturbances to the mechanisms by which cerebral cortical activity is regulated by subhemispheric systems (Dawson and Lewy 1989a,b).

All the above observed or inferred abnormalities of brain and mind would result from underdevelopment or a functional defect arising early in development, in the first half of infancy or even in early foetal or late embryo stages (before the fifth month of gestation). This strengthens the case for regarding autism as a genetic disease of brain growth, or a consequence of early infection.

A claim that autism is caused by atrophy of the left cerebral cortex, identified because that is the part of the brain where critical parts of the mechanism for language are located, is not supported by psychological or physiological and anatomical studies (Fein *et al.* 1984). On the other hand, the left hemisphere does undergo a spurt of neocortical differentiation at the stage autistic symptoms become evident at the close of infancy (Thatcher, Walker and Giudice 1987), and it does appear to be more susceptible to damage in autistic or retarded subjects. After reviewing the evidence, Fein *et al.* (1984, 1986) reject the idea that autism is primarily a language disorder consequent on left hemisphere pathology, and they point out that some symptoms, including deficient awareness of prosody in speech, and of emotional expression in general, and repetitive, compulsive behaviour would rather indicate faults in the right hemisphere.

In contrast to Fein *et al.* (1986) and Rogers and Pennington (1991), Damasio and Maurer (1978) appear to want to distance themselves from Kanner's view that autism is primarily a disorder in social behaviour and to ascribe the syndrome to 'an organized collection of primary defects that we described under disturbances of motility, disturbances in attention and ritualistic and compulsive behaviour, as well as under disturbances of communication' (p.782). However, they admit that the mesocortical structures they believe to be defective in autism, 'relay limbic system information back to the neocortex', and they continue – 'thus, appropriate affective labelling of stimuli in the process of learning, as well as appropriate affective recognition of the same stimuli later in life, may depend on the integrity of this way station' (p.783). It is not clear why they do not admit socio-affective deficits as primary when the same limbic structures are so crucially involved in affective expression and affective awareness (Heilman and Satz 1983).

Conclusion: Developing Humanness is Essentially Interpersonal

We can summarise the argument of this chapter as follows:

(1) Infants are ready from birth to establish communication with their caretakers by means of emotional or motivational expressions and sensitivities, imitating and making utterance-like messages. With appropriate support from an identified and affectionate caretaker, they communicate at this proto-conversational level elaborately and efficiently before they begin manipulative testing of 'object concepts'. Indeed, reactions to a mother's vocalisations, and learning to identify her by voice, starts before birth. Subsequently, the child's cognitive development and 'processing' of experience, which advances rapidly after the development of strong head support and effective reaching and grasping at four months, are regulated by emotions in play with other people, whose interests and actions are complemented and imitated by the child. After infancy, toddlers develop representations, conventional and role-based play as they learn language. They also develop cooperative skills with peers, copying gestures and tasks and sharing lively and imaginative communication.

(2) Of these developments, the ones that develop after the end of the first year, which normally lead a child towards proficiency in the culture's meanings and its 'mother tongue', are impaired in autism. It would appear, therefore, that this developmental disorder originates in failure of the cerebral systems that regulate a child's motivation for learning meanings in communication.

(3) Present knowledge of brain abnormalities that accompany autism, or that produce autism-like disorders in monkeys and in adult human beings, are compatible with the above interpretation. They are not

supportive of the view that the emotional and interpersonal aspects of autism are consequences of primary failure in sensory, motor or linguistic processes. Nor do they support the hypothesis that the central deficit in autism is the lack of a cognitive capacity to 'represent mental states', although such a deficit does appear to follow from the primary fault in immediate awareness of changing relationships to other persons and their feelings, and how to cooperate with them through communication.

CHAPTER 9

Communicating and Playing with an Autistic Child

How Autism Might Begin

Given that an infant, even one only a month or two old, can join in a 'conversation' of feelings with a caregiver, a meeting of motives for expression that needs contributions from both that person and the baby, it follows that the communication could break down by defect in the person-recognising 'conversation regulator' of either party. For the infant, this is an argument that predicts disorders of communication due to faulty sensitivity for the mother's feelings or abnormal reaction to what she does. On the mother's side, emotional illness that suppresses free expression of feelings and reduces responses to other persons' feelings (postnatal depression, for example) should interfere with her support of her infant's readiness for affectionate and playful contact. Indeed, there is evidence that a depressed or psychotic mother cannot support protoconversational play, and that this is disturbing for the infant, and it can have lasting effects (Cohn and Tronick 1983; Fraiberg 1980; Murray 1988, 1992).

In the same way, but in the opposite sense, it is likely that infantile autism, which can be differentiated from the emotional problems resulting from maternal emotional withdrawal, is a disorder in the child's capacity for perception of emotions and for interpersonal recognition, as many child psychiatrists and psychologists accept (Hobson 1989, 1993a; Rogers and Pennington 1991).

Autism is a disorder that becomes increasingly critical when the child develops motivation to attempt more elaborate mental exchange in the early stages of language acquisition. To explain the characteristic cognitive disorders of autism and the peculiarities of language development in autistic children we must, therefore, consider how development of an infant's knowledge of the world, problem-solving and use of words all depend on sharing of communication with others, and on the emotional regulation of this sharing.

It may be concluded, further, that information on this critical phase of early child development, information that emphasises both the social or interpersonal and cognitive aspects, will be an essential component in training for teachers who are destined to work with autistic children of whatever age; that is, that such training is important for teachers working in preschool, primary and secondary levels, wherever they are concerned with autistic children.

We know that infants developing normally are highly motivated to engage in interactions with their mothers and other adults, and as they grow older, we see them become increasingly competent in the comprehension and expression of language. These developmental milestones appear deviant in autistic children. Evidence on how development deviates can be found in retrospective studies of infants later diagnosed as autistic, in empirical studies of autistic children's verbal and non-verbal communication, and in the analysis of playful interactions between autistic children and their mothers.

The Earliest Stages

It is difficult to know if autism is manifested at birth. There is anecdotal evidence about the behaviour of autistic children in early infancy taken from retrospective parental reports and video data. It seems that the pattern normally observed in the pre-linguistic stage of development is distorted in autism. Some mothers report that there was something abnormal with their child since he/she was born, and others that they recognised a problem developing slowly as the child progressed through the first three years. Approximately one-third of the children show normal behaviour early in life and a regression appears just before the age of three years. For example, Eriksson and DeChateau (1992) analysed videotapes of an autistic girl filmed from birth and observed that although she was developing normally during the first year, later she became withdrawn without any apparent medical or biological reason. Some autistic infants cry rarely without demanding any attention. However, others cry very often, they even scream, and they have feeding and sleeping problems. There is a lack of interest in social contact and in the human voice. They smile, but not in response to social approaches. In the final part of their first year they do not show exploratory behaviour of their environment and they do not engage in shared activities with their parents. They are self-content to manipulate a specific object over a period of time and they can be fascinated with certain sensory experiences (Wing 1976).

There are several studies that report features of the autistic syndrome very early in infancy and the effects of the children's behaviour on their mothers. Massie, in an early study, reported features of the mother's behaviour with their infants who later became autistic. He claimed that mothers of 'psychotic' (that is 'autistic') children were relatively insensitive to their child's smiles and eye contact in the period from birth to six months (Massie 1978a). In analysis of interactions in the first six months, mothers and babies showed lower frequencies for holding, and mothers showed lower ratings for touching and mutual eye-to-eye gaze compared with normal mother–infant interaction (Massie 1978b). It is likely that such features of mothers' behaviour are reactive to the strange behaviour of the babies.

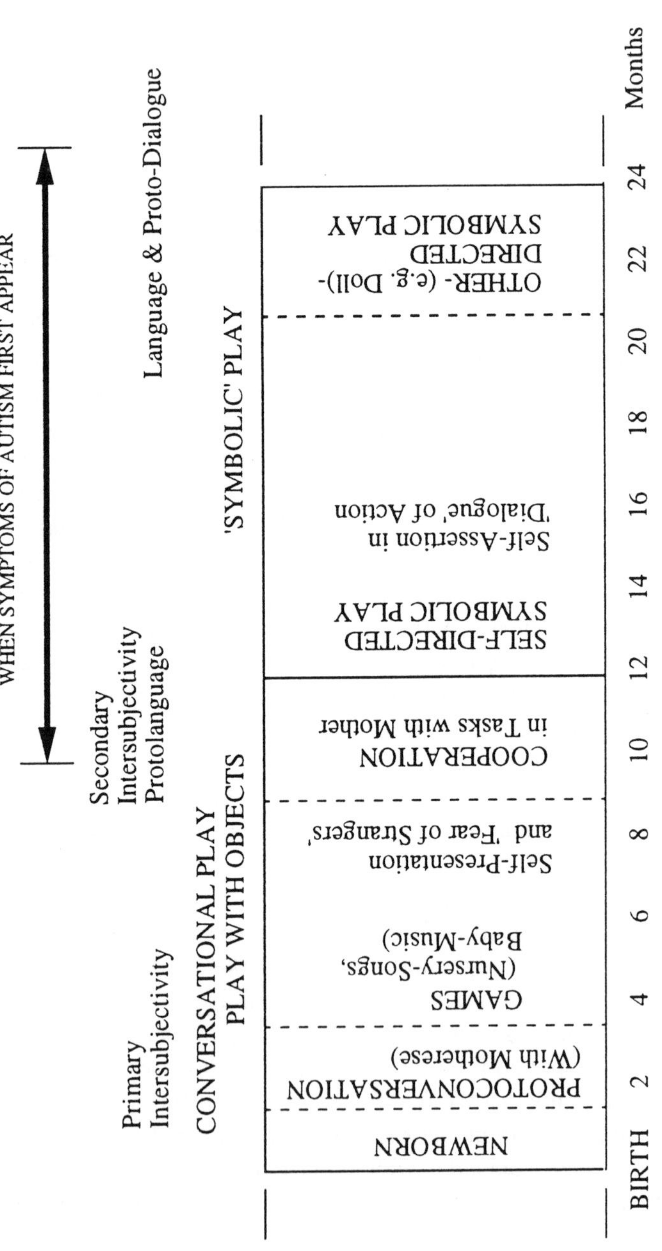

Figure 6: Charts of developments in communication and play in infancy and during preschool years

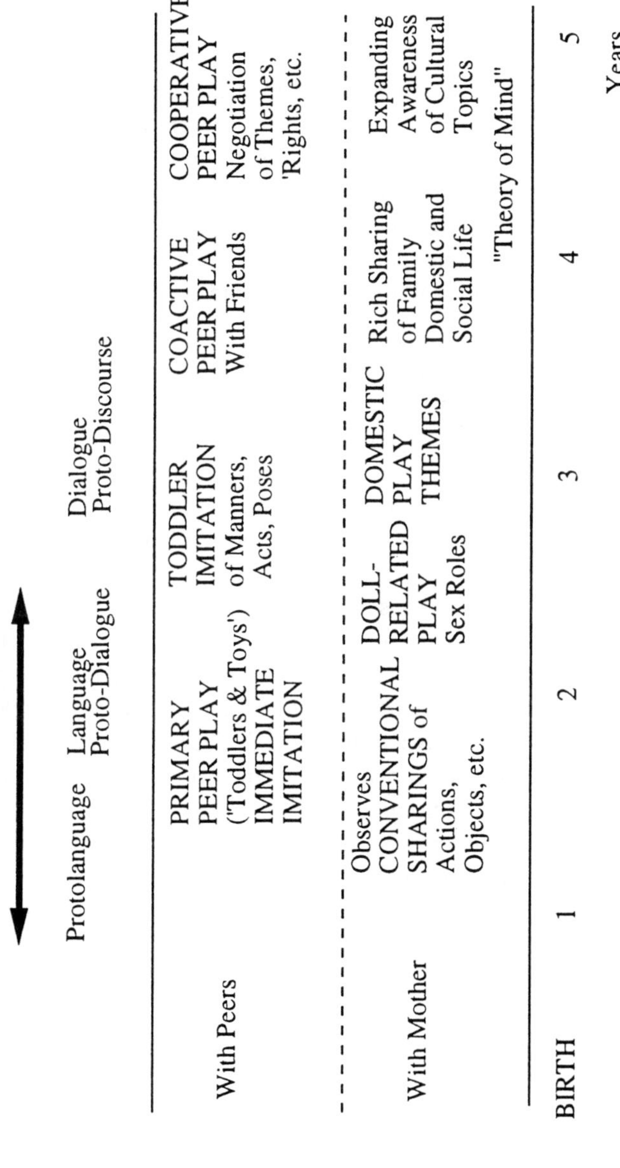

Figure 6: Charts of developments in communication and play in infancy and during preschool years (continued)

Sparling (1991), in analysis of a prospective case study, reported that abnormalities in expressive and receptive communication, and in eye contact during interaction with the mother, could be observed at three months, even though the mother's interactive style was characterised as of high 'quality' and 'appropriateness'. Kubicek (1980) described the organisation of two mother–infant interactions involving a normal infant and his fraternal twin brother who was later diagnosed as autistic (Twin A). These recordings were made when the infants were between 3 and 16 weeks of age. She reported that:

> ...[the] system of mutual exchange, based on subtle differences in facial expression and body movement, never occurred in the interaction between the mother and Twin A. Twin A failed to provide his mother with positive feedback, which is considered essential for establishing a 'normal' mother–infant interaction... Furthermore, he did not respond differentially to subtle changes in maternal behaviours, making it difficult for her to respond appropriately... (Kubicek 1980, p.109)

Other studies give information about the development of a possible autistic disorder later in infancy. Adrien, Faure, Perrot, Hameury, Garreau, Barthèlèmy, and Sauvage (1991) analysed home movies of children later diagnosed as autistic. They observed that in the first two years problems with social interaction, emotional disorders, abnormal visual and auditory behaviours, atypical behaviour and disorders of tone and motor behaviour appeared. In another study of ten cases in the same age range, it was revealed the same kind of behaviours were identified as differentiating autistic from normally developing children. These behaviours were described as poor social interaction and poor communication (no social smile, lack of appropriate facial expressions and gestures), restricted adaptation to environmental situations (hypoactivity), reduced motility (calmness and hypotonia), depressed emotional reactions (no expression of emotions) and abnormal attention (poor concentration) (Adrien, Perrot, Hameury, Martineau, Roux and Sauvage 1991).

The above studies argue that the interaction which takes place between autistic infants and their mothers does not follow the pathway of the reciprocal, rhythmically timed and synchronised communication that is typical of the normally developing baby. Later, as the infant grows older and the acquisition of skills for verbal and non-verbal communication is expected, much clearer impairments emerge in the autistic population. All diagnostic descriptions specify an impairment in communication – verbal and non-verbal, receptive and expressive.

Development of Communication and Language in Toddlers with Autism

Ricks (1979) investigated the way in which preverbal autistic children, between their third and sixth birthday, and normally-developing infants in their first two years of life, conveyed emotional meaning in four different types of sounds, to express request, frustration, greeting and pleasant surprise. He found that parents of autistic children were able to recognise their own child and normally developing children from their sounds, but they were not able to identify the sounds of other autistic children. Thus, the signals given by preverbal autistic children were perceived as idiosyncratic. They lacked the universal features observed in the normal infants and toddlers.

Autistic children have problems with comprehension of language. The severity of their problems is influenced by the content of language and the context in which a concept is expressed (Garfin and Lord 1986). Their expressive language is also both deviant and delayed (Cunningham 1968). Typical peculiarities include both immediate and delayed echoing of speech, reversing the person ('I' or 'me' vs. 'you') that pronouns refer to (Kanner 1943; Rutter 1978), stereotypic utterances, often repeated with no discernable meaning (Rutter 1978; DSM-III-R 1987), abnormal prosodic patterns (Tager-Flusberg 1989) and inappropriate metaphors (Kanner 1946). If speech is present, it is not used spontaneously and functionally in conversation (Rutter 1978; DSM-III-R 1987).

Autistic children who do speak do not often exhibit severe problems in the phonological and syntactic development of the language. It is the semantic and functional use of words, in appropriate relation to the pragmatic or social context, that constitutes the basic deficit (Tager-Flusberg 1981). Delayed language production is manifested in the use of speech spontaneously and functionally in conversation (Rutter 1978) and in using language for clearly depicted purposes of communication (Cunningham 1968). Autistic individuals have difficulties in giving, requesting or sharing information (Cunningham 1968; Hurtig, Ensrud and Tomblin 1982), in conversational turn-taking (Prizant and Schuler 1987), and in speaker–hearer relationships (Baltaxe 1977).

Clearly the problem goes beyond language in the limited sense of use of words. Deficits in non-verbal communication are also reported (Kanner 1943; Ricks and Wing 1975). Autistic children do not anticipate by reaching out when they are to be picked up (Ricks and Wing 1975; DSM-III-R 1987) and they show abnormalities in eye-to-eye contact (Hutt and Ounsted 1966; Rutter 1978; DSM-III-R 1987), in imitation (Rogers and Pennington 1991), in comprehension and expression of facial expressions (Hobson 1983, 1986a, 1986b; Snow *et al.* 1987; Yirmiya *et al.* 1989) and gestures, including pointing (Curcio 1978; Ohta 1987; Attwood, Frith and Hermelin 1988).

Getting at the Essential Problem in Autistic Intersubjectivity

If we are to understand why autistic children have deficits in social relationships and communication, we should first be clear what constitutes 'communication', and we should observe the interpersonal and realistic or practical world in which communication takes place. Human life depends on rich cooperation between the mental activities of conscious, feeling and intending persons; that is, on 'intersubjectivity'.

There are many ways to begin an analysis of how far children cooperate socially, depending on how mental life is conceived. McHale (1983) defined communication in terms of mere physical proximity or aggregation; children were considered to be part of a group if they were within five feet of one another. On this criterion, autistic children may communicate much less than other children, but they do not completely lack communicative interest. In terms of Speech Act Theory (Austin 1962), which analyses the *communicative intentions* of language users, autistic children can, again, be viewed as interactive to some degree, since they do use verbal and non-verbal communication intentionally to reach certain goals with other persons' aid (Wetherby and Prutting 1984; Wetherby 1986). In the framework of the theory of *pragmatics in language*, defining the effects of utterances or gestures between people, what they do to each other with language, the abnormal language of autistic children can still be seen to have a functional role, though a limited one.

For example, a single, apparently meaningless, repeated utterance of a four-year-old boy was found to be used effectively as a tool to engage his conversational partner in interaction (Coggins and Frederickson 1988). The deficiencies in speech acts and pragmatics of high functioning autistic individuals are subtle (Loveland *et al.* 1988). On the other hand, when communication is studied in terms of the use of '*joint-attention*' or '*shared focus*' (Mundy *et al.* 1986; Sigman *et al.* 1986), autistic children appear characteristically impaired. They show a marked inability to engage with and direct another's attention and they do not use postures or gestures such as pointing to help other people share what they are experiencing or thinking about (Jordan 1993). Moreover, those individuals who do share attention more are also more advanced in their use and understanding of language (Loveland and Landry 1986; Mundy, Sigman and Kasari 1990). Thus it would appear that the central problem in communication of autistic children has to do with the autistic child's recognition of the 'interpersonal' functions of language (Lyons 1977), rather than with the cognitive and rational systems involved in the comprehension or expression of words and the formulation of grammatical constructions. The problem concerns the child's interest and concern for communicating, and any loss of linguistic capability is apparently a secondary effect.

The difficulty that autistic children have in understanding others and in interpersonal motives for *cultural learning* (Hobson 1993; Tomasello *et al.* 1993) does not mean that they are insensitive to others and unaffected by who other persons are. It is reported that autistic children change the form or content of their communications depending on their social partners. Freitag (1970 observed that autistic children show less positive response to an encouraging or supportive adult than normally developing children, but McHale *et al.* (1980) found a higher level of communicative behaviour among autistic children when a teacher was present. Another study (Bernard-Opitz 1982) revealed that an autistic boy communicated verbally more frequently with his mother and a clinician than with a stranger, and the level of the communication was higher when the mother or the stranger responded to the child's initiations.

Autistic children show *imitation* and they may be highly sensitive to other persons' imitations of what they do. In a study of play (Tiegerman and Primavera 1981), it was found that the frequency and duration of object manipulation was higher when the experimenter imitated the child's behaviour. Nadel's work (Nadel and Peze 1993) confirms that autistic children, though they are abnormal in the reciprocation of imitative behaviours, can imitate, and an autistic child can become more communicative when their partner imitates them, developing communicative exchange through imitation (Tiegerman and Primavera 1984). Nadel and Fontaine (1989) emphasise the special temporary role of imitative behaviour in the development of communicative understanding in infants and toddlers, and Nadel (1992) and Nadel and Peze (1993) show that the same developmental succession can be seen, but at later ages, in autistic children, who, while they cannot communicate well, do show social interest and do watch others.

Richer (1978), who accepts an ethological approach based on research into the instinctive controls of animal communication and the theory of motivational conflict, observed that autistic children's avoidance is often followed by, and may seek, an adult's approach. Clark and Rutter (1981), seeking to better understand the conditions that favour teaching of autistic children, investigated the way certain types of social approach involving a high degree of structure combined with low interpersonal demands facilitate interaction of autistic children with others. A more recent study (Landry and Loveland 1989) reports that autistic children did not show more attention-seeking behaviour when in a situation that was directed and structured by an adult.

Thus the social impairment in autism appears not to reside mainly in a lack of social and emotional responsiveness of the child, or in imitative tendency, but to reflect a specific failure in comprehension of how to reciprocate with other people (Sigman and Mundy 1989). This interpretation of autistic children's behaviour with others, which draws a distinction between the sensitivity of the autistic child to other known persons and the difficulty that the child has in exchanging interests and point of view, is supported by studies that examined the *attachment behaviour* in autism. It was shown that autistic children exhibit social responses to separation from and reunion with their caregivers like other children, and that they direct more social responses to their mothers

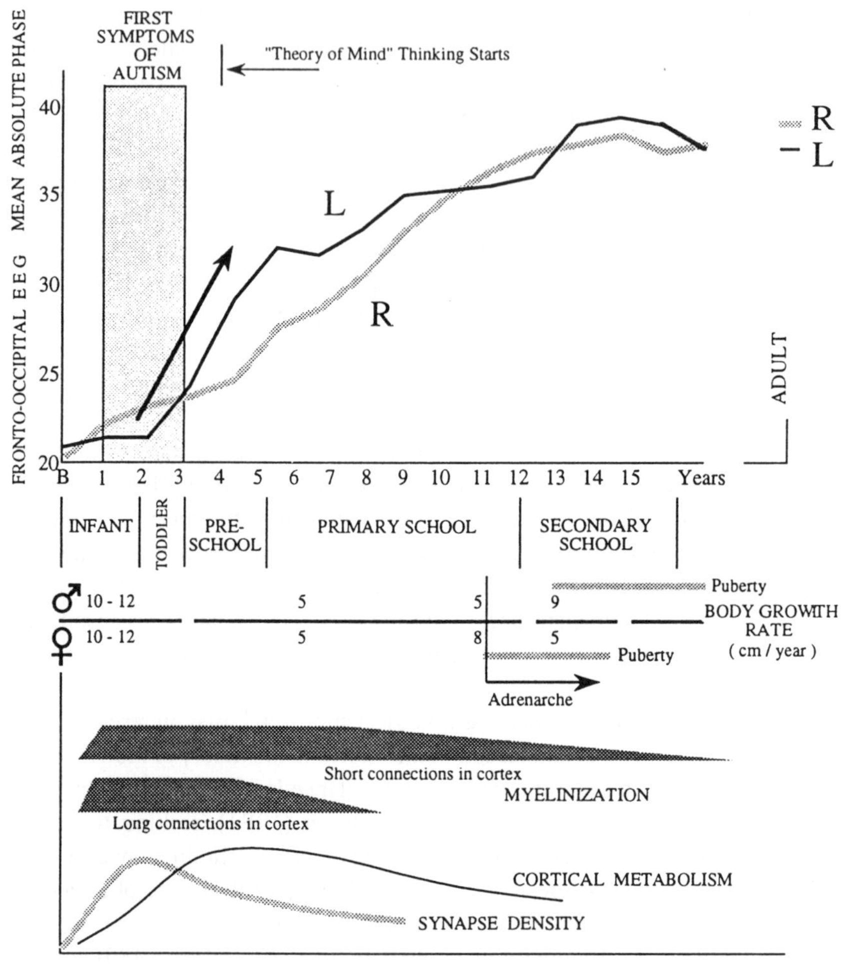

Figure 7: Chart to show the great growth of the brain in preschool and early primary years. Connections in the left cerebral hemisphere (L) grow rapidly as the vocabulary of speech develops from two to six years. The right hemisphere connections (R) develop earlier, in infancy, when communication is preverbal

than to strangers (Sigman and Ungerer 1984b; Shapiro, Sherman, Calamari and Kock 1987; Sigman and Mundy 1989). In a comprehensive theoretical review, Rogers and Pennington (1991) find that autistic children demonstrate the same level of attachment to their mother or carer as mental age matched Downs Syndrome children, but are typically unable to join in reciprocal imitation. Teachers and parents, both, should be encouraged to believe that even a grossly avoidant autistic child may feel an affectionate attachment and may be sensitive to the feelings and attitudes of other identified persons.

As we have explained, it has been proposed that communication in autism depends primarily on the development of cognitive skills. This approach stems mainly from the Piagetian theory, in which development of the child's *sensorimotor mental schemes* for understanding objects of any kind is considered to be a necessary precursor for the acquisition of language. Curcio (1978) examined the sensorimotor development of mute autistic children and its relationship with the level of non-verbal communication. Those children with relatively complete sensorimotor functioning in '*object permanence*', gestural imitation, means used for obtaining environmental benefits and '*causality*', were claimed to be more inclined to exhibit spontaneous gestures of pointing or showing. However another study (Sigman and Ungerer 1981) found that autistic children with good sensorimotor skills, in particular good 'object permanence', may, nevertheless, be impaired in language.

Play of Children with Autism

The study of how autistic children play has been bedeviled by the same complexity of approaches as has the study of their communication. As with communication, play of children with autism is best understood by comparison with the normal course of development, which reveals how the motives for play involve the child in increasingly complex levels of communication and cooperation.

Research with infants has shown that two- to three-month-olds can communicate with their mothers with refined synchrony, reciprocity and complementarity of expressions and older babies gain increasingly elaborate capacities and appetites for play (see Chapter 8). By one year a baby is capable of cooperation in simple arbitrary tasks and has a well-developed sense of a performing social 'Me'. It seems clear that the development of the representational capacity which accelerates in symbolic play during the second year has its origins in the affective and cooperative pattern of communication with familiar persons that grows in the first year.

In autism both the affective responses and the cooperation are impaired, and the fault appears about the end of the first year or during the second year. The current literature supports the conclusion that this describes the heart of the disorder, but additional specific problems exist in the play of autistic children and these correlate with the difficulties the children have in communicating and learning meanings by instruction from other people.

A Bewildering Array of Theories and Measures of Play

A wide range of terms is used to describe kinds of play in studies of autistic children, as with normally developing children. This multiplicity of classifications does not help comparative study of how autistic children at any particular developmental level play. Some commonly-used categories are overlapping (e.g. 'simple manipulation' and 'sensorimotor' play), others are employed with different meanings (e.g. 'symbolic' and 'pretend' play) and still others are defined in an idiosyncratic way and used by few studies. It seems that this variation in usage is due to the differing aims and theoretical backgrounds of the projects.

Earlier studies looked for deficits of play in autistic children, for example describing their abnormally repetitive activities, but the latest studies are comparative, seeking to understand what autistic children lack by applying descriptions of play developed for understanding normal development. An increasing focus on 'symbolic' play has created a tendency for redefinition of 'symbolic', 'pretend', 'imaginative', 'representational', 'make-believe' or 'fantasy' play. Here we briefly discuss the most commonly-quoted studies to demonstrate how the multiple classifications of play confuse our understanding of how autistic children do, or do not, play.

(1) Wing, Gould, Yeates and Brierly (1977) classified play into three classes; '*non-symbolic*' play includes repetitive manipulation of objects; '*stereotyped*' play is symbolic play that is characterised by stereotypies, repetitive acts and lack of innovation; '*symbolic*' play or other relevant activity includes symbolic activities, making car noises, pretending to drive into a garage, and functional activities such as brushing a doll's hair.

(2) Ungerer and Sigman (1981) and Sigman and Ungerer (1984a) used the most extensive coding system for recording play in autistic children, based on play behaviours they observed in normal development. Their coding scheme comprises four categories, as follows:

   (a) *Simple manipulation* is described as each instance of mouthing, waving, banging, fingering or throwing of a toy.

   (b) *Relational play* includes combinations of objects, stacking objects and using an object as a container to hold another.

(c) *Functional play* refers to self-directed acts (e.g. brushing one's hair), doll-directed acts (e.g. brushing a doll's hair), other-directed acts (e.g. brushing the mother's hair) and object-directed acts (e.g. placing the cup on the plate).

(d) *Symbolic play* incorporates *substitution play*, as in the use of one object as if it were a different object (e.g. using a banana as a telephone receiver), *agent play* as the use of a doll as an independent agent of action (e.g. propping a bottle in a doll's arm as if it could feed itself) and *imaginary play* as the creation of objects or people having no physical representation in the immediate environment (e.g. making the phone ring).

(3) Baron-Cohen (1987), influenced by Leslie's (1987) theory of 'pretense', introduced the notion of 'pretend' play as a substitute for 'symbolic' play. He defined '*sensorimotor*' play as the use of objects with no attention paid to their function (e.g. throwing an animal), and '*ordering*' play, as in the imposing of some pattern in disregard of the meaning of the objects (e.g. piling animals up). More advanced forms of play are: '*functional*' play in which the child uses objects according to their function, and '*pretend*' play in which the child uses an object as if it were another object (e.g. using a banana as a telephone receiver), or attributes relevant properties to an object which it does not actually have (e.g. attributing heat to a cooker), gives animate properties to toys, or refers to absent objects as if they were present.

(4) Lewis and Boucher (1988) defined '*manipulative*', '*functional*' and '*symbolic*' play similarly to Baron-Cohen's definitions of 'sensorimotor', 'functional' and 'pretend' play. In addition, Lewis and Boucher used the term '*pretend*' play to refer to imaginative play including 'functional' and 'symbolic' forms. They introduced the use of unconventional toys and they included two new categories: '*no play*' to indicate absence of play, and '*intermediate*' play to record instances of play falling between the categories of 'functional' and 'symbolic'.

It is important to have in mind this somewhat chaotic variation in the categorical analysis of play behaviours in autism when we discuss the findings from the various experimental or comparative studies. Careful observations have often come to the conclusion that many kinds of play are less affected in autistic children than was expected. Obviously it will be necessary to distinguish the various possible motives for playful behaviour unambiguously when attempting to identify what autism affects most.

Problems in Interpreting Autistic Children's Play

Some features of the odd way autistic children investigate and imagine appear to be easily defined. Their play is typically dominated by fascination with the mere presence of objects and their immediate sensory features, or what they offer for manipulation, rather than their cultural or symbolic meaning (Eisenberg and Kanner 1956). Autistic youngsters also engage in many repetitive activities (Kanner 1943; Eisenberg and Kanner 1956; Tilton and Ottinger 1964; DeMyer *et al.* 1967; Rutter 1978; DSM-III-R 1987), do not make up combinatorial uses for objects (Tilton and Ottinger 1964; DeMyer *et al.* 1967) and symbolic or meaningful fantasy play appears to be poor or absent (Kanner 1943; Wing *et al.* 1977; Rutter 1978; Wulff 1985; Baron-Cohen 1987; DSM-III-R 1987). Even relatively able autistic children play in peculiar ways (Lewis and Boucher 1988). All would agree on these descriptions. However, further quantitative analysis of these apparently abnormal features has proved difficult.

Autistic children's 'sensorimotor' or 'manipulative' play has been found to be unimpaired in several studies (Ungerer and Sigman 1981; Sigman and Ungerer 1984a; Wetherby and Prutting 1984; Baron-Cohen 1987; Lewis and Boucher 1988; Stone *et al.* 1990). On the other hand, it has been reported that, with toys that would be expected to elicit varied exploratory behaviour, they prefer to repeat stereotypical behaviours (Hutt *et al.* 1964). Only one study has reported a relative absence of combinatorial use of objects for autistic children when they were compared with developmentally-delayed and non-delayed children matched for chronological age (Tilton and Ottinger 1964). A number of other studies that employed stricter matching procedures did not find that autistic children's 'combinatorial' or 'relational' play was particularly impaired in comparison with unaffected children of approximately the same cognitive level (Riguet *et al.* 1981; Ungerer and Sigman 1981; Sigman and Ungerer 1984a; Wetherby and Prutting 1984; Baron-Cohen 1987; Stone *et al.* 1990).

Surprisingly, the 'functional' play of autistic children has also been found to be unimpaired in both observational studies (Ungerer and Sigman 1981; Baron-Cohen 1987) and those employing experimental situations to elicit such play (Lewis and Boucher 1988). However, other studies report that, in spontaneous or free play sessions, the amount of 'functional' play of autistic children is lower than in control groups (Sigman and Ungerer 1984a; Lewis and Boucher 1988; Stone *et al.* 1990).

The findings on 'symbolic' play are even more contradictory. In free or spontaneous situations, some studies claim that 'symbolic' play is impaired in autism (Sigman and Ungerer 1984a; Baron-Cohen 1987; Lewis and Boucher 1988) and others that it is unimpaired (Stone *et al.* 1990). Autistic children have been reported to lack 'symbolic' play in structured, eliciting or modelling situations (Riguet *et al.* 1981; Sigman and Ungerer 1984a; Mundy *et al.* 1986). Others cannot support this claim (Lewis and Boucher 1988).

It is doubtful that the descriptive studies, especially the earlier ones, garnered sufficiently unambiguous or detailed data about the development of play in children who were also properly identified as 'autistic'. They drew their conclusions from clinical impressions (Kanner 1943; Wing *et al.* 1977), from observations of the play of children diagnosed variably as 'childhood schizophrenic', 'autistic type' or 'autistic with symbiotic features' (Tilton and Ottinger 1964), or from maternal questionnaires (DeMyer *et al.* 1967). Studies carried out in experimental settings have measured autistic children's play in the form of imitations of acts modelled by the researcher (Riguet *et al.* 1981; Ungerer and Sigman 1981; Mundy *et al.* 1987). Recent studies have tried to tackle questions about the autistic children's deficits in 'symbolic' play by employing tasks designed to measure their ability for comprehension of 'pretence' (Jarrold, Boucher and Smith 1994), or 'executive function' – the children's ability to plan thoughts systematically (Jarrold, Smith, Boucher and Harris 1994). Bishop (1993) reports that all autistic individuals perform poorly on 'executive function' tasks, while only a proportion of individuals fail 'metacognitive' tasks. She concludes that executive function problems, which are known to detect abnormality in prefrontal activity of the brain, are more central to autism. However, none of the experimental strategies or measurements of performance on specific tests can be expected to reflect the more investigative functions of play, which is typically flexible, spontaneous and socially interactive in preschool age children. In only one study, by Baron-Cohen (1987), has the spontaneous play of solitary autistic children been examined in detail. Interactive or interpersonal play has not been described in any of the above studies.

Other methodological problems concern diagnosis, the chronological age of the children and matching procedures. In the recent studies of play, children are most commonly diagnosed as autistic if they meet Rutter's criteria (e.g. Baron-Cohen 1987; Lewis and Boucher 1988), or DSM-III criteria (as in Ungerer and Sigman 1981; Sigman and Ungerer 1984a; Mundy *et al.* 1987; Stone *et al.* 1990). Findings in different studies might differ because the children do not have the same profile of autism. Furthermore, autistic children who have been examined for their participation in imaginative play were, in some cases, too old for this kind of play to be expected on normal developmental criteria, and, moreover, these 'too old' children were compared with much younger normal children (Baron-Cohen 1987; Riguet *et al.* 1981). In other studies young autistic children were observed without comparison to any control group (Ungerer and Sigman 1981; Mundy *et al.* 1987).

Procedures for matching autistic children with developmentally-delayed and/or normally developing children in the various studies have not been uniform and in many cases they are not adequate for clear conclusions to be drawn. Some studies have compared autistic children's play with that of children with developmental disorders, making no attempt to match the groups on other characteristics (Wing *et al.* 1977). Still others matched subjects for chronological age only (Tilton and Ottinger 1964; DeMyer *et al.* 1967; Stone *et al.* 1990). In other studies, autistic and non-autistic groups were equated only on tests measuring general intelligence (Sigman and Ungerer 1984a). The autistic children are matched with comparison groups according to their intellectual abilities to control for the effects of mental retardation. Ideally, this procedure allows the behaviour differences observed in the autistic children to be attributed to autism and not to mental retardation. However, it is more appropriate to match the autistic and comparison groups on language ability because language loss is often the most profound of their cognitive impairments, and language functioning correlates closely with the level of play. The importance of language has been accepted in some studies in which autistic children and other groups of children were matched on tests measuring verbal abilities (Riguet *et al.* 1981; Baron-Cohen 1987), but in these problems remain concerning the particular verbal test that was used.

A persistent problem in studies of autistic children's play arises from the varied definition of the term 'symbol'. A symbol is usually conceived as a representation in the mind, part of the mind work in one head, and the interpersonal emotions and the communication or cooperation normally involved in the creation and use of symbols, especially important for a young child, is overlooked. Thus a symbol is taken as, 'something that stands for, represents, or denotes something else, not by exact resemblance, but by vague suggestion or by some accidental or conventional relation' (Ricks and Wing 1975, p.192); or, 'as a representation of a representation, or as a "second-order" representation' (Baron-Cohen 1987, p.146). It is worth mentioning here that recent research on the relationship of 'pretend' play and children's performance on 'theory of mind' tests brought evidence that 'pretend' play does not require competence for understanding second-order mental representations (Lillard 1993). On the other hand, an autistic child's deficit in social negotiation, or in reciprocity of feelings and ideas in communication with other people, may be expected to impair the process of symbol-formation and thus the development of language. In an analysis of this learning of meaning, symbols are more usefully viewed as, 'experiences and actions with interest and usefulness given to them by the motives for cooperative awareness' (Trevarthen and Logotheti 1987, p.4).

An Attempt to Resolve Confusions About Autistic Play

We are led to the conclusion that the level of verbal ability of a child is an important component of the motivation and intelligence that makes advanced kinds of play possible. Does this level depend on motivations for sharing all kinds of experience, verbal and non-verbal?

In a study set up to directly examine interpersonal factors in children's symbolic play with their mothers (Papoudi 1993), verbal or less-affected

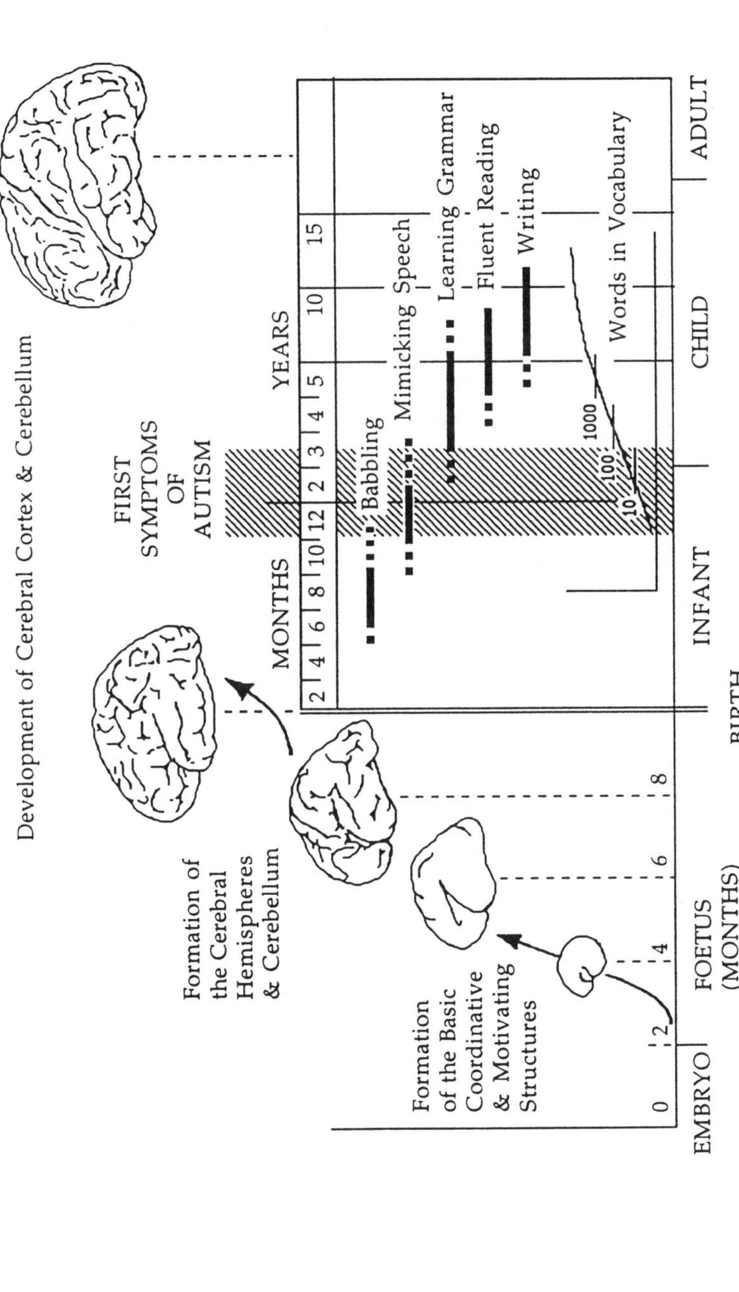

Figure 8: Brain growth and the postnatal development of language showing the period in which the first symptoms of autism appear. The developmental causes of autism will have begun much earlier, in the foetal or embryo stages, or possibly in a genetic fault before conception

autistic children of preschool age were matched with developmentally delayed and non-developmentally delayed children on the Reynell Developmental Language Scales. The mean verbal age of all the children was 27 months. 'Symbolic' play, involving pretense, occurred during moments of communication in all three groups with no significant differences between them. However, when these autistic children were compared with a group of autistic children with less verbal ability, significant differences were revealed. The signicant factor was the level of verbal ability, and this correlated with other aspects of readiness for communication.

The latter group, with poor language skills, were usually out-of-contact with their mothers. They failed to initiate symbolic acts that were directed to their mothers and failed to share objects with them. It may be concluded that motives for cooperative awareness are affected to a varying degree in autism, and that the severity of this basic impairment in capacity for sympathetic interaction is related to the level of linguistic and interpersonal skills that a child can reach. These findings support a theory which suggests that a minimum of interpersonal skills for communication by non-verbal means are essential motivation for learning verbal communication as well as for the development of representational play and other symbolic processes.

How Mothers May React to Autistic Children's Limited Sharing

Study of mother–infant communication leads to the hypothesis that the origins of symbolic play are to be found in affective and cooperative communication for which an infant has innate motivation. Some studies of autistic children and their mothers support this idea of development.

A conspicuous feature of autistic children's behaviour is infrequent initiative in 'sharing of attention'; they rarely point to an object, hold an object up for the mother to see, or bring an object to her (Sigman *et al.* 1986). They also do not readily share emotion (Mundy *et al.* 1986; Snow, Hertzig and Shapiro 1987; Yirmiya *et al.* 1989; Dawson *et al.* 1990; Kasari *et al.* 1990). In a natural reaction to this unusual and disturbing 'unavailability' or remoteness, mothers of autistic children may physically hold their children on task (Sigman *et al.* 1986), and they are directive in their speech, attempting to initiate cooperation even when the child is unresponsive, a strategy which is often counterproductive (Papoudi 1993). Children with different degrees of autistic impairment and language ability have different patterns of communication with their mothers (Mundy *et al.* 1987; Nadel 1992; Nadel and Peze 1993; Papoudi 1993). Mothers will therefore encounter differing degrees of difficulty when they attempt to share play.

It seems likely that mothers behave as they do in response to the puzzling ways their autistic children behave. They may behave automatically in ways that do not give the child the specially responsive and directed kind of response and example that is needed to help development. The more impaired the child is in 'sharing of attention', the more the mother is directive (Kasari *et al.* 1988). Mothers also adjust their speech down to the child's language level, using 'baby talk' or speaking as would normally be appropriate for a one-year-old when addressing a much older child, for example. The less well children do, the more mothers use directives and short utterances and the more they reinforce motoric rather than spoken behaviour (Konstantareas *et al.* 1988). On the other hand, the fact that mothers often appear 'asynchronous' in their responses to the acts and expressions of their autistic children, and are unable to set up 'dialogues' or maintain 'joint-attention' with them (Shapiro, Frosch and Arnold 1987), indicates that they may not be as sensitive to the capacities that their children do have, or as ready to make appropriate adjustments of their communicative behaviour, as they could be. This interpretation leads to a philosophy of intervention that encourages mothers to use a more accepting kind of approach (Chapter 10). It is important to note that the medical diagnosis of autism may in itself cause a mother to feel like 'giving up' in communication with her difficult child (Eikeseth and Lovaas 1992), which further indicates the need mothers have for helpful information on the nature of the disorder in communication and how best to cope with it.

There are many possibilities for applying forms of play systematically to improve the communication of autistic children; in groups, with pairs of children and with individual children interacting with an adult; at school and in the home. Treatments which attempt to use playful and imitative behaviours to encourage autistic children to be more responsive and cooperative are described in the next chapter.

CHAPTER 10

What can be Done?

Education for Autistic Children

The theory of intervention for autism has changed many times in the 50 years since Kanner gave his insightful appreciation of the disorder and its causes. His clear view was that the autistic child's pervasive aloneness and incapacity to share interests and plans with other persons through any medium of communication (and especially in a fluent and adaptable form of language that can serve the necessary negotiations of sense, feeling or purpose) was in the child from birth. He therefore thought it would need some treatment of the faulty brain or, in lieu of that, some radical modification of the human environment that would open the 'fortress' that the child's mind seemed to create for itself and make a bridge over which the child's motivation could be supported to serve an effective learning.

However, soon Kanner's discovery was absorbed into the psychoanalytic way of thinking, and treatment was directed to removal of the supposed cause of an adaptive withdrawal of a child from a cold and intrusive parenting. The advice was to separate the child from the parents, and to give loving, therapeutic attention in a foster home where people trained in psychodynamic therapy could direct the reconstruction of the child's damaged emotions and self-image.

In time, with the evident failure of psychodynamic methods, and the resentment of parents who knew they were not the primary cause of their child's aberrant behaviour, there was a vigorous counterattack. The fault, now back in the child, was perceived as a defect in sensations, in perception, in intelligence, in cognition or ability to analyse objective situations rationally. Behaviour modification techniques, suitably communicated in ways that had been found to work, but that had not been described or analysed, gave positive results. The autistic child could be taught, provided a way was found to give appropriate reinforcement, in a form acceptable to the child as reinforcement.

A policy of schooling in which the environment was changed to take account of the need that every autistic child has for a stable structure in the world and stability of conditions for observing, acting and transforming what the child perceives to be in the world proved effective both in helping the child to learn and in giving encouragement and relief for parents. It was firmly accepted that the primary condition in the child was not an emotional illness like the psychoanalytically-trained psychiatrists thought, but there was still a confusion.

All through the 1970s and 1980s a battle was joined between those who said the disorder was social and those who thought it was one of cognition or intelligence not specially concerned with social 'objects'. We now see that this dichotomy or choice is artificial and profoundly confusing. Motivation for learning in children, for their cognitive development, is necessarily affected by, indeed regulated and directed by, motives for communication, and therefore by the 'social environment'.

A seeming breakthrough came in the 1980s with the demonstration that 'high-functioning' (i.e. the verbally and rationally most competent) autistic children had a peculiar and marked inability to imagine and adjust to states of mind in others. They could not understand stories or fictional dramas in which they had to get into the heads of the protagonists to decide what, given the described circumstances, they, the characters and not the child onlooker, would believe, know, want and so forth. This theory does not apply to, and cannot make good sense of, the behaviours of the majority of autistic children who are either too young or too 'low functioning' to participate in the subtle textual and rational problems of 'theory of mind' tests. Nevertheless, the 'theory of mind' approach, emphasising as it does how a child must be able to imagine how other persons imagine and intend, may be a real help to parents and teachers, helping them conceive the difficulties the child faces in finding the 'other's' behaviour comprehensible and unthreatening.

Some, with increasing support from research on autistic persons' universal shortcomings in tests of perception of persons and their feelings and motives, began to claim the following:

- The disorder is not just a defect in language, which is very variable.
- Person perception is affected in all its aspects, leading to difficulties in all social contacts and relationships, but in varying ways that lead to the recognition of types of autism.
- General cognitive faults, in perception of any objects or events, cannot alone explain the disorder.
- IQs are usually below normal, but different in different individuals and generally higher in non-verbal components, which are in some cases above the normal range while language-related intelligence is clearly reduced.
- Emotional and affective reactions to persons are not absent and attachments do form.

- Changes occur with age which tend to increase the orientation of the child to others, without loss of oddness and incomprehension of others ideas, feelings, purposes, etc. Social gaucheness persists even in remarkable gifted 'high-functioning' individuals.
- There are specific deficiencies in imitation and in sharing of purpose or point of view which greatly handicap negotiated learning.
- 'Non-verbal' expressions of eye contact, voice quality and hand gestures are reduced and deviant leading immediately to difficulties in communication.
- Many different approaches to intervention can bring improvements in availability of an autistic child to other persons, and they can be taught.
- It is not possible to understand the interlocking problems of an autistic child and their difficulties in educational settings without comparisons with normal development and with other kinds of developmental disorder.
- Nonlinguistic and paralinguistic forms of communication, including special forms of game-playing and controlled musical improvisation therapy/training offer highly effective means of transforming the autistic child's 'availability'.

The Benefits of Early Intervention

Intervention approaches should be commenced at as early a stage as possible with autistic children for several reasons. First, one of the best predictors of outcome in this population remains the level of functional language use at 30 months. Second, early intervention should minimise secondary behavioural difficulties that often arise as a consequence of entrenched inappropriate obsessions and rituals of the children that can interfere greatly with learning. Until recently, early intervention has been highly problematic as early diagnosis was difficult and often children were not identified until approaching school entry. There are now a number of assessments, such as the CHAT and IBSE described above, that promise to facilitate early identification.

A wide range of early intervention methods is available, from those which are targetted specifically at the autistic preschooler (Strain, Jamieson and Hoyson 1986; Simmeonson, Olley and Rosenthal 1987), to the more general range targetted at the developmentally disabled which can also be of use for autistic children (see Tingey 1989, and Meisels and Shonkoff 1990, for an excellent introduction to this literature).

In the following summary a rough categorisation of methods of intervention depending on their theoretical orientation is attempted, but there is considerable overlap and the more successful approaches appear to be eclectic, adaptable to the needs of the individual and to involve the family in the training of the child. Gradually the narrower behavioural approaches are giving way to those that acknowledge the importance of special methods to facilitate communication and close interpersonal attention.

Behavioural and Cognitive Approaches to Therapy or Teaching

The most extensive research on the teaching of autistic children has been carried out on the use of behavioural and cognitive–behavioural methods. Of course, structured interventions lend themselves to quantitative appraisal. A large number of research and clinical groups have adopted this theoretical framework. Lovaas at UCLA (Lovaas 1978, 1987), the Autistic Project group at the Maudsley Hospital in London (Howlin and Rutter 1987; Howlin and Yates 1989), the Groden Institute, Carr's group at Stony Brook, New York State, and Schopler's TEACCH program in North Carolina are perhaps the best known. Some of these approaches will be described briefly under specific headings below.

Behaviour modification approaches have focused on two major areas:

(1) To improve acquisition of specified skills and in curricular teaching (see Clements 1987; Repp 1983; Schreibman 1988 for useful introductions to this kind of training, and also specific approaches detailed below under the TEACCH and Home Based Teaching programmes), and to the systematic teaching of language skills (Carr and Durand 1985; Howlin and Rutter 1987; Howlin 1989; Jordan 1993). There have been significant successes, but there is a problem with generalisation of skills teaching to other behaviours and this has not been directly addressed within this literature.

(2) Behavioural approaches have been used successfully in the management of specific behaviour problems which interfere with learning processes, such as aggressive outbursts (see Clements 1987), stereotypy and self-injury (see Murphy and Wilson 1985 for an excellent overview) and obsessional behaviour (Marchant *et al.* 1974).

A range of behavioural methods have been used successfully with autistic children, the common emphasis being on the development of a consistent, responsive environment which minimises the apparent benefits of solitary activity and of 'problem' behaviour, and maximises the benefit from the child's perspective for cooperative activity. This goal is often achieved through the use of external, nonsocial rewards, with the social development arising as a consequence of the child's interest in a particular reinforcement that is a tangible object or an activity desired by the child. Preferably, the child will be included in an appropriate peer group, and a consistency of responsive adult supervisors or teachers is essential. Negative reinforcement, punishment, is now not accepted, on the grounds that it is both inhumane and unnecessary.

There are now several papers in the clinical literature which demonstrate statistically and clinically significant treatment effects of early intensive behavioural treatment of autistic children (Harris *et al.* 1991; Lovaas 1987; McEachin, Smith, and Lovaas 1993). The most promising of these studies, from the Lovaas group, (McEachin, Smith, and Lovaas 1993) claims that a high proportion of autistic children can be successfully integrated in mainstream schools if such approaches are adopted. The critical discussion that follows this report guardedly accepts the authors' conclusion, but advises independent replication of this small-scale study to prove that the method is so successful. Early detection of autism has only recently been feasible, and it may transpire that the critical factor here is the age of the child when behavioural intervention is begun. Similar approaches, although helpful in management, prove to be markedly less successful with older autistic children as regards ultimate developmental outcome.

It is unclear at this point whether any of the effects of the behavioural methods that have been developed are specific to autistic children. It seems likely that all are of more general applicability. However, it is also the case that functional analysis and a single-case, client-centred approach are fundamental requirements for an effective behaviour modification technique.

Some workers using behavioural training methods have successfully pioneered recruitment of the family and peer network as co-trainers of the autistic child (Charlop and Walsh 1986; Jenson and Young 1985; Strain *et al.* 1986; Strain 1987; Simmeonson, Olley and Rosenthal 1987). Supervised involvement of the family is certainly important, both to increase the regularity and hence the effectiveness of therapy and to help reduce family anxiety. Training methods instituted by experts, and kept entirely in their control, run the risk of disempowering the child's principal companions and caregivers.

Berard Auditory Therapy

This method of auditory training employs systematic desensitisation or habituation of the child to particular frequencies of sound that have been causing the child distress and interfering with everyday life in the family. It relies on the finding that selective auditory attending with heightened sensitivity to certain kinds of sound (hyperacusis) is common in autistic children. There has, however, been no systematic assessment of its efficacy.

This and the other approaches which attempt to correct for auditory abnormalities in the autistic child drew their theoretical rationale from a model developed by Goldfarb (Goldfarb 1961) to explain a range of commonly observed problems such as the spinning, rocking, motor stereotypy, selective attention and hyperacusis seen in autistics. He hypothesised a primary abnormality of vestibular (inner ear) function. However, this explanation for autistic problems has not stood up to empirical scrutiny.

The Groden Institute

The Groden Institute in Providence, Rhode Island, offers a full-service, real-life provision for autistic children and their families. The centre is structured on behavioural lines. The methods and interdisciplinary working of the Institute are clearly described in a recent volume on its practice (Groden and Baron 1988).

Daily Life Therapy (The Higashi Approach)

Dr. Kiyoto Kitahara (1983/1984) at the Musashino Higashi Gakuen School in Tokyo has, over the past 25 years, developed an approach to working with autistic children for which considerable success has been claimed. With the opening in 1987 of the International Boston Higashi school, which caters for 70 children from six countries, the method has received a high press profile. As yet, however, it awaits systematic investigation (Quill, Gurry and Larkin 1989). The principal difference between the Japanese and US schools is in the limited integration and lack of parental participation in the latter because many of the parents live far from the school.

The Daily Life Therapy approach concentrates on a small number of basic methods. As far as possible, curricular activities are group-oriented and highly structured with an emphasis on learning transmitted from child to child through imitation. There is considerable emphasis on physical activity in groups – running three times per day for twenty minutes, gym for one hour each day and daily outdoor sports activities (football and basketball) for one hour. The academic curriculum focuses primarily on movement, music and art. It is known that high levels of physical exercise can be beneficial in the autistic population, particularly in reducing levels of self-stimulation and thus improving attention and learning potential (Watters and Watters 1980).

Many parallels can be drawn between the Higashi approach and others which are more familiar in European settings. For example, in its use of rhythmic intention and structured peer modelling, it is similar to the Peto method of Conductive Education for working with cerebral palsy (Trevarthen and Burford 1995).

The Doman-Delacato Method

The Doman-Delacato approach is essentially the same as the approach to working with any developmentally disordered population. The assumption is made that as ontogeny (development of an individual) recapitulates phylogeny (evolution of the race), working methods have to reflect an evolutionary order of development of behaviours; hence the well-publicised emphasis of this school of therapy on practicing supposedly ancestral locomotor patterns such as swimming or swinging from the arms (brachiation).

There has been no systematic appraisal of Doman-Delacato Methods with autistic children (Delacato 1974), and the method has been extensively criticised (see Cummins 1988 for a comprehensive review). On current evidence, this method cannot be recommended as an option for the education of autistic children.

Facilitated Communication

In this movement-training approach an adult therapist or 'facilitator' supports the hand of the autistic individual during communicative activities involving typing or other means of producing symbols. Its developers have claimed that autism is, in every case, primarily a form of communicative apraxia or inability to make movements as intended. The claim that the communicative purposes and thoughts of autistic individuals can be revealed if sensitive support is given to attempts at execution of directed hand movements has received widespread interest from media and from parents.

The only controlled evaluation of this method indicates that the effect may only be demonstrated when the facilitator knows what the individual is being asked, and that it disappears when he or she is attempting to aid while wearing headphones and a blindfold that prevent this knowledge (see Prior and Cummins (1992) for a recent discussion of this approach).

Clear evidence is not yet available to reach an objective decision on facilitated communication, and in Australasia, Canada and the USA debate is heated over its efficacy or otherwise. The current editorial position of the *Journal of Autism and Developmental Disorders* seems the most balanced opinion at present:

> As of now it appears that 'Facilitated Communication' has the potential for becoming a useful though not new technique for some people with autism most likely found in the group known to be precocious readers, good with computers, signs, and other forms of communication. Current promoters of this technique have been unwilling to differentiate those clients for whom a facilitator is useful from those who can learn spontaneous communication on their own. (Schopler 1992, p.337)

Treatment and Education of Autistic and Related Communication-Handicapped Children (TEACCH)

This state-wide public health program, run from the University of North Carolina, Chapel Hill, USA has been in operation for over 30 years. Highly effective materials have been developed to aid in the assessment and education of autistic children (Schopler and Reichler 1979; Schopler, Reichler and

Lansing 1980). Currently there are approximately 130 classes for children, and several centres for adolescents and adults in North Carolina run on TEACCH principles.

The focus of TEACCH in schools is on the development of appropriate communication skills and personal autonomy rather than on reducing problem behaviours. The approach is client-centred and structured around an assessment protocol; the Psycho-Educational Profile or **PEP** (see Mesibov, Troxler and Boswell 1988) for children, and the Adolescent and Adult Psycho-Educational Profile or **AAPEP** for adolescents and adults.

TEACCH integrates ideas from a wide variety of different methods to provide a complete program of service for the autistic individual and their family. Components of TEACCH are only adopted once there is research evidence for their efficacy. Furthermore, since no specified intervention may be necessary or can be sufficient with any particular individual, tailored solutions are adopted in every case. This is a well-researched and validated system designed to maximise quality of life for individuals with autism (Schopler, Mesibov, and Baker 1982; Schopler *et al.* 1981; Schopler *et al.* 1984; Schopler and Olley 1982; Schopler and Reichler 1971).

Workshops on TEACCH methods are frequently run in the UK and a number of other European countries and it has been actively adopted in a number of centres for autistic children.

Metacognitive or 'Theory of Mind' Training Approaches

A large body of data has been amassed by psychologists on the 'Theory of Mind' deficits that can be demonstrated in high-functioning autistic children. Autistic children appear to have a fundamental difficulty with interpersonal 'perspective taking', which is specific to this disorder, and not shown in normal or otherwise developmentally disabled controls matched in mental age with the autistic subjects. There is evidence for developmental progression with age in the autistic population.

There is, to date, no published test of the efficacy of intervention strategies based on the metacognitive or 'theory of mind' model of autism. Several unpublished studies are cited in Baron-Cohen and Howlin (1993). It appears that it is possible to train verbal autistic children to pass at least the 'first order' model of mind tasks, such as the 'Sally Anne' test of Baron-Cohen *et al.* (1986). However, the evidence to date seems to indicate that there is only limited generalisation of these abilities, and that the effect on everyday functioning is likely to be slight.

Speech and Sign Training

Since more than half of the autistic population will never develop spoken language, there is only a limited relevance for this group of formal, structural speech therapy input that attempts to improve production skills of prosody, timbre, articulation, grammar, etc., or that seeks to increase awareness of speech and language. Autistic children who do not speak benefit most from programmes that emphasise prelinguistic, interpersonal and cooperative aspects of communication (Hermelin and O'Connor 1985; Howlin 1989). Treatment of this kind may result in the child attempting to speak.

It is well recognised that high-functioning autistic children with good vocabularies and fluent speech exhibit marked abnormalities of language use, with semantic and pragmatic difficulties, and overly concrete interpretation of speech (Jordan 1993). Such children would be the most likely to benefit from systematic speech therapy sessions to address their linguistic problems. However, it should be recognised that the proportion of children for which this should be a central aspect of their educational programme is small.

Attempts to use a hand sign language to improve communication with autistic children, on the supposition that they have a specific defect in auditory comprehension and monitoring of speech (e.g. Konstantareas, Webster and Oxman 1979), have not been successful. However, in an integrated programme in which the use of gestural communication is part of a plan to increase communication by all possible means, American Sign Language or Makaton (a system developed by simplification of the vocabulary of British Sign Language; Walker 1980) has proven of some use in establishing appropriate communicative vocalisation, with decrease in echolalia and other non-communicative utterances (Carr 1979, 1982; Jordan 1993). The performance of autistic children with signs matches their use of speech; in both there is a specific failure in using signs for gaining social contact and for sharing ideas.

Interventions to Obtain Closer Affective Engagement[1]

Holding Therapy

Holding therapy, also called 'ethologically based' therapy, was developed by Martha Welch (1983) on the theoretical foundations of the Tinbergens' identification of autism with a motivational conflict behaviour (Tinbergen and Tinbergen 1983). The parent is encouraged to take the child on their lap, surrounded with their arms and to use positive affective expressions combined with eye contact to overcome the child's avoidance of an affectionate approach. If the child struggles and protests or becomes enraged, even this is praised. Inappropriate behaviours, such as echolalia, are ignored.

It is claimed that holding can lead to a reduction of avoidance and promote positive orientation and gentle affectionate touching (Richer 1983; Zappella *et al.* 1991). Zappella *et al.* (1991) identified ten children as autistic by DSM-III

---

1 Music Therapy is reviewed in the next chapter.

criteria and showed they had no neurological or biochemical abnormalities on routine testing. Assessments were made by analysis of videos of each child with the parents, with the therapist and alone. Following treatment as described, two improved rapidly with the disappearance of autistic behaviour, six improved to various degrees, and two showed no change.

Holding Therapy had the following aims:

- to obtain rich, extensive, emotionally directed communication
- to increase cooperative interactions.
- to reduce motivational conflict and increase affiliation, attachment behaviour, exploration and play.
- to give parents a direct control of their child.

Parents were to be the main agents of these changes in the child's behaviour.

Intensive Movement Therapy, Basic Communication Therapy

Work in Scotland shows that communication by non-verbal means through body contact and movement is highly successful in obtaining communication with mentally handicapped children, including those who are so profoundly affected as to have little learning or voluntary activity, and no symbolic communication (Latchford 1989; Burford 1988, 1992; Trevarthen and Burford 1995). This highlights the power of intensive, direct interpersonal contact and transfer of motivation such as obtains naturally between carers and infants (Knight and Watson 1990; Knight 1991). Hogg (1991) reviews improvements in the care and education of handicapped adults by an approach that recognises the need for basic or direct communication in an integrated curriculum. The principles of this approach, which can be related to music therapy, also apply to the improvement of interpersonal contact with autistic children.

The Option Method

The Option method developed from one couple's efforts to help their autistic son (Kaufman and Kaufman 1976). Many of the ideas used in this approach can be seen to parallel principles which underly the procedures of behavioural intervention, and particularly those used in 'Gentle Teaching'. Exaggerated responses and imitation are employed to engage the child in an interesting and interested social environment. Use of a therapy room is advocated, designed to offer as little distraction as possible, with diffusers on the windows, a diffused artificial light source, and only one adult working with the child at any one time. Materials not in use are placed out of the child's reach, and these can only be obtained by the child through communication with the adult.

The strong emphasis on imitation in this approach is supported by research showing that imitation of the behaviour of the autistic child by the mother on a regular basis significantly increases gaze at the mother's face and creative toy play (Dawson and Galpert 1990), without relation to measures of social maturity (Vineland scale), IQ or severity of autistic symptomatology. This is a significant change because autistic children usually look significantly less than normal children do at others during interaction (Volkmar and Mayes 1990), and they show clear evidence of joint attention deficits (Mundy and Sigman 1989a). The work of Nadel (1992; Nadel and Peze 1993) supports the conclusion that an autistic child can use imitation, and especially being imitated by a partner, as a bridge to closer cooperation in communication.

To date, several books are available on the Option method of work with specific children (e.g. Kaufman 1981). There has, however, been no systematic evaluation of this approach.

Family Education, Involvement of Parents

Home-Based Teaching

The Home-Based Teaching Project (Howlin and Rutter 1987; Howlin and Yates 1989) is a clinical programme, based in the Department of Child Psychiatry at the Maudsley Hospital in South London. It provides an outreach approach for young autistic children in families throughout the south of England. Treatment programmes are individually tailored to the needs of each child, with three main foci: fostering of language development; facilitation of social development; and treatment of behavioural problems that interfere with learning and development, such as obsessional and ritualistic behaviour.

This approach has been intensively investigated, comparing the progress of children in the programme against matched waiting list controls. It has been shown to be highly successful in many instances.

An important conclusion is reported as follows:

> ...by focussing the analysis on the relationship between changes in children and parents, it became apparent that the association was bidirectional. Parental intervention can be successful in changing many different aspects of children's behaviour, but the extent to which this intervention is effective will depend very much on the abilities and handicaps of the individual child. The art of successful intervention would seem to lie in helping to encourage the most effective forms of parent–child interaction. (Howlin and Rutter 1987, p.185).

Video Interaction Analysis and Video Hometraining

The technique of the Video Tape Recorded Playback (VTRP) is now widely used as an adjunct to behaviour therapy with emotionally disturbed patients and families in which there are difficulties of relating and communication. The client's or family's behaviour is videotaped and later played back for them to observe and appraise. Video playback allows a person or each member of a family to experience and become aware of their actions and their effects on other persons (Berger 1978). The use of this technique varies in: (1) the amount of the material replayed (the whole session or selected parts), (2) the conditions under which playback occurs, and (3) the timing of the playback (immediate or delayed)(Hugh and Rosenthal 1981).

> Video is a vehicle for discussion: it permits detailed observation; it records events that would otherwise go unseen; it has a distancing effect; it trains in observation and interpersonal skills. (Evans and Clifford 1976, p.129)

Video Hometraining, developed by Harrie Biemans in the Netherlands, is a method of intensive help for families with disturbed children that uses guided viewing of video recordings of communication in the home. The duration of the home training depends on the severity of the problem, on the level of the communication in the family and on the personal needs of the family. The aim is to teach the parents and the other members of the family (e.g. siblings and grandparents) how to achieve successful communication with a disturbed child. For this to be possible, it is important to know the characteristics of successful interaction. Biemans and Van Rees began to use Video Hometraining at ORION, a day care centre in the South of Holland in 1982. Better results were obtained when help was provided in homes rather than at the institution. In 1984, experimental programmes started at different places in Holland to help parents and children at home. In 1987, the Netherlands Government approved the establishment of SPIN,[2] the Foundation for the Promotion of the Intensive Home-based Treatment in the Netherlands, which was established in 1988.

Video home trainers help families where children are in trouble or causing concern: aggressive children, children with learning difficulties, neglected and sexually abused children, children with psychosomatic problems, children of neglected parents, parents that want to keep their child at home instead of sending him or her to a residential centre, and families who have problems in raising their children. Home training is not used when the child lives away from home; while other kinds of treatment are given to family members; while the parents continue to neglect, reject or abuse their children; when parents and children reject the home training; when unattended marital problems exist; and when children suffer from severe personality disorders. It is integrated with the work of other services.

Once the institution (assessment unit, day care centre, residential centre, children's home) decide that the family needs home training, the parents are informed and the first appointment is arranged. The home trainer visits the

---

2 SPIN, Witte Vrouwensingel 27, 3581 GC Utrecht, The Netherlands

family and a tape of the normal communication in a family is shown to introduce the method and the principles of home training. A very high proportion of the families, 80 to 90 per cent, agree to cooperate with home training.

Home training lasts three to four months on average, and there is a follow-up three months later to check if the family keeps the principles. The home trainer usually visits the family once a week, but visits may be more frequent at the beginning if the problems are severe. The home trainer films routine family life (e.g. dinner time, play situations, bath time and bedtime) and the next week reviews the film with the parents and older siblings. The filming situation is decided by the family, or it can be arranged at the home trainer's request.

The home trainer can model communication with the child for the parents to have a real paradigm of how a positive interaction can be applied. He can film himself during modelling and review this tape with the parents on the next week's meeting. The home trainer can also help the interaction of the family behind the camera; when he feels that there is a conflict or one member of the family has been neglected during the filming situation, he intervenes and tries to bring a balance using the principles of the scheme of successful contact that is outlined in Table IX, trying to achieve an increase of sympathetic or 'Yes' responses.

Table IX Scheme of Successful Contact During Video Analysis

'Yes' row	*Positive initiation or response*
attention	turn towards someone look towards someone
approval	friendly posture friendly intonation saying 'yes' friendly facial expression
conversation	chat name what the child is doing say what the child is allowed to do initiate mention/discuss ask
turn-taking	give turns, take turns
cooperation	give or take and object give help or ask for help
guidance	take initiative state what it is happening make proposals make plans search for solutions

Once the film has been made, the home trainer views it by himself frame-by-frame, determines which elements should be mentioned to the parents and discusses with his supervisor about how he should proceed. Having decided which items of the contact scheme should be increased, he uses still video pictures to show these to the parents, presenting some 'small' positive move as 'big' so that he can persuade them that they are doing well and that they should work on that more in the future.

Home trainers are social workers, psychologists and family therapists who take extra training in the method. The home trainer has first to learn the principles of the contact scheme and to execute the patterns of the successful communication while reviewing the tape with the family. The principles are learned by discussion with those already experienced so the home trainer can teach them to the members of the family who are seeking assistance.

Van Rees and Biemans (1986) showed in a demonstration video summarising video home training that a child with primary autism can respond to, and benefit from, a carefully adjusted and sustained regime of communication and play in which the mother benefits by guided interpretation of her behaviours and the child's responses. Review of videos of interaction with an autistic child can help parents or teachers gain insight into the child's behaviour and the adequacy or efficacy of their own behaviours.

Although tending to withdraw from attempts of others to break into their separateness, autistic children can be attracted to gently regulated responses that are timed and measured to match any moves they themselves make in relation to others, and contact can be established and extended this way (Nadel 1992; Nadel and Peze 1993). Communication by rhythmic movements with gently exaggerated attunement of vocalisations and touching to the child's behaviour, by music, by imitation of the child's gestures or sounds, and reaction to the child imitating, can lead to period of strong mutual engagement. All of these types of intervention can be made objective with the aid of video analysis, and video feedback can enhance their efficiency.

Medical Treatments for Neurochemical Abnormalities in the Brain

A wide range of drugs, vitamins and other biologically active substances have been administered in attempts to treat the brain condition of autism directly. Initially, interventions were prompted more by substance availability than by any clear rationale. Various medications were applied because they had proven effective or popular in treatment of mainstream adult psychiatric disorders. Phenothiazines, used successfully in the treatment of schizophrenia (Fish, Shapiro and Campbell 1966), lithium, used successfully for bipolar disorder (Gram and Rafaelsen 1972), and haemodialysis, used with no apparent benefit in the treatment of schizophrenia (Varley *et al.* 1980), have all been tried. Neither phenothiazines nor haemodialysis were of any demonstrable help to autistic children, while lithium proved to benefit the small subgroup who show autism coupled with bipolar affective disorder. For detailed reviews of this largely unproductive era of drug research, the reader is referred to Campbell (1975, 1989).

More recently, pharmacotherapies have been implemented and evaluated with more rigour and more thorough theoretical rationale. Treatments have been adopted with one of two justifications – either they are based on a research-based model of the underlying pathophysiology of autism, with the hope that an intervention targeting the cause will improve the condition of the child overall, or they have been focused to relieve specific symptoms such as overactivity, mood-swings, self-injury or aggression. The discovery of identified neurochemical abnormalities in autistic individuals, such as abnormal levels in the blood of the neurohormone endorphin (Gillberg *et al.* 1990), raised urinary homovenillic acid (HVA) (Garreau *et al.* 1988) and raised blood levels of the neuro-transmitter serotonin (Schain and Freedman 1961; Piven *et al.* 1991), has led to a number of drug studies being conducted on the basis of a more sound clinical reasoning.

Serotonin and the use of Fenfluramine

One of the earliest and most robust neurochemical abnormalities reported in the autistic population has been raised urinary serotonin, a neurotransmitter that has important functions in regulation of motivation and mood. This was first documented by Schain and Freedman in 1961, and has been consistently replicated in a significant proportion (approximately 30 per cent) of cases in subsequent reports. This finding led to considerable interest in the potential use of fenfluramine with autistic children. Fenfluramine is a weight-reducing medication which lowers levels of 5-hydroxy indole acetic acid (5-HIAA) in fluids of the brain, and thus both blood and urinary levels of the neurotransmitter dopamine. As a serotonin antagonist it might thus directly alter the system that is causing the abnormalities of urinary serotonin observed. A range of improvements have been observed (see Campbell 1988; Sloman 1991 for reviews) including improved social behaviour, improved attention span and reductions in motor restlessness. There are, however, a range of undesirable side effects, including weight loss, lethargy, sleeping problems and gastrointestinal upset which on balance mitigate against widespread use of this treatment. In open trials, most patients have been discontinued from longer term use because of developing problems with appetite, weight or drug intolerance. Several of the more recent studies have found that there is often little change in autistic symptomatology despite normalisation of urinary serotonin.

Haloperidol

Haloperidol has been used in the treatment of autism because a number of biochemical indicators show abnormalities of the dopamine neurotransmitter system in the brains of autistic children. A number of early studies had suggested that haloperidol, which has strong antidopaminergic properties, could be useful in helping the autistic child. The first well-controlled, randomised, double-blind trial (Campbell *et al.* 1978) claimed significant improvement over placebo in reducing autistic withdrawal and motor stereotypy in a population of 40 cases. Subsequent work by the same group has demonstrated that treatment with haloperidol can result in marked improvement in cognitive functioning and reduction in motor restlessness. Detailed double-blind, placebo-controlled studies have shown consistent improvements in activity level, stereotypy and aggression (Cohen *et al.* 1980). Given the apparent efficacy of this treatment, it is unfortunate that approximately 22 per cent of reported cases developed a drug-related movement problem even with low doses.

The Opiate Hypothesis – a Potential Role for Naloxone and Naltrexone

Panksepp was the first to propose that abnormalities in the systems that employ the natural opium-like substance endorphin may be implicated in autistic behaviour (Panksepp 1979). This was based on his observations of opiate-addicted young animals of a variety of species, which often showed signs that he felt were directly analogous to autistic behaviour in humans children. In particular, the animals showed decreased pain sensitivity, reduction in crying, poor clinging to the mother, low desire for social companionship, and extreme persistence in certain behaviours in the absence of external rewards. A number of subsequent theoretical papers have advanced a rationale for the use of opiate antagonists as part of the treatment for the 'subpopulation of autistic children having elevated brain opioids.' (Panksepp and Sahley 1987). Deutsch (1986) makes the same point.

There is some evidence that **naloxone**, a short acting intramuscularly administered drug that blocks the action of the natural endorphin system, can reduce motor stereotypies and self-injurious behaviour (Barron and Sandman 1983; Richardson and Zaleski 1983), and that it can also result in improved interpersonal functioning (Sandman *et al.* 1983). The varied results reported with naloxone may have been due, in part, to the need to inject it several times each day to achieve therapeutic levels. Subsequent research has used **naltrexone** which has the considerable advantages of being long acting and orally administered.

Campbell *et al.* (1988) have carried out one of the best designed studies to date of the effects of naltrexone on autistic children. Eight boys, 3.75 to 6.5 years of age with moderate to profound levels of mental retardation, took part in a study to assess responses to different dosages. A low dose (0.5 mg/kg/day) reduced fidgetiness and uncooperativeness; a higher dose (2.0 mg/kg/day) markedly reduced stereotypies and increased relatedness to people. Six of the eight subjects were judged to be responders.

Gillberg and his colleagues have reported significantly raised levels of endorphins in the brain fluids in approximately half of autistic individuals, but in none of their normal or neurological controls (Gillberg, Terenius and Lonnerholm 1985; Gillberg 1988b). Those autistic children with higher levels of endorphin were more likely to be self-injurious and they had higher levels of motor stereotypies and significantly decreased sensitivity to pain. In this small sample only the last result reached statistical significance.

It is clear that more detailed evaluation of endorphin antagonists such as naltrexone is required before their use is widely adopted in clinical management. The reported data from small groups of patients indicate that there is considerable promise in this line of research. For the present, any such treatments attempted should be closely monitored using single case research methods.

Megavitamin Therapies

Megavitamin treatments invoke the possible benefit of vitamin B6 in the treatment of autism. This concept stems from the discovery of the Institute for Child Behaviour Research that the common factor across families who claimed improvement in children on vitamin supplements was the inclusion of B6 in the supplement.

A number of trials have been conducted, most notably by the Lelord group in France (LeLord *et al.* 1981; Barthèlèmy *et al.* 1988), and there is clear evidence of benefit in a significant proportion (14 per cent of cases). Children who are younger, of higher IQ, with better initial language and with raised pre-trial urinary HVA (Homovanillic Acid) levels seem to derive particular benefit.

Conclusions

The central fault in the autistic child's brain is one that prevents the normal motivation for learning and being taught through shared attitudes, experiences and purposes. We need, therefore, a type of intervention that will systematically facilitate as much cooperative, negotiated and culturally-relative learning to occur as possible, and that is deliberately monitored with attention to the autistic learner's moment-to-moment motivational and interpersonal response. In this effort a wide variety of techniques for increasing interpersonal understanding, joint motivation and, in the end, cooperative awareness and skill in communicating, have been found to be effective, including improvisational music therapy (considered in the following chapter) and video monitoring of communicative behaviours with feedback of results of the evaluation, as described above.

The psychoanalytic approach, dismissed by many seeking a more objective, simpler or 'biological' explanation of the disorder, encourages an openness to the autistic person's real subjective experience, of life and of other persons, their speech, their actions and their expressions of emotion. For this reason it is prone to over-interpret responses of the child, attributing psychological abilities that are difficult to substantiate. In a modified form that recognises the inherent person-related motives of the human infant, and that acknowledges that autism is a real pathology of the mind, not just an avoidant adaptation or an immature responsiveness, a training in psychoanalysis can give a therapist enhanced insight to a child's confusions and fears, and can lead to a constructive education to increase the child's awareness and his or her capacity to regulate feelings with other persons' participation.

As with all young children, it is parents or their substitutes in intimate and consistently active relationships who have the key position in at least the early stages of this learning. Any educational or therapeutic provision for autistic children, however expert, must be child-and-family based, involving the parents as collaborators with teachers or therapists and co-beneficiaries in a changed communicative relationship with their child.

Behavioural skills training and cognitive enrichment techniques seeking to change the child will work only if the intersubjective, person-presenting aspect is adjusted to the child's special, reduced or deviant communicative needs. This requires careful and monitored management of any group in which the child is taught.

Although there have been advances in drug treatment of autistic children over the past two decades, and there are now a range of targeted interventions, no 'magic bullets' have been found. This is perhaps unsurprising given the heterogeneous manifestations of the disorder and its undoubtedly complex underlying pathophysiology. Some doubt that there is any value in using drug therapies with the autistic population (Sloman 1991). It cannot be imagined that such fundamental ways of intervening with the brain activity actively will ever replace the need for psychological and empathic forms of treatment.

The quest for improved interventions and advice to parents can be supported by research on the normal development of communication through infancy and preschool stages to school, as discussed in Chapter 8. We would repeat that early intervention, as soon as possible after the autistic symptoms are recognised, is important, and communication in infancy and preschool ages offers the best model for the kind of one-to-one teaching that autistic children respond to best. Information on these aspects is the best way to counteract the discouragement parents will feel on receiving the diagnosis of autism for their child (Eikeseth and Loovas 1992).

CHAPTER 11

Music Therapy for Children with Autism

Music therapy is now recognised as an appropriate and efficient way to help children with autism develop their capacities for emotional communication and social interaction (Baron-Cohen and Bolton 1993; Aarons and Gittens 1992). The development of music therapy spans some 40 years, and it is now an established profession in the UK health and social services. Various kinds of music therapy are practised in over 50 countries, with many different client groups and in a variety of settings (Maranto 1993).[1] In special schools, child and family centres, child development and assessment units and other specialist teams, music therapists are increasingly contributing to the multi-disciplinary assessment and treatment of children and young people with emotional or psychiatric problems, learning disabilities and a wide range of complex communication difficulties, including autism (Bunt 1994; Davis, Gfeller and Thaut 1992; Heal and Wigram 1993; Wigram 1995). Strong support, and demand, for music therapy comes from parents and carers. The relevance of music therapy as part of the developmental curriculum for a child with special needs is, however, not yet fully recognised within some sectors of the education service in the UK.[2] Warwick (1995), a leading British music therapist, presents a convincing argument for music therapy in special education: she makes clear distinctions between music therapy and music education, and describes the role that the music therapist can play within the multi-disciplinary team.

What is Music Therapy?

> Music Therapy provides a framework in which a mutual relationship is set up between client and therapist. The growing relationship enables changes to occur, both in the condition of the client and in the form that the therapy takes. (APMT 1995)

---

1 The World Federation of Music Therapy provides an international forum for discussion and collaboration among professional music therapy organisations.

2 This is under discussion in the Association of Professional Music Therapists, the professional body of qualified music therapists in the UK.

There are many theories to explain the therapeutic effects of music, but the main forms of practice use music to reach and affect the emotions,[3] and to offer a means of stimulation in emotional communication. This can benefit clients of all ages with emotional, cognitive, physical and/or sensory difficulties, engaging their awareness, motivation and feelings at their foundations.

> Music is essentially an emotional experience and can be as wide and varied in its content as the human emotions themselves. (Nordoff and Robbins 1971a, p.49)

Early publications by pioneer music therapists, Alvin (1968; revised edition, Alvin and Warwick 1991), Gaston (1968), and Nordoff and Robbins (1971a, 1977), emphasize the self-organising powers inherent in spontaneous musical engagement of the emotions when this is directed to give both supportive structure and freedom in expression to the client or patient. Creating experiences of relationship in music, developing self-expression through emotional involvement and enhancing communication remain primary goals in contemporary music therapy.

Improvisational music therapy (Bruscia 1987, 1989, 1991), in which the therapist encourages spontaneous musical expression, is a mainstream clinical orientation, basic to many of the training courses, and it is a form of music therapy widely used in the treatment of autistic children (Alvin and Warwick 1991; Brown 1994; Bunt 1994; Nordoff and Robbins 1971a, 1971b, 1977; Warwick 1995; Wigram 1995). A notable alternative is the work of Thaut (1980, 1983, 1987, 1988, 1992), who, in his significant contribution to research and teaching, takes a more directive 'behavioural' or educational approach.

Why or how improvisational music therapy carried out by a trained practitioner can help an autistic child is examined in this chapter. In addition, and in response to the increasingly early identification of autism, and to the growing numbers of referrals of very young children with autism and other complex communication disorders now being reported nationwide in the UK (Aarons and Gittens 1992), a case study of individual music therapy with a three-and-a-half-year-old boy with Kanner's autism is presented to illustrate the particular value of this medium as an early intervention. Although there is enormous variety and individuality in the ways people of all ages, developmental stages and abilities across the autistic continuum respond to music therapy, some commonly recurring features will be found in this case material. We should note, however, that the creative and clinical resources of music therapy do not

---

3 The power of music to affect the emotions has been widely documented in aesthetics, philosophy and the neurosciences (e.g. Buck 1984; Critchley and Henson 1977; Dewey 1934; Evans and Clynes 1986; Langer 1953; Meyer 1994; Wallin 1991; Zuckerkandl 1976).

apply only to young autistic children, or to those, such as this little boy, who are without verbal means of expression. The therapy that lies in music and in musical communication may benefit the emotional well-being of the autistic person at different stages of life (Brown 1994; Bryan 1989; Pedersen 1992).

The 'music' inherent in all our human functioning can be traced in the rhythms and sympathetic responses of infants. New infancy research findings integrated with clinical observations and research in improvisational music therapy contribute to a richer understanding of how taking part in musical interaction, and being influenced by aesthetic properties of music itself, helps autistic children to gain a self-awareness and relatedness to others that is cohesive rather than fragmented, and how they become more able to respond to other people in everyday social interaction.

Music and the Emotions: Dynamic Forms of Feeling in the Music Therapeutic Process

A comprehensive account of music therapy would draw from many disciplines, including music ethnology, phenomenology and aesthetics, music psychology, psychoanalysis, neurosciences and philosophy, and from developmental psychology. At the root of musical responses is the power of music to express and to influence emotional states. This connection between music and the emotions can be discussed only briefly here.

The rhythms of walking, breathing, heartbeat, autonomic functions, and indeed all kinaesthetic or motion-sensing aspects of expression through movement, with the tonal inflections of our voices (whether in laughing, crying, or speaking) all form a musical hierarchy or orchestration of self-regulation and self-organisation, which are directly linked to feeling states. Tone and rhythm are intrinsic to our innate human functioning and they are cultivated in music.[4] Thus human expression can be objectively perceived as essentially musical. Musical 'data' provide an individual musical 'blueprint' or dynamic 'gestalt' which objectifies essentially how we are at any moment, how we function and how we relate in the world (Aldridge 1989; Alvin and Warwick 1991; Brown 1994; Nordoff and Robbins 1971a, 1977).

An improvisational music therapist is able to 'read' or apprehend these 'dynamic forms of feeling' (Langer 1953) as they unfold in the musical relationship, and can respond to them accordingly (Pavlicevic 1990, 1995; Robarts 1994). Music therapists are highly skilled musicians, trained to use music creatively with clinical objectives that are perceived within the musical

---

4 The function of musical expression in self-regulation of motive states and in the 'activation of basic integrative processes' has been described in the infant developmental research of Papousek and Papousek (1979, 1981). This work testifies to the significance of certain fundamental processes in music therapy that appear to activate processes that are present from birth.

and other dynamic forms of the therapeutic relationship. Musical dynamic forms may manifest across different modalities of expression, both 'sounded' in speech and singing (or on musical instruments) and silent in motor-kinaesthetic responses of gesture and dance. As they arise within the client, within the therapist, and between client and therapist, these dynamic forms of personal and interpersonal expressions are objectified, enhanced and developed within the music. The therapy that lies in music is thus directly connected to the inherent 'musicality' or innate responsiveness to music found universally in everyone, whether they are musically educated or not. This universal musicality appears to survive considerable intellectual or neurological impairment, indicating music's deeply rooted biological origins (Alvin and Warwick 1991; Bunt 1994; Evans and Clynes 1986; Nordoff and Robbins 1971a, 1977; Wallin 1991). Every individual, no matter how profoundly mentally handicapped or emotionally disturbed, can show some form of response to music.

Concerning the sense of self and self-in-relationship, music therapy addresses the fundamentals of what it is to be a human being reacting to other human beings, and it offers a context in which the motives of the self can be nurtured, and the emotions can be experienced, expressed and brought into play in communication. In work with autistic children, musical experiences of this kind can engender self-experiences and developments in emotional communication which, in many cases, are reported not only to carry out into everyday life, but to have a significant impact on the overall mental development of the child. (Alvin and Warwick 1991; Brown 1994; Edgerton 1994; Nordoff and Robbins 1971a, 1977; Robbins 1993; Warwick 1995). We see such a progress in the case history presented below.

The Phenomenological/Psychodynamic Debate in Improvisational Music Therapy

Two major philosophical and theoretical positions influence current music therapy practice: the phenomenological and the psychodynamic. On the one hand, the phenomenologists claim that the therapy lies 'in the music' and in the 'person' or the 'musical being' of client and therapist (Aigen 1995; Ansdell 1995). They tend to regard psychodynamic conceptualisations as inappropriate to the creative–aesthetic and emotional–physiological phenomena at the core of the music therapy process. There are elements of 'absolute expressionism' in music therapy viewed from this perspective (Meyer 1994). On the other hand, there are those music therapists whose understanding of the music therapy process is underpinned by a range of psychological, psychoanalytic or humanist and 'client-centred' theories which directly influence their clinical practice (Dvorkin 1994; Heal 1994; Heal Hughes 1995; Lecourt 1991; Priestley 1994; Rogers 1994). Their various orientations seem to relate more closely to the position of 'referential expressionism' (Meyer 1994). This author (JZR) finds many useful correspondences between a phenomenological approach to music therapy and a psychodynamic perspective that encompasses the theories of 'self psychology', 'object relations', and that integrates these with the findings of the new infancy research (Robarts 1994; Robarts & Sloboda 1994). As mentioned earlier, the paradigm shift in psychoanalytic and developmental perspectives which was heralded by Daniel Stern's book *The Interpersonal World of the Infant* (Stern 1985) has particular relevance for music therapy and supports its increasing recognition within modern special education and healthcare services.

Research in Improvisational Music Therapy: Finding Appropriate Methods

The claim that music therapy can help individuals with autism still rests mainly on the profession's own substantial and rigorous clinical documentation, and on the recognition of its benefits by parents, carers and other professionals. A common criticism by those without direct experience of the efficacy of music therapy is that the improvements reported to arise from improvisational music therapy and their generalisation to other settings have not been substantiated by controlled research studies. In response, experienced practitioners point out that while each child's (or client's) individuality and the subtle aspects of emotional expression and creativity within the dynamics of relationship are paramount considerations in music therapy, these features do not lend themselves readily to measurement by scientific research methods that are designed to compare treatment groups and to make 'blind' assessments of behaviours defined a priori. In recent years, this dilemma has begun to be addressed: on the one hand, by psychological researchers whose collaborations with music therapists have produced some convincing results within a quantitative perspective (Aldridge 1991, 1993a, b, 1994; Aldridge, Gustorff and Neugebauer 1995; Pavlicevic and Trevarthen 1989); and by practitioner researchers who have adopted qualitative methodologies to examine the relationship and various phenomena of the music therapy process (Aigen 1993, 1995; Forinash and Gonzalez 1989; Lee 1995; Payne 1993; Rogers 1995; Smeijsters and Van Den Hurk 1993). Some of these studies have included elements of quantitative research methods (Rogers 1993). The move from old to new paradigm research models is demonstrated in Wheeler's text, *Music Therapy Research: Quantitative and Qualitative Perspectives* (Wheeler 1995) and by recently documented music therapy research in Europe (Rogers 1995; Smeijsters *et al.* 1995). The potential for quantitative appraisal within a qualitative design is demonstrated by such studies as Thaut's (1988),[5] which compared autistic and normal children's spontaneous playing of a xylophone, but not within the dynamic interaction

5 Thaut (1988) concluded that: 'The low performance on complexity and rule adherence of such (autistic) children suggest an inability to organise and retain complex temporal sequences'.

typical of music therapy. Appropriate research methodologies and designs for research in improvisational music therapy may be offered by the sophisticated recording and microanalytic techniques developed by infant developmental reseachers, whose interests have many parallels with those of music therapist researchers.

Two recent quantitative studies in improvisational music therapy research with autistic children (Muller and Warwick 1992; Edgerton 1994) are discussed below.

Links between Early Communication and the Music Therapy Process: Implications for Helping Autistic Children

For music therapists who are examining intersubjective aspects of their work, the microanalytic methodology and descriptive design of recent infant developmental research, especially that on the first communications of infants with other persons, holds much interest. Many of the basic principles of music therapy practice are represented in research studies that record and measure the musical elements of infant perception and expression (Papousek and Papousek 1979, 1981; Trehub *et al.* 1977, 1989, 1991) and the microanalytic descriptions of timing, phrasing and prosody in interaction between mother and infant (Stern 1977, 1985; Trevarthen and Hubley 1978; Trevarthen 1979; Trevarthen and Marwick 1986; Beebe *et al.* 1985). The spontaneity, immediacy and adaptability of the dynamic and improvisatory relationship in music therapy seem closely related to the 'mutual influence structures' described by Beebe *et al.* (1985), and to the 'dynamic interpersonal motives' of early communication (Trevarthen 1993a, b). This concept of the infant's motivation, described by Stern (1986, p.67) as beginning in the 'domain of emergent relatedness...the coming-into-being of organisation that is at the heart of creating and learning' (p.67), is most pertinent to the music therapy process. Such immediate interpersonal experiences appear to be vital in the normal development of symbolisation and language, and they have special significance for autistic children. Research in adult attachment (Main 1994) suggests that the principles of dynamic sympathy apply through adult life, giving meaning and coherence to relationships and the sense of self. This comparatively new focus on the developmental function of empathic modes of interaction (Alvarez 1992; Emde 1983, 1990; Schore 1994; Tustin 1986, 1994) has provided an impetus to a more informed understanding of music therapy as a medium for emotional communication with wide clinical application.

The similarities between the musical-emotional improvising in the music therapeutic relationship and mother–infant communication have been noted by many music therapists (Agrotou 1988; Heal Hughes 1995; Robarts 1994; Pavlicevic 1990). Infancy research, in its investigation of the beginnings of relationship, social interaction and communication, uncovers a spectrum of rhythmic phenomena and expressive tones that requires musical terminology to provide accurate and appropriate description. Microanalytic studies of mother–infant interaction demonstrate in detail the musical improvisatory features and phrased infra-structures of basic emotional communication, 'mother and infant both adjusting the timing, emotional form and energy of their expression to obtain intersynchrony, harmonious transitions and complementarity of feelings between them in an emotional partnership or "confluence"' (Trevarthen 1993a, p.57). It is this very intersynchrony, flexibility and creative reciprocity that is absent in the autistic child, and which the music therapist seeks to help the child experience and assimilate to whatever extent she or he is able to do so.

'Protoconversation' of mother and infant (Trevarthen 1979, 1980) seems to invoke 'innate musicality', a rhythmic, phrased activity which provides, or is, the fundamental organisation of dynamic cerebral processes underlying perceptual, affective, motor and cognitive expression. Infant and mother share a hierarchy of vocal elements in phrases and polyrhythmic gestures (Lynch *et al.* 1995), exchanging their parts with split-second timing (Beebe 1982). The sharing of affective states or moods that precedes development of higher, more cooperative levels of relatedness between mother and infant (Trevarthen and Hubley 1978) can be very powerfully realised in music therapy. 'Vitality affects', 'affect attunement' and 'temporal feeling shapes' described by Daniel Stern (1977, 1985, 1994) are clinical realities in the musically empathic therapeutic relationship, as are the 'prosodic envelopes' in which the infant perceives and sympathises with the form of communicative exchanges (Papousek and Papousek 1979, 1981). Such observations are particularly relevant to developmental objectives pursued in music therapy. They help explain the steps that therapy will tend to follow.

Dyadic, emotional and dynamic patterns of communication are shown by infancy research to form the foundations of psychological and cognitive development, social adaptation and personality integration (Beebe *et al.* 1985; Brazelton, Koslowski and Main 1974; Condon and Sander 1974; Papousek and Papousek 1981; Schore 1994; Stern 1977, 1985; Trevarthen 1979, 1984, 1993a, d):

> the motives and emotions excited between mother and baby, that live only in their communication have a primary directive and organising role in cognitive and psychological growth. (Trevarthen 1993d)

Infancy research has also demonstrated the adverse impact on the child's development when this fundamental vitality of communication between infant and mother is disturbed or inhibited by innate or environmental factors (Murray and Trevarthen 1985; Murray 1992). In the case of the child with autism, the dynamic forms of the child's expressive-responsive behaviour are either imperceptible or idiosyncratic and therefore hard to 'read'. The emotional partnership of mother and infant becomes increasingly distorted; mutuality of emotional communication becomes difficult to engage and entrain. The lack of self-synchrony and inter-synchrony in the autistic child (Condon 1975; Evans 1986) has been described by Hobson (1989) as 'a biologically based impairment of affective–conative relatedness with the environment' (p.42) and by Grotstein (1980) as the lack of a filter for incoming and outgoing stimuli. Secondary or acquired emotional and cognitive handicaps are likely to compound the almost inevitable dysfunctions in the primary relationship (Sinason 1992).

In spite of the serious impairment of their inter-synchrony of expression with other persons, autistic children's responsiveness to certain forms of music and musical stimuli (Rimland 1964; Sherwin 1953; Thaut 1980, 1984) shows that some of the infantile foundations of their innate musicality remain unimpaired. It is not surprising, then, that such a deeply rooted biological response to music, when appropriately engaged, can begin to build new experiences of affective-conative relatedness for the children. In the education and treatment of children with autism, improvisational music therapy may assist the autistic child in many specific ways: entraining responses, giving a sense of temporal flow to develop a cohesive sense of self; expanding his/her capacities in social interaction; helping assimilation of change and variation, while offering creative strategies instead of the autistic child's obsessive, fixated behaviours; helping to resolve problems of self-regulation, habituation and the modulation of states of arousal (Dawson and Lewy 1989b; Frith1989). Above all, it is the emotional, aesthetic power of music (hard to convey in words) that can offer a depth of shared emotions or 'communion' of the kind that unites people, regardless of abilities or disabilities.

The Literature on Music Therapy and Children with Autism

Though research is needed to understand the process of music therapy, there is a significant body of clinical documentation showing how autistic children gain in communication and social interaction through the use of either structured or more freely creative techniques. Case studies give detailed evidence that music therapy can have highly beneficial effects on motivation. Some of the most substantial clinical documentations of the improvisational music therapy technique are those of Alvin and Warwick (1991), Warwick (1995) and Nordoff and Robbins (1971, 1977).

The general principles of music therapy for children with autism are recorded by Alvin and Warwick (1991) who describe their experience of free improvisational music therapy used to develop a trusting relationship, self-expression and social interaction. These authors emphasise the qualities of musical sound, and the therapeutically-defined silence and space in which the autistic child may acquire new experiences of him or herself. The case material presents individual children across the autistic continuum, with varying degrees of learning difficulties and idiosyncratic or avoidant behaviour, and provides moment by moment accounts of the process by which these children were engaged in musical–emotional communication. Warwick (1995) describes her highly original approach working with mothers and their autistic children in their homes. She gives a detailed account of how one mother gradually takes up some of the musical–relational and confrontational 'strategies' observed in the music therapy sessions, and, moreover, how she became more aware of her feelings towards her son. Music therapy was concluded when this mother was ready to assume the function of the music therapist. In this same paper, Warwick (1995) describes a research project (Muller and Warwick 1992), which set out to measure the effects of mothers' involvement in music therapy. While results showed increases in turn-taking and in musical activity, as well as decreases in stereotypic behaviour in the children, the mothers' participation in the music therapy process was not shown to have any notable influence. Attempts to assess generalisation of communication and shared play outside the therapy setting were inconclusive in this study. The measured results of this study contrast with the descriptive evidence of the clinical case material.

A controlled research study by Edgerton (1994) supports the claim that improvisational music therapy can increase autistic children's communicative behaviours, and suggests that generalisation of skills to other settings does occur. Further research is required to confirm that generalisation of communication skills occurs, and to provide closer analysis of musical phenomena – the microstructures and dynamic forms – and to identify precisely the intra- and interpersonal development in improvisational music therapy.

In the 1960s and 1970s, pioneering music therapists Nordoff and Robbins seemed to approach this level of microanalysis (although without the advantages of computer-driven technology). Combining their creative gifts and professional experiences – Paul Nordoff as composer and pianist, Clive Robbins as an educator of children with learning difficulties – they developed an original musical-therapeutic approach and began detailed empirical research into musical improvisation as therapy with autistic children and other children with a wide range of emotional and learning difficulties. They initiated several successive projects, the first being funded by the National Institute for Mental Health and carried out in association with Ruttenberg and his colleagues at the Daycare Center for Psychotic Children, University of Pennsylvania.[6] They identified the improvisational musical phenomena and recorded how these influenced the intra- and interpersonal development in these children. Nordoff and Robbins' many case studies, recorded on audio and later on videotape,[7] provide valuable

6 This early research in improvisational music therapy coincided with infant developmental researchers' identification of 'musical' improvisatory phenomena in mother–infant 'protoconversation' and games (Beebe *et al.* 1979; Stern 1974a, b, 1977; Trevarthen 1974).

7 Archive material of The Nordoff-Robbins Music Therapy Center, New York University and of The Nordoff-Robbins Music Therapy Centre, London.

documentation of the impact of their improvisational approach and techniques with autistic children. Their publications, *Therapy in Music for Handicapped Children* (1971a), *Music Therapy in Special Education* (1971b) and *Creative Music Therapy* (1977) – a new revised edition is in press – describe in detail the developmental and emotional growth of these children within and outside the music therapy setting.

In group music therapy, Nordoff and Robbins' use of creatively improvised as well as structured music-making drew autistic children into a shared musical-emotional experience. Sometimes this was developed further in improvised or pre-composed musical plays or stories. In individual therapy, a six-year-old very remote autistic girl was gradually engaged by carefully improvised music that picked up her fleeting responses and met her mood. This mode of contact in music helped her overcome her tendency to avoid communication. As a lively, rhythmic 'What's that?' song was improvised for her, her use of words, including appropriate use of personal pronouns, increased (Nordoff and Robbins 1968). A second case study demonstrates the progress in music therapy of a five-and-a-half-year-old emotionally and behaviourally disturbed autistic boy. Musically matching and meeting the emotional intensity of the boy's screaming heightened the child's awareness of himself and led to 'singing-crying' responses which began to show features of musical relatedness in pitch and in melodic and rhythmic patterns. Positive developments included spontaneous enjoyment, playful babbling conversational exchanges, development and appropriate use of words, improved emotional stability and adaptability to new situations, including improved response to speech and language therapy. The musical relationship was one of acceptance and careful nurturing, as well as challenge, expectation and confrontation, intended to support the child's potential abilities and thereby diminish pathological or habitual features of response. Nordoff and Robbins give eloquent accounts of the flowering of the children's individual personalities and their unique personal expression through this creative music therapy approach.

A further original aspect of Nordoff and Robbins' work was their conception that the resistive responses of the child were often 'a corollary to participation'. 'Often, in a child's behaviour, resistiveness enfolds a developing response so closely as to require a most subtle transmission of musical experience' (Nordoff and Robbins 1977, p.190). They observed that the character of the child's 'resistiveness' changed with the level of participation. Within the musical relationship, working with 'resistiveness' was thus viewed positively as a means of meeting the child in the 'here and now' of relationship and seeking through this relationship to resolve and integrate the varied pathological aspects of the child's self-expression. A responsive 'self-structure' is implicit in Nordoff and Robbins' musical and relational perspective. Evaluation or rating scales were developed to assist a therapist trained in Nordoff–Robbins techniques to assess evolving clinical situations and to define clinical goals. The first scale shows the hierarchical organisation (presented in two columns and ascending in seven parallel points) of both resistive and participatory responses in the child–therapist relationship; a second scale charts musical communicativeness across three modalities of vocal and instrumental response and body movements. The 'lower' levels of this scale comprise 'evoked' responses, that is those that precede intentional communication, and that are of prime importance in the development of a musical relationship where the child's perceptual and/or motivational capacities are impaired. In Nordoff and Robbin's scheme, evoked levels bear many similarities to the interpersonal phenomena of Stern's 'emergent sense of self' (Stern 1985), which continue within more highly-developed, intentional forms and superstructures of communication. A third scale registers the structural-expressive elements of musical response.

The case studies of other music therapists record results similar to those already cited. Stevens and Clark (1969) reported increases in 'pro-social behaviours' (adaptive, adjustive and socially acceptable behaviours); Saperston's (1973) study of an eight-year-old autistic boy demonstrated increases in awareness of and interaction with his environment, improved eye contact and increased vocalisation; Mahlberg's (1973) study of a seven-year-old boy in music therapy as part of a composite treatment programme, which included speech and occupational therapies, highlighted increased self–other awareness, showing affection and initiating 'caring acts'. Increases in attention span and development of vocal imitation were found by Saperston (1982). The episodic patterns of play of a ten-year-old girl with autistic features in music therapy was analysed by Agrotou (1988), drawing parallels between mother–infant communication and the music therapy process, and showing increases in communication and spontaneous shared play. A study of a small group of autistic adolescent boys and girls by Bryan (1989) illustrates the impact of a slow tempo in helping the group play together. A psychoanalytically oriented account by Levinge (1990) of a two-and-a-half-year-old girl traces the development of her sense of self and use of 'You' and 'I'. Howat (1995) provides a detailed session by session description of the ways in which music therapy helped a young autistic girl during significant changes in her life.

The significance of music therapy for a young blind autistic girl, with a complex medical condition necessitating many operations in infancy is described by Robbins (1993); this child's musical responsiveness which developed in therapy, brought joy, creative self-expression and a more normal autonomy in relationships, which she could not achieve in any other way due to the nature of her needs and dependency. Robbins highlights the role of dance within creative music therapy, in developing this child's spatial awareness and self-confidence. Toigo (1992) provides a comprehensive account of the many ways in which music therapy can address the problems of autism, referring to the writings and experiences of Dr Temple Grandin, who herself has described her autistic sensitivities and perceptions in her work as an academic and inventor.

In a philosophical and clinical paper, examining why music can provide a medium for change and emotional well-being, Brown (1994) discusses some of the underlying emotional-behavioural problems secondary to autism, and in five case studies describes very specific individual difficulties and idiosyncrasies revealed by the musical phenomena.

The role of music therapy in the context of multi-disciplinary evaluation where diagnosis is required for children presenting a wide range of learning and communication difficulties is discussed by Wigram (1995). Several case studies illustrate his assessment procedures and make important distinctions between assessment and treatment in music therapy.

The Essential Motivating Power of Music as Therapy

Used creatively and improvisationally, and with clinical musical perception, music evidently can meet, engage, and support a child in spontaneously evolving interaction. As their experiences of sympathetic relating and of self-regulation in coactivity progress, autistic children appear to find both security and freedom in the music. Music as therapy evidently offers a context in which to build a sense of self-in-relationship, and this leads to developments in communication (e.g. a wider range of emotions and use of words) and interactive play. In the immediacy and creative variation of music and of the musically attuned relationship, shared meaning and symbolisation can grow.

Nordoff and Robbins (1971a) offer detailed interpretations of the process of clinical musical improvisation with autistic children:

> The flexibility of the therapist's playing searches out the region of contact for that child, creates the emotional substance of the contact and sets the musical ground for interactivity. The timing of his playing – the tempo, its rhythms and pauses – attentively follows, leads and follows the child's activity, supporting the experience it carries; his capacity for musical expressiveness in his playing and his singing is at the service of the child's involvement... His improvising is free of any restrictions of conventional musical form for it must constantly meet the changing forms of the child's response. (p.144)

They describe the extensive range of emotional experience that music, spontaneously improvised in relationship to a child, can offer:

> ...in addition to the 'conventional' range of emotions, all kind of moods and nuances of feeling can be realised, all subtleties and progression of change, all degrees of intensity. There are experiences of *form* and *order*...and the forms that are creatively, expressively realised. There are the basic elements of *tempo* and *rhythm*, fundamental to music and fundmental to our extramusical organisation and life. The *melodic element* contains all the above as well as the evocative

> concurrences between speech and music – these also make directly possible in *song* the setting and expression of thought forms and ideas that have personal significance for a child. (Nordoff and Robbins 1977, p.2, original emphasis).

Music is both sound and silence. Actively experienced silences (Nordoff and Robbins 1977) can be provided in the improvisational music-making context as a 'space' in which self-awareness may begin to emerge. The therapist needs 'to respect the child's silences and to give space, both physical and emotional in which the relationship should develop' (Warwick 1995, p.216). At first the music therapist sensitively supports and fosters the tiniest impulses, in order to find initial contact.

The tensions and resolutions of social–emotional interaction give rise to bodily and emotional experiences described as a 'sense of self' (Stern 1985; Trevarthen 1993c). For the autistic child, cohesion and entrainment of responses at a somatic-affective level can be engendered by music within a dynamic relational framework, which sets up new patterns of experience and of reciprocity (Rider and Eagle 1986). At a fundamental level of sensory-motor-affective functioning, music can provide a medium in which the autistic child can experience and explore a sense of equilibrium and healthy autonomy through a range of emotional-developmental levels adjusted to that individual child's needs and personality.

The musical-emotional-aesthetic features and the temporal (rhythmic) organisation of the interpersonal relationship provide vital information to the music therapist. From moment to moment, and from session to session, he or she can perceive how to further the child's development and how to address the child's individual strengths and needs. Many music therapists record their sessions on audio or videotape for later evaluation of the musical–dynamic content.[8] This ensures continuity and consistency of clinical direction with each client. Whilst 'meeting' and supporting the child in the music, the music therapist is thus gathering and synthesising detailed information about the child's emotional or developmental level and potential for inter-responsiveness, where he or she is comfortably able to function in empathic reaction.

Indicated in the above paragraphs is the path that the musical relationship may take after initial musical contact with the child; from primary motivation to emotional communication, mutuality, shared meaning and symbolisation – developments which will be examined later in the case study concluding this chapter.

---

8 Audio and video recordings are kept as confidential clinical records, case studies for teaching or training purposes (with signed consent of the parties concerned), or otherwise are erased.

Working with Avoidant, Habitual and Stereotypic Expression in Music Therapy

Habitual or stereotypic behaviour patterns may be the autistic child's way to regulate states of arousal and interest precipitated by the complex, often overwhelming, stimuli of social–emotional communication. As described above, avoidance or remoteness can be addressed musically and emotionally, by meeting the child's mood and mediating a carefully measured expression of feelings in communication. Through musical imitation or enhancement, through sound and silence, the therapist may support, heighten and bring out a new feeling-tone – may bring about a change in subjective experience, transforming the child's preoccupations, or those 'sensation-dominated states' or 'auto-sensuous barriers' described by Tustin (1986, 1994). Furthermore, the music improvisational enhancement can introduce a vital quality, which either reflects the child's behaviour through matching tonal or rhythmic aspects of the child's expression, or offers a complementary or contrasting mood. This provides a relational context, a basis for musical-emotional interaction.

Progressing from the first levels of response evoked or influenced by the music, subsequent changes in feeling states may be nurtured through use of clinically-directed musical techniques intended to heighten self-awareness and shared emotional communication. Such forms of self-experience and relatedness through the medium of music may help an evasive or remote child tolerate affective contact, whereupon two-way communication can be developed at the child's pace and in the child's own individual style.

In the case of a child whose habitual or ritualistic behaviours are deeply entrenched, a more directive, intrusive intervention by the therapist can prove helpful. Such intervention, far from being insensitive or uncreative, requires very fine, careful perceptions by the therapist as to the child's inner capacities and strengths (or state of 'ego-development'). Intervention in therapy, whether behaviouristic or psychodynamic, tends to generate heated debate, and a directive approach by the therapist is not generally accepted. Tustin (1986) and Howlin and Rutter (1987), however, agree with the behaviour therapist Lovaas (1987), that autistic children often need active help to leave their habitual behaviour patterns. Autistic children often become 'wound up' in sensory, ritualistic, sometimes self-injurious actions and experiences and they need assistance to find different forms of self-experience, leading to a relatedness with others, which they usually cannot create for themselves. This perspective is expanded by the child psychotherapist Alvarez (1992) when she describes the therapist acting as an 'auxiliary ego' in work with children who have significant 'ego-deficits'. Autistic children frequently need help of this kind.

Discovering security in predictable musical patterns as well as experiencing the tension of unresolved anticipation in musical interplay can help an autistic child deal with the variety and change in the routines and rituals of everyday life with other people. Maintaining a balance between the familiar and the novel is an important aspect of flexibility and adaptability of response, an aspect of freedom in self-expression and social interaction. In music therapy this can begin to be fostered to lead the child towards more creative and interactive forms of expression.

Experiencing and Experiencing with

In music therapy, vitality of expression and (finely-judged) moments of change are brought into the experiencing of the autistic child by means of rhythm, harmonic progression, changing intensities, melodic movement and repetition of motif – and much more besides. Timbre (musical overtones giving characteristic 'colour' and 'texture' to sounds), as well as the tactile and visual qualities of the musical instruments, have a vital part to play in engaging the autistic child's spontaneous involvement in a comprehensible world of dynamic form and change. From this experiencing in and for the self, the child is helped to experience with the other.[9]

When spontaneity recedes into perseverative patterns of play, or when a lively sharing 'collapses' into habitual, stereotypic preoccupation, the dynamic musical contact must first return to a basic subjective (rather than intersubjective) experiencing – simply perceiving sound, silence, timbre, musical mood – enhancing the child's bodily sensing of self in 'lived' or 'experienced' time, as Langer (1953) described it. This corresponds to Neisser's 'ecological self', or the self-with-body in the field of stimulation, taking information about the changing relations with the environment (Neisser 1993). This is the basic ground of being or experiencing, to which musical relationship with an autistic child frequently needs to return. The music therapist carefully adjusts the musical-emotional components (e.g. harmonic textures or sonorities, sustaining of tones within melodic phrase or contour), including interpersonal temporal patterns, meeting the clinically/musically perceived needs of the child to bring about moments of relatedness, however fleeting or fragmentary. It is through this cathexis of basic emotional communication in music that a sensation of 'I', 'You' and 'It' can begin to evolve and form as a relational entity.

---

9 To bring the child's experience into the realm of personal, social and cultural values is perhaps the most fundamental task of music improvisation in therapy for autistic children, who are so devastatingly impaired in this respect. The significance of this level of consciousness is described by R. P. Hobson (1991) as follows: '...children arrive at knowledge about the nature of persons...through experience of affectively charged interpersonal relations' (p.44); and the phenomenon is further examined by R. F. Hobson (1985): 'Experiencing is a spontaneous activity in which elementary shapes emerge, are related, dissolved, and re-combined. They are elaborated in diverse forms. I shall term that process symbolical transformation (p.84)...The activity of symbolical transformation...weaves a pattern of significance, of "meaning in life". The key to this sense of *meaning*, especially in the dialogue of personal relationships, is the living symbol.' (p.85)

In working with autistic children, the dynamic musical processes in therapy bring valuable and fascinating glimpses of how a sense of self emerges and how that sense of self can be maintained from moment to moment in a fullness and richness of being.

Case Study of 'Colin', a Three-and-a-Half-Year-Old Boy with Autism

In the following case study of Colin we shall see how musical improvisation can develop social-emotional communication and symbolisation.[10] In particular, musical improvisational processes which constitute 'temporal and emotional organisation' will be identified in their role of providing the autistic child with the kind of creative and self-regulating emotional experiences that can assist development of empathic communication and social interaction.

The dynamic forms of the musical improvisation were carefully clinically adapted to meet and support the child's responses. In this way, emotional contact was made, sustained and developed through music. Change was instigated and supported by musical means that heightened Colin's self-awareness. The creative resources of the music therapy interaction helped him progress through early developmental patterns of spontaneous shared play. Patterns of more flexible inter-responsiveness were fostered musically, helping to diminish some of the restrictions imposed by his autism.

Colin's Early History

Colin was a placid baby who was thought to be developing normally until the age of one and a half years, when his lack of progress in language and abnormalities in social development caused concern. He was then communicating by gesture only in a limited way, and did not babble, but rather screeched. He related to family members, but showed strong aversion to the voices of strangers. Colin had temper tantrums if his routines were upset, but, oddly, he did not cry if hurt or if toys were taken away from him. He showed no awareness of danger. He was physically energetic, often spinning himself around in circles, or jumping up and down, flapping his arms. He showed no 'symbolic' or imitative play, except with a telephone, with which he could echo speech-like sounds.

The diagnostic impression of Colin when he was three years old was given as 'autistic disorder with onset in childhood, accompanied by language delay and learning delay'. He was referred to music therapy for help with his emotional-behavioural and social communication difficulties.

---

10 Colin's music therapy sessions were recorded on audio tape, and, with the exception of the first two sessions, on video as well. A colleague operated the video camera in the therapy room as unobtrusively as possible.

Colin began individual music therapy when he was three and a half years old. He received forty-six sessions of thirty minutes each over a period of eighteen months. His mother played an important supportive role in his therapy sessions until the final months of treatment. The sessions took place at the same time and place each week, and he was carefully prepared for any holidays or other breaks in regularity of treatment.

At the age of four and a half, after a year of music therapy as his only formal therapeutic input, Colin was diagnosed by a leading authority as having autism in the classic form described by Kanner (1943). However, his imaginative play was described as being unusually advanced in view of the overall results of his specialist psychological-developmental assessment. The speech and language therapist who later treated Colin made a similar observation.

The music therapy room in which Colin was treated is a purpose-built, sound-attenuated room, dedicated to music therapy. It measures about six metres square and has no inessential equipment or other distractions.[11] An upright piano (well-maintained and in tune), stands in one corner of the room, and various large and small professional and ethnic percussion instruments are available, sometimes displayed on a low wooden bench. A lockable cabinet contains a collection of the smaller instruments, beaters, and the audio recording equipment. (A room adjacent to the therapy room stores the large percussion and tuned instruments, such as conga and temple drums, bass metallophone, tenor xylophone, tubular bells, a range of cymbals on stands, and Chinese temple-blocks).

SESSION 1: WORKING MUSICALLY WITH RAGE REACTION – MAKING CONTACT THROUGH THE MUSIC[12]

Colin entered the therapy room, holding his mother's hand. The room contained a snare drum (with the snares removed to soften the sound), a cymbal (14 inches in diameter) on a stand, a pair of small beaters or drumsticks, a tambourine, two handchimes (on a wooden bench), and two small chairs, one larger chair, an upright piano and piano stool.

On seeing me, Colin threw himself onto the floor, where he lay prone and motionless. I remained where I was, by the bench. I tentatively tapped a few beats on the tambourine and paused. Colin showed no response or reaction. His mother sat down quietly on a chair some distance away from him. I began to sing softly, while trying to gauge his mood, and immediately Colin screamed and 'drummed' his feet on the floor, his rage soon escalating to a full-scale

---

11 Music therapy with autistic children, or with other children and adolescents with emotional and behavioural difficulties, is almost impossible in a large hall or playroom where there is no contained or defined space, or in a room where there is the distraction of equipment for general play or physical education.

12 The therapist continues the account, referring to herself in the first person.

temper tantrum. To meet the intensity and match the tonal–rhythmic emotional characteristics of Colin's screaming and kicking, I began communicating with him from the piano, using intense, full-bodied and sometimes dissonant harmonies in a minor key. This seemed to resonate with and acknowledge some of the emotional tension and pathos in his sounds. After repeating this twice and pausing for about the same phrase-length between playing, I noticed that Colin's screaming was not only in the tonality of the music, but was showing more clearly defined tonal–rhythmic elements of the music with which I had matched his initial sounds. His 'drumming' feet had begun to acquire an emotionally expressive organisation in the music.

I lengthened my pauses between playing, whereupon Colin initiated a further 'drumming' of his feet as if requesting the the dialogue should continue. Soon his screaming became more clearly pitched, and showed a further communicative exchange of two notes possibly evoked or influenced by a quiet two-note motif I had played within the intensity of musical response to his rage. Through dynamic contrasts and temporal–emotional organisation of this kind which met Colin's mood and matched salient features of his emotional expression, a musical relationship began to form between us.[13]

In the increasing spontaneity and confidence of this exchange I sang 'hello'. From the comparative steadiness and regularity of our 'conversation', Colin's rage revived anew, his screams glissando-ing in an ascending scale to the tonic (high 'doh') of my/our music's tonality. Here we see the musical phenomenon of 'being in tune' with someone presenting at an evoked level (as opposed to a focused, intentionally aware response), assisting the child's self-organisation and self-regulation, even when 'beside himself' with rage. As further episodes of conversational feet-drumming and vocalisation ensued, I began to overlap my responses with his, so that his responses would not be too exposed in the pauses and would be 'camouflaged' to avoid possibly overloading his newly heightened self-awareness. Later in the session Colin showed interest in spinning the cymbal. His emotional communication with me was replaced by the 'auto-sensuous' visual and tactile pleasure of this activity. At the end of the session he left the therapist room quietly with his mother.

---

13 Papousek and Papousek (1981, p.206) emphasise the *instructive* function of the parent's imitation of the infant's sounds, which, they claim, provide the infant with a 'biological mirror' or a 'biological echo' allowing him or her to compare auditory products on both sides... This is an important condition for the development of the *infant's initiative capacity* and hence for the development of both language and self-concept. Parents commonly imitate infants' expressions, and this is used conversationally to regulate the interpersonal contact, calming or exciting the infant and encouraging creative messages as seems appropriate to the infants' changing moods and interests (Trevarthen 1979; Kugiumutzakis 1993).

INTERPRETATIONS:

(1) This first session revealed Colin's capacity for two-way communication, not only imitating but initiating contact. This is not unusual in a first music therapy session with an autistic child, and the child's retreat into more perseverative and self-stimulatory behaviours in subsequent sessions is also a common clinical experience.

(2) Colin's mother was able to resist comforting her son in his rage and possible distress. When we spoke later, she said she had wanted to console him, but then had realised that 'something was going on in the music'. Her role in the early sessions was to support (and console) Colin when necessary, but to allow as much contact as possible to take place through the music. In this way communication could be developed within the musical–emotional framework. Regular contact between Colin's mother and myself was maintained away from the therapy room, and away from Colin, throughout his treatment, to discuss his progress and share information.

(3) Tonality forming a background for incipient (evoked) musical-emotional relatedness is a musical phenomenon as influential as pulse in creating a basis for empathic relationship and entraining inter-responsiveness.

(4) The temporal structures using rhythmically placed rests or silences were particularly important in developing Colin's intentionality in musical–emotional dialogue and correspond to the 'burst-pause' neonatal patterns of interaction described by Brazelton and Cramer (1991) and the phrases identified in infant vocalisation by Lynch *et al.* (1995). The lengthening of the pause creates tension and anticipation for the child in interaction, very similar to the scaler timing process ('elastic band') described by Stern (1977, pp.91, 92). The tempi of intercommunication with Colin occurred within the 'magic range' of timing in mother–infant interaction, at approximately 66–200 beats per minute (Beebe 1982); that is, from a slow, relaxed tempo to a very urgent one.

The key aims of therapy were determined by these initial sessions, as follows:

(1) To help Colin increase his tolerance of dynamic forms of sensory–affective stimuli in communication.

(2) To develop his vocalisation and vocal dialogue.

(3) To increasing his capacity for self-expression and self–other awareness.

(4) To develop spontaneity and flexibility of his play in interaction.

(5) To find means whereby he could be more easily diverted from habitual, ritualistic, perseverative or obsessive behaviours.

SESSIONS 2–7: TRANSITION TO MORE PLAYFUL VOCAL COMMUNICATION

The second session was similar to the first, but there was a noticeable increase in stereotypic and avoidant behaviour, such as hand-flapping and cymbal-spinning, interspersed with fleeting moments of vocal communication within temper tantrums. His habit of lying on the floor seemed to 'ground' him emotionally as well as physically, and his responses were often similar to those of a baby. As he tended to roll away if I or his mother approached him in his withdrawn state, communication through music was essential as a medium for making emotional contact. Although hard to sustain any flow of vocal dialogue, my singing of two- and three-note tonal motifs elicited an almost gurgling-singing response from Colin; he now seemed to accept my voice, but otherwise seemed to be enjoying being quite calm in a world of his own.

INTERPRETATIONS:

These sessions mark a settling-down period. The musical setting and myself, no longer novel, did not elicit the temper tantrums and rage reaction which had successfully transformed into carefully regulated dialogue. Colin may have experienced the improvised music and the therapist partly as 'intrusive', partly as something about which he felt 'OK'. The balance between these two facets of response to music therapy interaction continued to be important for Colin's development, and the experience of negotiating with his feelings, from the extreme to the near imperceptible levels of expression, taught me a great deal about the role of more intrusive, yet creative musical intervention with autistic children. This less interactive period helped develop a sense of mutual acceptance and trust between Colin and myself.

SESSIONS 8–17: MORE SELF-AWARENESS, INITIATION AND INTENTIONALITY IN SHARED MUSICAL-EMOTIONAL COMMUNICATION; PROGRESSING THROUGH EARLY DEVELOPMENTAL PATTERNS OF PLAY

In session eight Colin showed intermittent interest in playing the cymbal, rather than spinning it. My playing music in the wholetone scale enhanced the overtones of the cymbal, making as direct a connection as possible with Colin's auditory experience of his own actions. The 'on-goingness' of this scale (which has no harmonic cadences to stem the flow) helped to sustain his playing for nearly four minutes in his characteristic 'action-pause' episodes. He would walk away after each period of six to eight seconds of engagement. This pattern of withdrawal seemed to be his way of modulating his excitement in the experience of shared play, which, while following and supporting him, was not solely on his terms. My use of 'active silences' (Nordoff and Robbins 1977; Alvin and Warwick 1991) offered a musically-contrived encouragement for him to initiate a beat. This he did very tentatively on the drum, becoming rather excited and beating faster, accelerating until he could hardly maintain his rather immature grip on the beater. After a brief pause, I initiated on the piano a similar 'accelerando' within Colin's tempo range, which he spontaneously followed on the drum, looking directly across at me as he played, his excitement still evident.

DEVELOPMENTAL PATTERNS OF PLAY: OBSESSIONAL–REPETITIVE PLAY AND THE USE OF ANTICIPATION–RESOLUTION ('ANACRUSIS')

Colin's obsessive play and prevaricating behaviour began to increase. His interests now included jumping from a low ledge that covered the heating system, lying on the floor and pushing or kicking away any musical instruments nearby, picking up and throwing beaters repeatedly, or lying on his back and kicking the door (which he did at home). He liked running and bumping himself against the wall, before running back to his mother and bumping into her in the same manner. In this particular young child, this behaviour seemed to represent a practising of early developmental phases of play. He seemed to be checking out physical boundaries and exploring the various basic self-experiences involved in losing and finding. At the same time, he was impervious to any alternative games or variations offered by myself or his mother.

Although I matched aspects of his activity in the music, or listened in silence to enable him to 'listen' to himself, he became increasingly caught up in the momentum of his activity. In order to help him out of this vortex of separate activity and re-enter shared play, I enhanced certain elements of his expression, in such a way as to provide some shaping or modulation of his auto-sensory experience. I created sequential musical phrases on an ascending scale which formed an external temporal–affective framework, into which Colin's repetitive activity might be drawn.[14]

Using a melodic phrase on the up-beat (known in musical terminology as the 'anacrusis') as a preparatory, tension/attention-creating device, I then resolved the tension with a slight hesitation on an accented beat. I sometimes shaped the 'anacrusis' both vocally (in a descending melodic phrase and gesturally, raising my arms above my head before bringing them down in a slow arc onto the drum nearby, concluding the movement with a slight rubato preceding a sudden sforzando beat to coincide exactly with his jump and landing on the floor. This device of anticipation and resolution-with-surprise was a temporal and emotionally/physically regulating, self-organising structure which caught his attention, especially when his mother matched her son's landing and my strong beat with a clap of her hands, so that all three of us finished 'together'. Colin now looked at his mother, then at me, prior to each

14 The research of Trehub *et al.* (1977, 1989, 1990a) shows the early development of the infant's capacity to process rhythm and melody, particularly structural elements such as sequence, confirming that the 'global processing strategy' underlying language acquisition is already intact in infants. Infants enter language through rhythmic and prosodic communication (Bruner 1983; Trevarthen 1987a; Lock 1993; Lynch *et al.* 1995).

jump – finally his activity became a shared experience, and for a time at least it seemed important to him that this was so.

His confidence seemed robust enough for me to assess his capacity for flexibility and adaptability by 'stretching' an interaction. I retained certain musical elements of the anacrusis by developing a hierarchy of sequential phrases, but shortened the final one to catch his attention. The first time the shortened phrase was used, Colin looked disconcerted and stared blankly past me for a moment, before he somehow accepted the 'new' shape of interaction, responding with a one second time lag. Without this kind of shaping of inter-responsiveness, Colin would return to flapping his hands, throwing sticks, picking them up again and becoming 'stuck' in perseverative activity. I had to 'animate' the play in ways that did not overwhelm him, that struck a balance between structure (e.g. the temporal–affective organisation of the 'anacrusis') and freedom (e.g. periods of silence, or the introduction of variation, creative developments from familiar to unfamiliar elements of music). He seemed unable to discover and maintain a flexibility of motivation alone.

INTERPRETATIONS:

(1) In these sessions, the 'temporal feeling shape', described by Stern (1994) as 'a temporal contour of feeling that unfolds during a moment in which a motive is in play', was used to counter aspects of Colin's obsessive habits of play. The emotional dynamic and a cohesiveness introduced in this way enabled Colin to accommodate change and respond to me at his 'immature' level of functioning.

'Temporal-affective contouring' proved to be a powerful 'self-regulator' for Colin, helping him accommodate to and assimilate a variety in patterns of emotional and social interaction in this early play, and it laid the ground for more complex aesthetic forms of music-emotional communication that were to develop later.

(2) Here the 'temporal feeling shape' is applied in therapy for a child who does not yet have a motive for play. The playful feeling, and especially its communicative aspects, had to be externally aroused and then regulated within the musical contour or 'feeling shape', giving form to his subjective and intersubjective (shared) experiences. Colin began to laugh at our interactions. His mother commented that she had never seen him laugh so normally.

In music therapy this strategy can be particularly useful as a 'cueing' device to secure a dynamic structure for the child, whose attention needs to be focused or whose emotional awareness is being held or entrained. Where self-organisation is immature and poorly regulated, or the emotions labile – for example, in very young or developmentally delayed children, and in emotionally disturbed or

> traumatised children – the presentation of a musical 'anacrusis' or a feeling contour leading to a stressed beat can provide an invaluable (and infinitely variable) aid to regulation and a means to facilitate trust and emotional engagement in shared play.
>
> Autistic children seem to derive particular benefit from such emotional regulation, and seem to require a much more carefully prepared and often more exaggeratedly intense expression of this than children with other learning and developmental difficulties. Maximum clarity of structure in the 'feeling shape' seems to be needed, often using more than one expressive modality.[15] Above all, timing and the use of silences are critical devices to sustain the musical/emotional connection.

SESSION 18: SUSTAINING SELF-EXPRESSIVE VOCAL AND CROSS-MODAL FORMS OF EMOTIONAL COMMUNICATION

This session marked an important shift in Colin's capacity to participate coactively. After several episodes of musical dialogue, which were entrained by the 'anacrusis' technique, Colin began to sustain the flow of the musical conversation with the support only of a steady andante accompaniment in a D major and minor tonality, which I played at the piano.

At first he was preoccupied in taking his shoes and socks off, but then Colin looked up at me as I sang about what he was doing: 'Colin's (pause) SOCK!' and 'taking it (pause) OFF!'. As usual Colin's attention was engaged and held by certain familiar aspects of the temporal–affective structure, and even more so when the resolution (or cadence) of the phrase was withheld, creating an increase of tension (and attention) that accompanies anticipation. This time I sang the 'anacrusis' allargando (i.e. at a much slower tempo), adding further tension by widening the melodic intervals within the contour or phrase. Colin's face and vocal sounds expressed heightened pleasure in his recognition and naming of 'sock' (at the phrase end), as he held it up in his right hand. Moments later, passing his sock to his left hand, he held it up with a deft movement, and echoed an approximation of the word 'off'. There followed several episodes of sustained preverbal musical communication, involving babble sounds and open vowel sounds in short rhythmic exchanges, as well as in intersynchronous cross-modal forms of communication.[16] The spontaneous vocalisations and variations in vocal exchange which Colin initiated were very encouraging developments. His facial expression and physical attitude registered occasional surges of pleasure and surprise (at himself and the musical dialogue, it seemed

---

15 This concurs with the research study of Thaut (1988). See footnote 7.

16 This sequence on video provides a fascinating record of Colin's processing across a spectrum of emotional and cognitive states in preverbal and verbal communication. Similar sequences are described by Warwick (1995).

to me). His need to modulate the intensity of his new level of emotional comunication manifested in periodic withdrawing, sometimes to the door (and its satisfyingly round handle), sometimes to his mother, bumping up against her or almost throwing himself onto her lap.

The session ended with Colin sitting on his mother's lap beside me at the piano, and touching the keys with his bare feet. As one of his feet was about to strike a cluster of notes, I gently delayed its descent so that it then 'played' in time with the stressed beat of 'bye-bye'. Colin then played the two-beat motif with his hands, turn-taking within the 'bye-bye' song. Colin then sang bye-bye ('dye-dye') several times in turn with me and glancing at his mother and myself with pleasure and understanding.

After the session his mother and I discussed the use of short phrases and placing the 'key word' at the end of phrase in helping Colin begin to develop more fluent interaction and to motivate him to use words.

INTERPRETATIONS:

This session was significant for its development of vocalisation in prosodic, pre-speech forms of turn-taking. Rhythmic and melodic contouring were important factors in sustaining phrased vocal exchanges.

SESSION 21: DEVELOPMENT OF VARIETY AND FLEXIBILITY IN INTERACTIVE PLAY

Now Colin often became fractious and difficult to engage. However, when his tempestuous mood was met by my playing short 'volleys' of dissonant chord clusters (using a scale form with flattened second and sixth intervals) in an intense crescendo and in the tonality of his gurning sounds, he gave a half-smile. It seemed as if this music had 'struck the right note' for him. The intensity of the harmonies created a physical–emotional experience, involving cycles of successive tensions and resolutions. Having engaged Colin's interest, I offered a complete change of mood by introducing a playful arpeggio (or ascending/descending patterns of intervals) on the piano. Colin soon joined in, imitating my rather exaggerated prodding movements with his index finger – a new experience for him. He then accepted successive variations in pattern and phrase length, which shortened or lengthened randomly and were too swift and spontaneous for him to echo or imitate exactly as the interaction gained momentum. This resulted in increased freedom from slavish copying and provided exposure to new musical experiences which he himself began initiating almost in spite of himself. Colin enjoyed this new game. It seemed to comprise the right balance of the expected and unexpected stimulating his emotional involvement from moment to moment, the structural elements giving him the means to contain his excitement.

SESSION 24: DEVELOPING THREE-WAY COMMUNICATION

Colin had begun to jargon communicatively. At the beginning of this session he seemed to be trying to request his mother to play one of the reed horns. A three-way interaction with his mother and myself developed and continued in the subsequent months of therapy. His vocal range increased particularly during his playing of the reed horns. His intentionality in vocal communication became much more consistent and playful in character, showing his desire to sustain the shared play with less reliance on adult support. He became able to communicate with more than one person at a time and this was noted outside of the music therapy sessions. It was possible to work more directly with any resistive or avoidant behaviour, for example, by offering 'yes–no' games, which posed questions, and encouraged his close attending to the meaning of what I was asking him. Colin's use of words increased to short phrases, uttered somewhat stiltedly, as if he were retrieving newly acquired language and needing to concentrate while using it to communicate.

SESSION 40: MISSING HIS MUMMY IN THE SESSION; EXPRESSING SADNESS, ANGER AND UPSET

Colin had begun to attend school and could separate easily from his mother, but he had become used to her being with him in the music therapy room and found it difficult to break this pattern. Both his mother and I felt it might be a good time to try to effect this separation while encouraging more flexibility in the therapy sessions.

Colin entered the therapy room reluctantly, his lower lip quivering. As I sang to him, he responded: 'No want Jackie!' and proceeded to knock over several small chairs in the room. Without reacting to this I responded to his mood, playing a slow pulse in a minor key in the mid to bass register of the piano. Reflecting his feelings musically and verbally, I sang about how he felt in the room without his mother. His pleased glances of recognition and understanding alternated with ambivalent angry–sad glowering expressions. Both the music's pulse, its sonorities and harmonies and my verbal reflecting of his feeling states seemed to contain his feelings. His increased emotional stability and ability to self-regulate his feelings also seemed to help him reflect on himself in this unhappy situation. He played and sang a tearful goodbye at the piano, becoming more lively in response to my offering our familiar arpeggio patterns of play.

INTERPRETATIONS:

In this session, as emotional tensions and their resolutions were addressed both in the music and verbally, phenomenological and psychodynamic ways of working in the therapy were combined.

I made use of the following psychodynamic ideas:

(1) Bion's (1959, 1962) concept of the 'alpha function' of the mother who contains and transforms the baby's emotions when they threaten to overwhelm him.

(2) Winnicott's concepts of the infant's 'going-on-being' as the mother provides 'holding', and of 'transitional objects and phenomena' that

support creative ideas (1965, 1971). I consider musical or sonorous phenomena as such 'objects'.

On the other hand, the phenomenological musically-defined elements of the therapy included:

(1) Application of changes in tone, rhythm and tempo to match or enhance Colin's vocal sounds, movements or gestures ('attunement').

(2) A 'pedal point' or steady pulse played on the tonic, dominant, or flattened second, to give a sense of continuity and support while meeting Colin's mood and holding his attention.

(3) The use of marked silences to evoke Colin's creative potential for self-experience and reflection.

SESSION 43: HIDE AND SEEK – FURTHER DEVELOPMENTS IN SYMBOLISATION

Colin began to use 'I' and 'You' in this session, and he spontaneously used my name and that of the video camera operator. He had begun to enjoy hiding behind either the curtains or the piano. This theme of losing and finding, of disappearing and re-appearing continued in different ways. Colin was greatly amused by the alterations in these tensions and resolutions, but gradually reverted to rather fixed temporal patterns in his play, the sense of shared experience receding. He needed constant musical intervention to maintain flexibility and a real sense of interaction.

SESSION 44: COLIN'S CAPACITY FOR COMPROMISE BETWEEN SOCIAL AND AUTO-SENSUOUS PLAY

Colin now more frequently and spontaneously initiated communicative play with me, vocally, with the other instruments (particularly the reed horn), and at the piano. However, in recent sessions he had become interested in the piano pedals, enjoying their feel, shape and taste as much as their action. He kept ducking down under the keyboard to touch and taste the pedals, coming up just in time, or almost in time, to complete the phrase in the 'Goodbye' song I was singing.[17] This was a good example of Colin's increased flexibility and capacity for what I perceived as a reasonable compromise between his autistic, sensory enjoyments, self-regulatory devices, and his taking part in a social world, which held as many joys as complexities for him. Our final goodbye in this song expressed both mutual enjoyment, affection and humourous exasperation – sentiments shared by the best of friends.

---

17 With Colin I tended to improvise such songs in response to his behaviour in the moment to ensure as far as possible, a really shared, spontaneous, alive experience rather than a conditioned, memorised repetition. Other children, particularly those who are emotionally disturbed, may need the security offered by repeated presentation of a familiar song, which may then become the basis for developing emotional expression and communication in improvisation.

Colin's parents reported that he was now relating more spontaneously to his siblings, although at times was almost too attached to his older brother. His school and speech therapy reports were very encouraging, particularly in respect of:

(1) his increased use of spontaneous language rather than gesture to express his needs and feelings;

(2) his social awareness and sense of being in a group with his peers;

(3) his symbolic and imaginative play continuing to develop well and in advance of his overall level of development.

Conclusion

Music therapy played a significant role in developing this autistic child's emotional, integrative and self-organisational experiences. Colin's case illustrates how the spontaneously created, clinically-oriented use of musical improvisation shares many of the dynamic (and musical–improvisatory) forms of mother–infant communication fundamental to psychological development and personality growth. The power of music to reach into the emotional experience and inner being of a child is the essence of music as therapy, which engages and influences the whole personality and potential of the individual, changing awareness, initiative and the capacity for learning and development.

CHAPTER 12

Psychoanalysis and the Management of Pervasive Developmental Disorders, Including Autism

Olga Maratos[1]

Psychoanalyst, Associate Professor of Clinical Psychology, University of Athens, Greece

The Psychoanalytic Approach to Autism

Psychoanalysts began studying autism as a different condition with special features soon after Kanner's famous article was published. Until then autism was described under the broadly-defined category of 'early childhood psychosis'. Most psychoanalysts do not enter into speculation about the aetiology of autism, although early articles on the subject, including some by Kanner (Kanner and Eisenberg 1956; Kanner 1973), hypothesised a probable relation between maternal depression, which may take the form of maternal withdrawal from caring and emotional involvement with the child, and a child's autism. The main psychoanalytic concern is the description of the child's mental functioning, affective states and the way he or she relates to people.

There are many different theoretical attempts to explain autism within the psychoanalytic school of thought. Margaret Mahler's theory, based on classical Freudian Ego Psychology and the school of Self Psychology, stressed the pathological way in which 'symbiotic' and autistic children interact with people and objects, and their inability to interact meaningfully (Mahler 1968). She thought of autism as a subgroup of infantile psychosis, with symptoms that become apparent quite early and certainly during the first year of life. Mahler

1 This chapter is based on a talk that Dr Maratos, a distinguished child psychologist known for her pioneering work on neonatal imitation, gave at the Department of Psychology, The University of Edinburgh in February, 1995.

also stressed the fact that these children seem to receive many sensations from the inside of the body and from the objects of the environment though the senses separately. It appears that the autistic child cannot integrate such sensory impressions into a meaningful whole, or into coherent objects.

Donald Meltzer, of the Kleinian school[2], described the autistic *state of mind*, which can be found in many children who suffer from early mental disturbances, as follows (Meltzer *et al.* 1975). He thinks that most autistic children are more intelligent than appears in formal tests and that they have an abnormally acute perceptual sensitivity and emotional sensibility. Meltzer has hypothesised a process which he calls 'dismantling', brought about by the suspension of attention to the whole function of an object and which allows the senses to wander each to the most attractive part of the object at any one moment. This scattering of awareness brings about a passive dismantling of the self, and the sense of wholeness and the continuity of being is thus destroyed. When this happens the child is dominated by primitive emotions, some of which may be painful. This is why Meltzer suggests that it is necessary for the therapist to try to mobilise the child's suspended attention in order to bring it back to a coherent relationship with objects, and with the child's own self.

Frances Tustin (1981) also stresses the predominance of disorderly sensations in the life of the autistic child, and she describes a number of distinct types of autistic states in autistic and psychotic children ('shell'-type, 'segmented', 'confusional', etc.). On the basis of her wide clinical experience with psychotherapy of autistic children, her descriptions of their behaviour, of the psychological defense mechanisms that these children use, as well as of the actual techniques she herself practiced with them in therapy, have all been extremely useful to child therapists.

French psychoanalysts have also helped in our thinking about autism: (1) by stressing the organising effect that language can have on children who do not themselves speak (psychoanalysts following the Lacanian school[3]); (2) stressing the importance in therapy of the use of specific words referring to the body, food, emotions, etc. (Genevieve Haag[4]); (3) the introduction into the psychoanalytic literature of the 'pictogramme' (Piera Aulagnier 1981) which is a theoretical concept referring to the link between the first mental representations and the somatic areas or zones, a link that forms a complex qualified

---

2 For a summary of the theory of Melanie Klein, see Segal (1964) and Hinshelwood (1991).

3 Jacques Lacan, a leading French psychoanalyst, reformulated Freudian theory to give more importance to language and he attributed less importance to psychic energy, affects and emotions in the functioning of the unconscious.

4 See footnote 2, p.162.

by psychic energy. Autistic children, Aulagnier believes, have severe difficulties in forming this iconic representation.[5]

Psychoanalytically-oriented psychotherapies with autistic children use a variety of psychoanalytic concepts and adapt the technique to suit each child's needs. The main concept of 'transference' is explored in attempts to relate with the child. Transference is the process by which the unconscious desires of the patient towards the other person are actualised during the psychoanalytic procedure; the desires and conflicts are usually considered to be repetitions of infantile prototypes. As with all children, play material is used during the therapeutic session. It is believed that the stability of the setting (that is, fixed days and hours as well as fixed length of the therapeutic hour), neutrality of the therapist and stability of interventions, all help the child build a basic trust in the other person. Special modification of the classical psychoanalytic technique for children may also be required with some autistic children. For instance, some kinds of food (milk or biscuits) or use of a potty may be employed on the assumption that somatic sensations and needs are important to children who interact in a primitive and disturbed way.

Finally, it should be stated that psychoanalytically-oriented therapy has considerable success with autistic children, usually after many long years of treatment. Some such children can and do get out of the autistic state of mind, as has been described in many reports on the outcome of individual psychotherapies published in the psychoanalytic journals. It appears that the psychoanalytic treatment has significantly facilitated improvement in these cases.

My Experience in a School for Autistic Children

Some 12 years ago, I and a few other professionals decided to do something to fill a big gap in the Greek mental health system; to start what we then thought was going to be a therapeutic nursery school for children with pervasive developmental disorders (autistic and psychotic children, without marked mental retardation). Our aims were to provide services for the children and their families, to promote research, to provide specialist training for professionals and to exert pressure on the state and the public so they would look on these early disturbances of mental development in a different way.

We worked for ten years with children from two to eight years of age, relying exclusively on donations from the private sector in addition to the fees the

---

5 The views of leading French psychoanalysts – Rene Diatkin, Genevieve Haag, Piera Aulagnier, Didier Houzel, etc. – are presented in the following journals: *Topique: Revue Freudienne* 1985 Nos. 35–36, with the subtitle 'Voies d'Entree dans la Psychose' ('Pathways to Psychosis'); *Journal de la Psychoanalyse de l'Enfant* 1988 No. 5, subtitled 'Psychoanalyse des Psychoses de l'Enfant' ('Psychoanalysis of Infantile Psychoses'). Paris: Editions Paidos/Centurion.

parents paid, which covered a quarter of the total cost of the unit. Half of the money paid by the parents was reimbursed by their social security funds. During the last two years our work has gained official recognition and we now obtain financial help from the Greek state and from European funds. I must stress that we first became known in Europe and the USA, and only later in Greece.

The unit is called *Perivolaki*, which in Greek means 'small garden' and has now 25 children from 2 to 14 years old, and over 20 professional workers including part-time therapists. It is a day unit, with two 'classes'. Parents are seen weekly during the first two years of the child's stay at *Perivolaki* and every fortnight thereafter. The average length of stay of a child at *Perivolaki* is four to five years.

How we Manage Autistic Children

At *Perivolaki* we observe the children, think about them a lot, and discuss their behaviour at staff meetings, along with our feelings, with a view to understanding whether their autistic behaviour is defensive, refusing interaction and relations because they don't make sense for them or because they are painful, or whether there is a pervasive lack of motivation for relating and communicating. We find both conditions present, at different times, in all our children.

Classroom activities are organised to provide many kinds of interactive situations with people and with objects. One teacher becomes, through mutual choice and effort, the preferred caretaker of each child. There are activities normally found in nursery schools, primary school classrooms, and in the home: drawing, painting, story telling, dressing-up, make believe activities, playing with puppets, educational toys, shopping, cooking and setting out lunch, videos, and so forth; plus music therapy (individually or in groups of two to three children), organised psychomotor activities, outdoor activities, and so on. For children who can cope we go on to activities preparing for reading and writing, even some arithmetic lessons, usually individually or with two or three children together.

Children also go out once a week to picnics, to the zoo, to other schools, the local library, the children's museum, the airport, and every week two children with one teacher are responsible for purchasing, preparing and setting the meals out for all the others. Nothing is imposed on the children, so that at any one moment one can see children who are quite isolated in the classroom, but an adult is always nearby, occasionally talking to them and confirming that they are not alone, and that they are wanted to join in with other children in whatever activity is going on at the time. During the month of June, the children go to the seaside for swimming three times a week with their teachers and this 'summer programme' is much loved by staff, parents and children.

Each child has individual psychotherapy two or three times per week. Obviously these children do not have psychoanalysis in the traditional sense of the word since they don't function at a symbolic or verbal level that is required for such therapeutic intervention. The classical technique is very much modified. In effect, it is really play therapy modified to suit the child's needs by a therapist who, working through this interaction with the child, uses his or her psychoanalytic training, empathy and compassion as aids. The main modification of technique that we have introduced has to do with what we call 'physical objects', such as milk, sweets, biscuits, a blanket and the potty. As mentioned, we find that these modifications are necessary because of the importance bodily functions have for these children. We also hold the child when that seems necessary, so there is some bodily interaction, which in the classic psychoanalytic approach would not be permitted. In spite of these innovations, we keep the main principles of set days and times, and length of sessions, which is called the 'setting' in psychoanalytic terms. The repetition of set days and times and length of sessions gives the children a sense of rhythm which seems to help. They very quickly recognise these aspects and ask for their therapy sessions in their own way. We give the children frequent verbal interpretations, and we use transference as our main tool for understanding the child. With children who can use drawing and symbolic play, we operate with a more traditional psychoanalytic technique.

Now about the parents. As I have already mentioned, cooperation of the parents is a necessary condition in order for a child to be accepted at *Perivolaki*, and it is clearly stated in the initial contract. At the beginning work with parents is done separately from the child. The couple sees the social worker and most of the session is usually spent talking about the child and themselves at home. Very often one of the parents may ask for more sessions and this is offered to him or her, but if there is a demand for therapy we recommend the couple or the individual to have psychotherapy outside *Perivolaki*. This is done to avoid the 'institutionalisation' of cases. The parents also meet with the teachers of their children individually or in a group with all the parents, three to four times per year.

When we come to know the child and the parents better, usually after the first two years' stay of the child at *Perivolaki*, we organise sessions with the whole family, parents and child together or even brothers and sisters together, where our aim is to help them interact with the child in such activities that we have singled out as the most successful in getting the child to communicate. This is actually a new development which seems to help a lot, but is still in an experimental stage.

Training of professionals at *Perivolaki* comprises the following: each year we accept five to six people, preschool teachers, teachers or developmental psychologists, in the classrooms for training. We also accept one or two social workers who take up cases under supervision. Every psychotherapist that joins *Perivolaki* also has supervision during his or her first two years at the unit. Finally, there is a seminar every fortnight on autism and childhood psychoses which can be attended by the staff members and by professionals that are interested. This year 30 people are attending the seminar.

In the 12 years of the unit's existence, over 300 children have been referred to us for differential diagnosis, over half of them from other specialist centres, with various diagnoses. Fifty of the children have been accepted to enrol at *Perivolaki*. Twenty-five children have left, some because they were too old to stay with us. We have follow-up data for these children. Three of them (12 per cent) were later diagnosed to have mild mental retardation with specific language disorder, in addition to autism. Another three children (12 per cent) still have what can be called nuclear autism of the Kanner type and they attend the only state school for autistic children that exists in the Athens area. Ten children (40 per cent) go to special schools, but have developed useful speech and are educable in spite of psychotic disturbances, in some cases delusions and hallucinations, and behaviour disorders. Last, but not least, nine children (36 per cent) go to normal school, and two of them are in secondary school. Most children continued their individual psychotherapy for many years with the same psychotherapist after leaving *Perivolaki*.

Out of the total of 50 children who were enrolled at *Perivolaki* only four (8 per cent) suffer from epileptic fits and are under a neurologist's control. In none of the children was a Fragile-X syndrome detected, and none of the children has any known brain abnormality. One boy was diagnosed as having Asperger's syndrome.

Two Clinical Examples

The two cases that follow are chosen to illustrate the way we think about the behaviour and the personal symptoms that an individual child may present at any one moment during his or her stay at *Perivolaki*, and the way we try to cope with them, both in the classroom and at individual psychotherapy sessions. The first child, Marco, is still at the unit and the incident described took place during his second year at *Perivolaki*. The second child, Diana, presented the behaviour described during the third year she was with us. She stayed at the unit for five years.

MARCO

Marco is classically autistic, looks like a two-year-old and has muscular hypotonia which is not identified with any known neurological disorder. He can say three to four words, all echolalic and out of context, except for the word 'hair', *mallia* in Greek, which he always says in an appropriate context.

Marco is obsessed with the hair of all adult women at *Perivolaki*, and with the hair of little girls in his classroom. He pulls hair, caresses it, touches it with his face and always prefers long hair. His obsession is such that he can stay immobile for a long time just looking at somebody's hair from a distance, and his perseverence with this interest is of such strength that when he is seated next to somebody, he takes great care to put himself in a position parallel to the other person so that he excludes any eye contact but remains close to them. The behaviour looks like a trick devised to prevent Marco from doing anything else but be near hair.

We discussed this peculiar behaviour many times at staff meetings, making different hypotheses about Marco's obsession and the pathological relation he has established with a 'part object', the hair but not the person. Sometimes Marco gets very excited when he pulls our hair and we have often thought of a Greek proverb, 'The drowning man grabs at hair'. We had learned from his parents that Marco's mother had long hair which she cut when Marco was nine months old in order to avoid the annoyance Marco's behaviour was causing her at that early age. It is remarkable that Marco's obsession with his mother's hair developed from around six months. We thought that perhaps Marco equated hair with his mother's body and when his mother cut her hair, he felt despair as if he had lost the whole mother.

Confirmation of this hypothesis came when his preferred teacher, who, by the way, he calls *Malli*[6] (though her name is actually Maggie), informed the children in her classroom that she was going to have a baby and would be leaving for a few months. Marco went into real mourning, crying almost constantly or having extremely depressed moods which caused many of the staff to feel despair. Marco tried to hold on to his teacher, and for the first time he articulated a sentence: 'Mallia, to go in mallia!' We thought at last that we had a solution to our puzzle about Marco's problem. *Mallia* means 'mother's belly' and maybe Marco wanted to be in her, like an embryo. This led us to handle Marco's behaviour towards her in a different way. We started talking to him more about his mother, and the pregnancy of his mother and of his teacher. We showed him carefully how hair is only a part of a body, we gave him material that looks and feels like hair, and we tried to have him play with bald dolls, dolls with hair, and so forth.

Marco stopped mourning but is still extremely interested in hair. The matter was, of course, taken up in his individual psychotherapy sessions. The parents were informed of our thoughts, and we discussed the whole issue in their meetings with the family therapist.

DIANA

The second example is of a six-year-old girl during her third year at *Perivolaki*. I shall call her Diana. When she first came, at the age of three and a half, she was very isolated, showing all the typical autistic symptoms: avoidance of

---

6 *Mallia* is the plural for hair in Greek and *malli* is the singular. Marco articulates the word *mallia* for many different objects, and also when he is alone without any apparent relation to a particular object or situation. He uses the word *Malli* only to name his preferred teacher.

eye-to-eye contact, stereotyped repetitive movements, silence, etc. After two years at *Perivolaki*, Diana was still inaccessible for social contact. However, she managed to cooperate in some educationally-oriented activities. We felt that she agreed to cooperate in these activities more to comply with her mother's wishes rather than her own.

During that time Diana, under great stress, as all of us asked her to do things, started coming to the unit carrying between her fingers hard plastic nails from an educational toy. She was picking them up and wearing them between her fingers in a very ritualistic way, as if the nails were extensions of her fingers, a habit which restricted the movements of her hands and made her impotent, putting at the same time a safe distance between herself and the external world. We thought of this peculiar behaviour as Diana's attempt to defend herself against the anxiety she felt when in contact with people, and at the same time it was an attempt to show some of the aggression she felt and a wish to dominate others.

Psychotherapy was focused for some time on that particular problem and the therapist put into words her feelings of anxiety, pain and aggression. Diana's motivation for relating to others and her actual interaction were ameliorated in the following months through psychotherapy and with the help of her mother. Her parents were divorced and Diana lived with her mother.

Diana eventually restricted the hard plastic nails to one hand, and she started touching people and objects with her other hand. Still later the nails were replaced by soft tissue paper. The behaviour persisted for a little over one year. Diana is now ten years old. She goes to a special school, speaks quite well and can read and write.

I would like to stress that these children have intense feelings which they express very well and which are immediately recognisable: joy, anger, anxiety, fear, panic, sadness, despair, depressive moods and frustration. Some are clearly related to specific situations, but for others it is much more difficult to find an explanation.

Problems of Diagnosis: a Need to Treat the Whole Child

We find that the category 'childhood autism' is on the one hand too restrictive to contain all the variations of disorders that affect many aspects of development in a child, and on the other hand too broad and descriptive to support any intuition into the psychological aspects of the disorder. To give an example: ICD-10 includes 'infantile psychosis' under the category of 'childhood autism' (F: 84. 0), which we believe is very misleading, because the differences are very marked and infantile psychosis is a very real category which might differ from autism in terms of the course it takes, prognosis and social adaptation. Another problem is the key statement for the differential diagnosis of autism from 'early childhood schizophrenia', that is 'absence of delusions and hallucinations'.

Children diagnosed as autistic, when older and when some of them are functioning at what we could call a post-autistic mental state, often have delusions and hallucinations. Considering even earlier stages, how can we know that those sudden laughs and panic-stricken reactions that a lot of autistic children have are not accompanied by hallucinations?

Because the category of 'childhood autism' in DSM-III-R and ICD-10, if compared to their earlier forms, includes many more children under the category of 'autism', both professionals and lay people have been led to regard the whole group of children so labelled as very severely and perhaps permanently handicapped, because of the connotations the term 'autism' carries.

In our experience autism falls into a category we could call 'affective or emotional communication disorders', or, following Gillberg (1991a), 'empathic disorders'. These disorders certainly have tremendous and lasting effects on the total mental functioning of the child. The problems we observe in cognitive, language, social and learning areas are, we believe, secondary to the emotional–affective or empathic disturbance, which may be congenital and which certainly becomes apparent in infancy.

A clear diagnosis is important because the therapeutic approach one chooses depends on the way one thinks about the disorder. Modern therapeutic approaches tend to replicate what we see in autism itself; namely a propensity to conceive mental functioning cut into pieces. Problems are identified in 'cognitive functioning', 'attention deficits', 'language' and 'communication'; organic deficits are found in glutin sensitivity, serotonin, Fragile-X chromosomes, etc. The therapeutic approaches tend to address one or the other aspect, as if we do not have to deal with a single individual whose pathology may or may not include other unidentified aspects as well. We fail to look at the child as a whole human being who cannot relate to other people and to inanimate objects in ways that are so natural for the normal child, or who has not the motivation to do so.

At *Perivolaki* all therapists and most of the permanent staff, special teachers and psychiatric social workers are trained in psychodynamic psychotherapy with adults or children. We find that the psychodynamic–psychoanalytic approach matches best the way we wish to view and understand autism. I would like at this point to remind you that psychoanalysts were the first to try to do something constructive with autistic children, by taking them in to a psychotherapy that may last ten or more years, and with some positive results. Most of all, psychoanalysts are the therapists most inclined to consider autism as an emotional disorder, a sub-category of early psychotic disturbances.

I am of course aware and very critical of the view of Bettelheim (1967) and some other psychoanalysts that autism is an environmental disorder, and of the blame some put on mothers of autistic children. However Bettelheim, the main advocate of such a view, has not received support from the majority of psychoanalysts. They were in fact the first to criticise his views. Kanner on the other hand involved the parents of autistic children only indirectly, by trying to describe their personality structure. As to Margaret Mahler's original claim that there is an autistic stage in normal child development, I would, as a developmental psychologist who has studied communication with newborns, be the first to dismiss it, as she did herself (Tustin 1994, p.5), because I know that babies are born with the motivation to communicate with others and are emotionally very well attuned to interactive situations from birth. The same criticism must be made of Melanie Klein[7] who claimed that there is a schizoid–paranoid position in normal development. Hana Segal[8] is also reviewing this description. I must however stress that many of Melanie Klein's descriptions are extremely helpful when one does psychotherapy with autistic children. Her concepts of 'early fantasies', 'part objects', 'defence mechanisms', and so on, are genuine clinical insights based on much experience. I would also like to remind you that Esther Bick (1964) managed to get mother–baby observation in the curriculum for training in child psychotherapy, a practice that is now disseminated across Europe and which started at the Tavistock Clinic when John Bowlby was its director (see Shuttleworth 1989).

At *Perivolaki*, we find that many new concepts advanced by psychoanalysts are very useful to our psychotherapeutic approach towards autism. Such concepts are Piera Aulagnier's 'pictogramme', Bion's (1962) concepts of 'beta-function' and 'maternal reverie' (pp.1–9), Winnicott's (1965) concepts of 'primary maternal preoccupation' (pp.52–4), 'false self' (pp.133–4) and 'transitional objects' (p.181)[9], as well as Meltzer's concept of 'dismantling' (Meltzer *et al.* 1975), Tustin's (1981) concepts of 'autistic shells' and 'autistic contours', etc.

Tustin, Meltzer and Winnicott, in the UK, and McDougall and Lebovici (1989), Diatkine and Haag (see footnote 2, p.162) in France have also something to say about autistic children. Some of them call them 'psychotic' and this may not be an acceptable term for a very young child, because it has connotations that lead us to think of very disturbed adults, condemned in mental hospitals. But when we talk of an emotional–social, or an empathic–motive disorder, are we not really saying what has already been said about some psychotic behaviour of adults or about psychotic personality structure?

Finally, I would add that while an emphasis on biological research is certainly scientifically necessary, I do not think that it will fundamentally alter the therapeutic approach that is based on analysis of mental processes. The belief that scientists are going to find a single biological or organic cause for autism may be convenient, because it relieves us from guilt feelings about our

---

7 See Segal 1964 and Hinshelwood 1991.

8 See Segal 1964 and Hinshelwood 1991.

9 See also Winnicott 1977.

inadequacy to understand autistic children and to offer them an efficient therapy. This belief, we should note, also allows parents to think that there is very little they themselves can do to help their children, and this in our view is a very unfortunate consequence that makes the child's situation more precarious. It is necessary for scientists and parents to cooperate in approaching the autistic child as a being with complex psychology.

I wish to repeat that in our therapeutic approach at *Perivolaki* we are not concerned primarily with aetiology. We follow medical doctors' orders if the child has epilepsy or if the parents choose to follow a specific dietary regime, but we strictly resist any practice of looking at the child's stools to see if they float or if they sink into the toilet! We also advise against taking the child around to various specialist places to run medical tests, or attempts to find new drugs to improve the child's availability to social contact.

To Sum Up

We think of autism as a state in which there is insufficient differentiation between stimuli coming from the inside of the body or from the environment. The child cannot construct representations of feelings. All stimulation is thus experienced as fragmented, as if it were coming from a 'part object', or a sensation coming from a fragmented body. Thus any bonds or relations that are formed are also fragmented and with 'part objects'. Whenever the children develop some speech this is also fragmented and may have delusional elements. These children's senses are very sensitive and fragile, so feelings coming from bodily sensations are very strong.

While the child lives within this type of autistic state there is no possibility of forming a sensible whole continuous experience either when alone or when in the presence of others. If a child becomes motivated to relate or to understand the continuity of his existence, that is to integrate experiences into a sensical whole, then we may see what Tustin (1981) has called 'confusional states' (pp.34–49), or what in traditional French child psychopathology is called 'symbiotic psychosis', or even the 'infantile psychosis' of ICD-9 which is lost in ICD-10. Asperger's syndrome or schizoid disorder of childhood might also be the same nosological entities.

If I were to make a comment about prognosis in one sentence, I would say that apart from early diagnosis and early intervention, the course of autistic disorder and the final outcome depend mostly on the way parents perceive and think of their child, on how much they are ready to cooperate with therapists and how much they can offer mentally and emotionally.

CHAPTER 13

Education for Autistic Children[1]

The Key Deficits Indicate the Most Appropriate Remedial Action

The recurring theme of our review is this: however varied its severity and whatever the precise forms of disability may come with it in different children, autism is a disorder of relating. Whether they speak or make inarticulate sounds, all autistic children communicate in a way that makes sharing of experience, and especially teaching, difficult. This means that the fundamental task of anyone, parent, teacher, playmate or friend, who wants to help the child to communicate and learn better, is to find a way to be as accessible and comprehensible to the child as possible.

We have seen that there are many different techniques for opening communication with an autistic child that work. All adapt to what the autistic child can perceive, understand and respond to. The great problem is that the reciprocal, imitative, playful and cooperative contact that is perfectly simple and easy for an unaffected young child, even one who has severe sensory or motor handicap, is extremely difficult for a child who is autistic. The partner who tries to communicate may decide that the child does not want to communicate. A change of approach may reveal that this is certainly not the explanation. However, what we take for granted about persons' awareness of other persons and how to negotiate and explore ideas with them just does not come naturally to the autistic child.

Finding the Right Balance of Contact

There are two ways to misread autism. One assumes that the avoiding child is better left alone to amuse him- or herself with repetitive ritualised explorations of simple experiences, or even more complex memory feats of an obsessional kind. The other tries to shape the child's behaviours by an imposed drill in

---

1 This final chapter is essentially as it was written in response to a commission of the Scottish Office Department of Education for a report on education for autistic children. This report, the origin of this book, was submitted to the Scottish Office in 1993 by the authors on behalf of the Edinburgh Centre for Research in Child Development of the Department of Psychology, The University of Edinburgh.

desirable habits, according to a prescribed programme and with simple forms of coercion. Either of these approaches, by failing to excite a minimal awareness of other persons' feelings and purposes, can make the isolation of the child worse. This is not to say that autistic children cannot respond to behavioural training. However, to transform an autistic child's habits requires attention to what motivates the child to act and to repeat learned acts. The best rule is to try to find how to meet the child in a dialogue of action and attention that develops and that leads the child away from avoidant or self-directed and repetitive behaviours. This is a difficult and delicate task, but positive emotional and other-seeking responses that can be elicited, when the teacher has the right measure of the child, are both reward for the teacher, and evidence of a constructive change in the motivation of the child. Autistic children that seemed completely cut-off can be revealed to have playfulness and to be happy when an affectionate relationship is found. This helps subsequent teaching or training.

Simple descriptions of autism are always misleading. It is not true that autistic children are unemotional, unaffectionate or incapable of forming attachments, even though they often seem to avoid direct or sustained recognition of other persons as persons, and they may treat someone to whom they obviously are attached, or parts of this person's body, as if they were just useful 'tools'. Autistic children are not unable to imitate, although the way they do so tends to be strange and rudimentary, depending on how severely their motives for communicating are affected. They tend to immediately imitate in an echoing kind of way, or they repeat previously experienced actions or expressions of others like a tape recorder, triggered by the context or by an association with an emotion-generating event of the past in a way that makes no sense in the communication of the present. The speech of autistic children is often characterised by immediate or delayed echolalia, repeating the words of others with no sense, except by way of simple sensory association that only they may experience.

It is not true that autistic children never play or that they all lack symbolic play. However, it is true that their play tends to be repetitive and ritualised, lacking creativity or invention. They cannot join in that unique kind of fanciful guessing and inventing that makes pretend play of young children such an effective way of exploring partners' imaginations and beliefs. This fits with the most difficult characteristic of the autistic child for a teacher; learning of ordinary culturally-significant roles and tasks is an immensely difficult task. The child neither has curiosity for the new meaning of what people say or do, nor does he or she respond easily to the kind of drill that helps most of us develop flexible and refined skills under guidance from someone who knows better.

Adjusting to Individual Needs

The learning difficulties of the individual autistic child correlate well with the degree to which their social or interpersonal responsiveness is impaired. Those that learn best, and who speak best, are generally those who orient more readily to others and who reciprocate and cooperate more readily in imitation and play. The deficit in understanding other persons and what they feel or intend is a fundamental block to cognitive development.

As autism is a developmental disorder, it changes with the age of the affected child. Clear symptoms appear in the second or third year and they change in severity and kind as the child grows up. As habit formation is in some ways a forte of the autistic child, it is important that practice of self-stimulatory, isolating or even self-injurious behaviours is reduced as much as possible. The one exception is in sexual behaviour, as mentioned below, because some autistic teenagers lose their habitual unwillingness to approach others and may make unwelcome advances that cause discomfort and strife in a group of children. All ritualised, self-stimulatory behaviours increase when the child is anxious, and anxiety is greater with strange people and in unfamiliar places or programmes. This argues for an environment that is stable and for consistency in caretakers and in the daily routine of care or teaching.

It is important to underline, as many studies have confirmed, that autistic children, even severely disturbed ones, can be brought to much more accessible and playful states by carefully measured communication that invites them according to their individual inclinations and that pays attention to their idiosyncratic ways of expressing themselves. Body contact play and even very vigorous group activity can lead to a freer and more sociable behaviour.

Monitoring Progress

Study of the precise ways that an autistic child accepts or rejects contact can help a carer or teacher greatly, making them aware of the kinds of joint activity that are most acceptable and encouraging to the child. Here review of video recordings gives invaluable help. Musical communication guided by an experienced therapist, often a very effective way of obtaining positive and evolving communication with an autistic child, can also easily be made into a record that can be studied to give greater appreciation of an autistic child's needs. These techniques are certainly valuable adjuncts in the training of parents and special education teachers in the art of supportive behaviour that works best with the individual autistic child.

We have summarised a number of assessment instruments that can be used to test a child's level of functioning and to chart progress. Many of these are designed to identify specific psychological difficulties and to give a profile of needs that can be a guide to treatment. These can give very helpful encouragement to a carer. It is important to emphasise, however, that expert assessment, advice or training on scientifically established principles should not be administered in a such a way that it reduces the confidence or decreases that understanding of the person, parent, carer or teacher, who will be responsible for day-to-day communication and care of the child or for continuous long-term teaching.

Finally, since autism is a rare condition, there will be few autistic children in any local community, unless they have been brought together from a large population. This means that parents of an autistic child have probably never seen one before and none of their family or friends are likely to have helpful experience.

These points have the following implications for policies and action.

Assistance for Parents and Parental Action

As an autistic child needs to be treated with carefully-measured and conscious attention to their responses, which is a demanding and often frustrating task, parents particularly need both advice and forms of relief. It is important for them to have ready access to organisations to which they can turn to receive advice and help, and that there is provision for care of the child outside the home by experienced persons from time to time. Parent self-help organisations that can disseminate knowledge, pool experiences and lobby for services are of great importance for such a difficult and rare problem of child care.

Home-based programmes have been developed which guide parents and other family members in establishing conditions that are favourable for the autistic child, helping learning and reducing the burden of care.

It will be necessary for local authorities to take the lead in establishing effective lines of communication between various specialists in educational psychology, medical diagnosis and therapy and to inform parents how they may obtain appropriate help.

Parents of autistic children have, in many places in the UK and overseas, set up mutual assistance and information-collecting groups or fora. It is also helpful if a similar coordination is organised among the professions who assume responsibility for different aspects of the care of autistic children. A survey of need is essential, to ascertain to what extent parents in different regions and in different socio-economic groups all have good access to the services and information that are available. Autism is such a rare condition that there will be very few autistic children in any community and most parents and families confronted with the problem of an autistic toddler will have never seen an autistic child before. It is therefore necessary for networks of communication and cooperation to be established to work out how to modify existing services and to add new ones to improve the care of these children.

Teacher Training and Educational Services

Provision for special teachers and school facilities must recognise that children with autism need special care from preschool ages. Early intervention needs to be regular, recognisable for families of the children and continuous, with recognition that the interruptions of the school year may limit the effects of treatment.

While it is generally true that professionals concerned with young children need more, not less, awareness of the important factors and processes of child learning, in comparison with those who are responsible for older primary and secondary school children, the peculiar characteristics of autistic children make understanding of the socio-emotional factors in early learning all the more important, and for a longer period of the child's life.

Teachers of autistic children need thorough training both in general principles of early child development, including the interpersonal aspects that recent research has brought to the fore, and in the special techniques for improving communication with autistic children. Autistic children cannot be adequtely treated under non-specific special education for children of lower than normal intelligence. They are not simply mentally handicapped and their learning difficulties are very different from, say, Down's syndrome children. Persons responsible for autistic children need training that pays special attention to the relationship between cognitive or intellectual development, skills learning and communication and the emotional regulation of personal relationships. The availability of cheap camcorders for video recording makes this method of diary-keeping a practical and valuable aid to training and monitoring.

It appears that little or no special training in care and teaching of autistic children is at present available for teachers in many areas of the UK. It would not be difficult for modules on autism, and other developmental conditions affecting children's communication and learning, to be incorporated in general courses on child development for teachers, nursery nurses and auxiliary or volunteer workers. However, it would seem necessary to establish a number of specialist posts to monitor services and teacher training as well as to aid parents through regular workshops.

Special units at preschool level based on the mainstream nursery schools would seem to be the most effective provision for children up to seven or eight years old, when the child can be moved to another form of provision. Continuity is of great importance for the maintenance of gains in learning for autistic children. The most difficult problems concern the more than half of autistic children at the lower end of intellectual and linguistic ability. Flexibility of provision is also essential, to permit transfer of children to the most appropriate available facility.

Organisation of the Environment and Care of an Autistic Child in School

The autistic child's behaviour can be 'channelled' by providing a standard environment with a fixed routine to which the individual child moulds and adapts. This is the strategy of the Higashi and the more behavioural programmes such as Schopler's TEACHH and the programme of the Institute of Psychiatry in London. Alternatively, the child's behaviour can be directed by providing an environment that is sensitive and responsive to the interests and patterns of the individual child, as with the Option method. The former approach, emphasising accommodation of the child to experiences, leads to concerns over situational specificity, seeking ways to lead the individual to adapt to a proposed environment. The latter approach, seeking to help the child assimilate the environment to his or her world view, can, if carefully planned and monitored, lead an autistic child to effective and self-motivated social participation and integration in a school class or residential community. Both result in the establishment of routines in behaviour which can become limiting due to the obsessional 'insistence on sameness' characteristic of autistic children. Both, therefore, can benefit from close attention to the limitations of awareness and motivation in the autistic child's communication with teachers and companions.

Liaison with Medical Services

Our review of pathologies associated with autism explains the importance for any child suspected to have autism or an autism-like disorder, of a detailed medical investigation, to make sure of the following:

(1) that the child is not presenting with a similar disorder that emerges before age three, such as Rett's syndrome, Batten's syndrome or developmental dysphasia;

(2) that an accurate estimation has been made of the nature and severity of any of the neurological disorders, such as epilepsy or ataxia, commonly seen in the autistic child;

(3) that, when autism has been diagnosed, sufficient evidence has been obtained to establish, as far as is possible, the organic basis to the condition – is there Fragile-X syndrome, tuberous sclerosis, etc.?

A thorough medical work-up can aid in the identification of medical and educational needs and prevent inappropriate treatment. There is always a need to adjust provision to areas of recognised difficulty.

Special Medical and Psychological Aspects of Care

A number of direct educational implications follow from the spectrum of medical and behavioural problems that are unusually common in the autistic population.

(1) Frequently an inability to learn self-care skills beyond infancy leads to an increased likelihood that toilet training programmes will be required in preschool, nursery and primary age settings.

(2) The relatively high frequency of epilepsy in this population requires staff to be trained in recognition and treatment of fits (e.g. in the use of Paraldehyde and rectal Valium). Autistic children require close monitoring if epileptic seizures are to be detected and appropriately treated.

(3) An input of regular and sustained occupational therapy will be required to help with motor and motor-planning difficulties.

(4) Access to professional advice will be required for the assessment and treatment of behavioural management problems, such as excessive obsessional routines, extreme tantrums and self-injurious behaviours.

(5) As autistic children reach the teens, carefully tailored expert advice on sex education, pitched at the level of social understanding of the individual, becomes essential. In most cases this will focus on training in self-stimulatory means of gratification to discourage overtures to other children, in contrast to the more typical other-directed programmes for handicapped individuals of similar developmental level who do not suffer from autism. Mentally handicapped young adults are normally guided to form stable relations and how to manage intercourse. Autistic teenagers tend to make inappropriate sexual overtures and they fail to understand why these are rejected. This causes recurrent difficulties, especially in a residential setting.

References

Aarons, M. and Gittens, T. (1992) *Autism: A Guide for Parents and Professionals.* London: Tavistock Routledge.

Abvitbol M., Menini C., Delezoide A-L., Rhyner T., Vekemans M. and Mallet J. (1993) Nucleus basalis magnocellularis and hippocampus are the major sites of FMR-1 expression in the human fetal brain. *Nature Genetics, 4,* 147–153.

Adamson, L. and Bakeman, R. (1985) Affect and attention: infants observed with mother and peers. *Child Development, 56,* 582–93.

Adrien, J. L., Barthèlèmy, C., Perrot, A., Roux, S., Lenoir, P., Haumery, L. and Sauvage, D. (1992) Validity and reliability of the Infant Behavioural Summarized Evaluation (IBSE): A rating scale for the assessment of young children with autism and developmental disorders. *Journal of Autism and Developmental Disorders, 22,* 375–394.

Adrien, J. L., Faure, M., Perrot, A., Hameury, L., Garreau, B., Barthèlèmy, C. and Sauvage, D. (1991) Autism and family home movies: Preliminary findings. *Journal of Autism and Developmental Disorders, 21,* 43–51.

Adrien, J. L., Lenoir, P., Martineau, J., Perrot, Haumery, L., Larmande, C. and Sauvage, D. (1993) Blind ratings of early symptoms of autism based upon family home movies. *Journal of the American Academy of Child and Adolescent Psychiatry, 32 (3),* 617–626.

Adrien, J. L., Perrot, A., Hameury, L., Martineau, J., Roux, S. and Sauvage, D. (1991) Family home movies: Identification of early autistic signs in infants later diagnosed as autistics. *Brain Dysfunction, 4,* 355–362.

Agrotou, A. (1988) A case study: Lara. *Journal of British Music Therapy, 2 (1),* 1 7–23.

Aigen, K. (1993) The music therapist as qualitative researcher. *Music Therapy, 12,* 1, 16–39.

Aigen, K. (1995) Aesthetic foundations of clinical theory. In C. Bereznak Kenny (ed) *Listening, Playing, Creating: Essays on the Power of Sound.* New York: State University of New York, 233–258.

Aitken, K. J. (1991a) Examining the evidence for a common structural basis to autism. *Developmental Medicine and Child Neurology, 33,* 933–938.

Aitken, K. J. (1991b) Diagnostic issues in autism: Are we measuring the emperor for another suit of clothes? *Developmental Medicine and Child Neurology, 33,* 1015–1020.

Aitken, K.J. (1991c) *An Investigation into the Biological Perturbations of Prematurity.* PhD Thesis, University of Edinburgh.

Akefeldt, A. and Gillberg, C. (1991) Hypomelanosis of Ito in three cases with autism and autistic-like conditions. *Developmental Medicine and Child Neurology, 33,* 737–743.

Aldridge, D. (1989) A phenomenological comparison of the organization of music and the self. *Arts in Psychotherapy, 16,* 91–97.

Aldridge, D. (1991) Physiological change, communication and the playing of improvised music: some proposals for research. *The Arts in Psychotherapy, 18* 59–64.

Aldridge, D. (1993a) Music therapy research I: A review of the medical research literature with a general context of music therapy research. *The Arts in Psychotherapy, 20 (1),* 11–35.

Aldridge, D. (1993b) Music therapy research II: Research methods suitable for music therapy. *The Arts in Psychotherapy, 20,* 2, 117–31.

Aldridge, D. (1994) Single-case research designs for the creative arts therapist. *The Arts in Psychotherapy, 21 (5),* 333–342.

Aldridge, D., Gustorff, D. and Neugebauer, L. (1995) A preliminary study of creative music therapy in the treatment of children with developmental delay. *The Arts in Psychotherapy, 21 (3),* 189–205.

Allen, D.A. and Rapin, I. (1992) Autistic children are also dysphasic. In H. Naruse and E.M. Ornitz (eds) *Neurobiology of Infantile Autism,* International Congress Series 965. Amsterdam: Excerpta Medica.

Alvarez, A. (1992) *Live Company.* London: Routledge.

Alvin, J. (1968) *Music Therapy for the Autistic Child.* Oxford: Oxford University Press.

Alvin, J. and Warwick, A. (1991) *Music Therapy for the Autistic Child.* Oxford: Oxford University Press.

Ansdell, G. (1995) *Music for Life: Aspects of Creative Music Therapy with Adult Clients.* London: Jessica Kingsley.

Anthony, J. (1958) An experimental approach to the psychopathology of childhood autism. *British Journal of Medical Psychology, 31,* 211–225.

Armstrong, D. (1992) The neuropathology of Rett Syndrome. *Brain and Development, 14* (supplement), S89–S101.

Asperger, H. (1944) Die 'autistischen psychopathen' in Kindersalter. *Archiv. fur Psyciatrie und Nervenkrankheiten, 117,* 76–136.

Association of Professional Music Therapists (1995) *A Career in Music Therapy.* London: APMT.

Attwood, A., Frith, U. and Hermelin, B. (1988) The understanding and use of interpersonal gestures by autistic and Down's syndrome children. *Journal of Autism and Developmental Disorders, 18,* 241–257.

Austin, J. L. (1962) *How to Do Things with Words.* Oxford: Basil Blackwell.

Bakeman, R. and Adamson, L. B. (1984) Coordinating attention to people and objects in mother–infant and peer–infant interaction. *Child Development, 55,* 1278–1289.

Ballotin, U., Bejor, M., Cecchini, A., Martelli, A., Palazzi, S. and Lanzi, G. (1989) Infantile autism and computerised tomography brain-scan findings: specific versus nonspecific abnormalities. *Journal of Autism and Developmental Disorders, 19,* 109–117.

Baltaxe, C. A. M. (1977) Pragmatic deficits in the language of autistic adolescents. *Journal of Pediatric Psychology, 2,* 176–180.

Barnard, P. J. and Teasdale, J. D. (1991) Interacting cognitive subsystems: A systematic approach to cognitive–affective interaction and change. *Cognition and Emotion, 5,* 1–39.

Baron-Cohen, S. (1987) Autism and symbolic play. *British Journal of Developmental Psychology, 5,* 139–148.

Baron-Cohen, S. (1989a) Perceptual role taking and protodeclarative pointing in autism. *British Journal of Developmental Psychology, 7,* 113–127.

Baron-Cohen, S. (1989b) The autistic child's theory of mind: A case of specific developmental delay. *Journal of Child Psychology and Psychiatry, 30,* 285–297.

Baron-Cohen, S. (1989c) Are autistic children 'behaviourists?' An examination of their mental–physical and appearance–reality distinctions. *Journal of Autism and Developmental Disorders, 19,* 579–600.

Baron-Cohen, S. (1990) Autism: a specific cognitive disorder of 'mind-blindness'. *International Review of Psychiatry, 2,* 81–90.

Baron-Cohen, S. (1991a) Precursors to a theory of mind: Understanding attention in others. In A. Whiten (ed), *Natural Theories of Mind: Evolution, Development and Simulation of Everyday Mindreading.* Oxford: Basil Blackwell.

Baron-Cohen, S. (1991b) Do people with autism understand what causes emotion? *Child Development, 62,* 385–395.

Baron-Cohen, S. (1992) Out of sight or out of mind? Another look at deception in autism. *Journal of Child Psychology and Psychiatry, 33,* 1141–1155.

Baron-Cohen, S. (1995) *Mindblindness: An Essay on Autism and Theory of Mind.* Cambridge, MA: MIT Press.

Baron-Cohen, S., Allen, J. and Gillberg, C. (1992) Can autism be detected at 18 months? The needle, the haystack and the CHAT. *British Journal of Psychiatry, 161,* 839–843.

Baron-Cohen, S. and Bolton, P. (1993) *Autism – The Facts.* Oxford: Oxford University Press.

Baron-Cohen, S. and Howlin, P. (1993) The theory of mind deficit in autism: Some questions for teaching and diagnosis. In S. Baron-Cohen, H. Tager-Flusberg and D. J. Cohen (eds.), *Understanding Other Minds: Perspectives from Autism.* London: Oxford University Press, 466–479.

Baron-Cohen, S., Leslie, A. and Frith, U. (1985) Does the autistic child have a theory of mind? *Cognition, 21,* 37–46.

Baron-Cohen, S., Leslie, A. M., and Frith, U. (1986) Mechanical, behavioural and intentional understanding of picture stories in autistic children. *British Journal of Developmental Psychology, 4,* 113–125.

Barron, J. and Sandman, C. A. (1983) Relationship of sedative–hypnotic response to self-injurious behaviour and stereotypy by mentally retarded clients. *American Journal of Mental Deficiency, 88,* 177–186.

Bartak, L. and Rutter, M. (1976) Differences between mentally retarded and normally intelligent autistic children. *Journal of Autism and Childhood Schizophrenia, 6,* 109–120.

Bartak, L., Rutter, M. and Cox, A., (1975) A comparative study of infantile autism and specific developmental receptive language disorder. I. The children. *British Journal of Psychiatry, 126,* 127–145.

Barthèlèmy, C., Adrien J.L., Roux, S., Garreau, B., Perrot, A. and LeLord, G. (1992) Sensitivity and specificity of the behavioural summarized evaluation (BSE) for the assessment of autistic behaviours. *Journal of Autism and Developmental Disorders, 22,* 23–31.

Barthèlèmy, C., Garreau, B., Bruneau, N., Martineau, J., Jouve, J., Roux, S. and Lelord, G. (1988) Biological and behavioural effects of magnesium + vitamin B6, folates and fenflouramine in autistic children. In L. Wing (ed) *Aspects of Autism: Biological Research.* London: Gaskell, pp.59–73.

Barthèlèmy, C., Hameury, I. and LeLord, G. (1989) Exchange and Development Therapies (EDT) for children with autism: A treatment program from Tours, France. In C. Gillberg (ed) *Autism: The State of the Art.* New York: Elsevier, *263–284.*

Bartlik, B. (1981) Monthly variation in births of autistic children in North Carolina. *Journal of the American Medical Women's Association, 36,* 363–368.

Bates, E. (1979) *The Emergence of Symbols: Cognition and Communication in Infancy.* New York: Academic Press.

Bateson, M. C. (1971) The interpersonal context of infant vocalization. *Quarterly Progress Report of the Research Laboratory of Electronics,* 100:170–176.

Bauman, M. L. and Kemper, T. L. (1985) Histoanatomic observations of the brain in early infantile autism. *Neurology, 35,* 866–874.

Beebe, B. (1982) Micro-timing in mother–infant communication. In M.R. Key (ed) *Nonverbal Communication Today.* New York: Mouton.

Beebe, B., Jaffe, J., Feldstein, S., Mays, K. and Alson, D. (1985) Inter-personal timing: The application of an adult dialogue model to mother–infant vocal and kinesic interactions. In F.M Field and N. Fox (eds.), *Social Perception in Infants.* Norwood, NJ: Ablex.

Beebe, B., Stern, D. and Jaffe, J. (1979) The kinesic rhythm of mother–infant interactions. In A. W. Siegman and S. Feldstein (Eds.) *Of Speech and Time; Temporal Speech Patterns in Interpersonal Contexts.* Hillsdale, NJ: Erlbaum.

Bellugi, U., van Hoek, K., Lillo-Martin, D. and O'Grady, L. (1988) The acquisition of syntax and space in young deaf signers. In D. Bishop and K. Mogford, (eds.), *Language Development in Exceptional Circumstances.* London: Churchill Livingstone.

Berger, J. (1990) Interactions between parents and their infants with Down Syndrome. In D. Cicchetti and M. Beeghly (eds) *Children with Down Syndrome: A Developmental Perspective.* Cambridge: Cambridge University Press.

Berger, M. M. (1978) Video feedback confrontation review. In M. M. Berger (ed), *Videotape Techniques in Psychiatric Training and Treatment.* New York: Bruner/Mazel.

Bernard-Opitz, V. (1982) Pragmatic analysis of the communicative behaviour of an autistic child. *Journal of Speech and Hearing Disorders, 47,* 99–109.

Berthier, M.L., Starkstein, S.E. and Leiguarda, R. (1990) Developmental cortical anomalies in Asperger's Syndrome: neuroradiological findings in two patients. *Journal of Neuropsychiatry and Clinical Neuroscience, 2,* 197–201.

Bettelheim, B. (1967) *The Empty Fortess – Infantile Autism and the Birth of the Self.* New York: The Free Press.

Bion, W. (1959) Attacks on linking. *International Journal of Psycho-analysis, 40,* 308–315.

Bion, W. (1962) Theory of thinking. *International Journal of Psycho-analysis, 43,* 306–310.

Bishop, D. V. M. (1989) Semantic pragmatic disorders and the autistic continuum. *British Journal of Disorders of Communication, 24,* 115–122.

Bishop, D. V. M. (1990) *Handedness and Developmental Disorder, Clinics in Developmental Medicine, 110.* London: Mackeith Press.

Bishop, D. V. M. (1992) The underlying nature of specific language impairment. *Journal of Child Psychology and Psychiatry, 33,* 3–66

Bishop, D. V. M. (1993) Autism, executive functions and theory of mind: a neuropsychological perspective. *Journal of Child Psychology and Psychiatry, 34 (3), 279–295.*

Bleuler, E. (1913) Autistic thinking. *American Journal of Insanity, 69,* 873–886.

Boesen, U. and Aarkrog, T. (1967) Pneumoencephalograpy of patients in a child psychiatry department. *Danish Medical Bulletin, 14,* 210–218.

Bohman, M., Bohman, I. L., Bjørck, P. O. and Sjøholm, E. (1983) Childhood psychosis in a northern Swedish county: some preliminary findings from an epidemiological survey. In M. H. Schmidt and H. Remschmidt (eds.) *Epidemiological Approaches in Child Psychiatry, 2.* Stuttgart: Thieme, 164–173.

Bolton, P., Pickles, A., Harrington, R., Macdonald, H. and Rutter, M. (1992) Season of birth: issues, approaches and findings for autism. *Journal of Child Psychology and Psychiatry, 33,* 509–530.

Boucher J. (1977) Hand preference in autistic children and their parents. *Journal of Autism and Childhood Schizophrenia, 7,* 177–187.

Brask, B. H. (1970) A prevalence investigation of childhood psychosis. Presented paper; *16th Scandanavian Conference on Child Psychiatry.*

Brazelton, T. B., Koslowski, B., and Main, M. (1974) The origins of reciprocity: the early mother–infant interaction. In M. Lewis and L. A. Roseblum (eds.) *The Effect of the Infant on its Caregivers.* London: Wiley Interscience.

Bretherton, I. and Bates, E. (1979) The emergence of intentional communication. In I. C. Uzgiris (ed) *New Directions for Child Development, Vol. 4.* San Francisco: Jossey-Bass.

Brodtkorb, E., Nilsen, G., Smevik, O. and Rinck, P. A. (1992) Epilepsy and anomalies of neuronal migration: MRI and clinical aspects. *Acta Neurologica Scandinavica, 86,* 24–32.

Brown, S.M.K. (1994) Autism and music therapy – is change possible, and why music? *Journal of British Music Therapy 8 (1),15–25.*

Brown, W. T., Jenkins, E. C., Cohen, I. L., Fisch, G. S., Wolf-Schen, E. G., Gross, A., Waterhouse, L., Fein, D., Mason-Brothers, A., Ritvo, E., Ruttenberg, B. A., Bentley, W. and Castells, S. (1986) Fragile-X and autism: A multicenter survey. *American Journal of Medical Genetics, 23,* 341–352.

Bruner, J. S. (1975) The ontogenesis of speech acts. *Journal of Child Language 2,* 1–19.

Bruner, J. S. (1983) *Child's Talk.* New York: Norton.

Bruner, J. S. (1990) *Acts of Meaning.* Cambridge, Mass.: Harvard University Press.

Bruscia, K. E. (1987) *Improvisational Models of Music Therapy.* Springville, IL: Charles C. Thomas.

Bruscia, K. E. (1989) *Defining Music Therapy.* Phoenixville: Barcelona Publishers.

Bruscia, K. E. (1991) The fundamentals of music therapy practice. In K.E. Bruscia (ed) *Case Studies in Music Therapy, 3–13.*

Bryan, A. (1989) Autistic group case study. *Journal of British Music Therapy, 3 (1),* 16–21.

Bryson, S.E., Clark, B.S. and Smith, I.M. (1988) First report of a Canadian epidemiological study of autistic syndromes. *Journal of Child Psychology and Psychiatry, 29,* 433–445.

Buck, R. (1984) *The Communication of Emotion.* New York: Guilford Press.

Buitelaar, J. K., Van Engeland, H., De Koegel, K., De Vries, H., Van Hooff, J. and Van Ree, J. (1992) The adrenocorticotrophic hormone (4–9) Analog ORG 2766 benefits autistic children: Report on a second controlled clinical trial. *Journal of the American Academy of Child and Adolescent Psychiatry, 31,* 1149–1156.

Buitelaar, J. K., Van Engeland, H., van Ree, J., and De Weid, D. (1990) Behavioural effects of ORG 2766, a synthetic analog of the adrenocorticotrophic hormone (4–9) in 14 outpatient autistic children. *Journal of Autism and Developmental Disorders, 20,* 467–478.

Bullowa, M. (ed), (1979) *Before Speech: The Beginnings of Human Communication.* London: Cambridge University Press.

Bunt, L. (1994) *Music Therapy: an Art Beyond Words.* London: Routledge.

Burford, B. (1988) Action cycles: Rhythmic actions for engagement with children and young adults with profound mental handicap. *European Journal of Special Educational Needs, 3*

Burford, B. (1992) Communicating through movement and posture. In W. MacGillivray, W.I. Fraser and A. Green (eds) *Hallas' Caring for People with Mental Handicap.* London: Butterworth Heinemann.

Butterworth, G. (1991) The ontogeny and phylogeny of joint visual attention. In A. Whiten (ed) *Natural Theories of Mind: Evolution, Development and Simulation of Everyday Mindreading.* Oxford: Blackwell.

Butterworth, G., and Grover, L. (1988) *The origins of referential communication in human infancy.* In L. Weiskrantz (ed) Thought Without Language. Oxford: Clarendon.

Campbell, M. (1975) Pharmacotherapy in early infantile autism. *Biological Psychiatry, 10,* 399–423.

Campbell, M. (1988) Fenfluramine treatment of autism. *Journal of Child Psychology and Psychiatry, 29,* 1–10 (Annotation)

Campbell, M. (1989) Pharmacotherapy in autism: An overview. In C. Gillberg (ed) *Diagnosis and Treatment of Autism.* New York: Plenum, 203–217.

Campbell, M., Adams, P., Small, A. M., Tesch, L. McV. and Curren, E. L. (1988) Naltrexone in infantile autism, *Psychopharmacology Bulletin, 24,* 135–139.

Campbell, M., Anderson, L. T., Meier, M., Cohen, I. L., Small, A. M., Samit, C. and Sachar, E. J. (1978) A comparison of haloperidol, behaviour therapy and their interaction in autistic children. *Journal of the American Academy of Child Psychiatry, 17,* 640–655.

Campbell, M., Rosenbloom, S., Perry, R., George, A. E., Kricheff, I. I., Anderson, L., Small, A. M. and Jennings, S. J. (1982) Computerised axial tomography in young autistic children. *American Journal of Psychiatry, 139,* 510–512.

Capps, L., Sigman, M. and Mundy, P. (1994) Attachment security in children with autism. *Development and Psychopathology, 6 (2), 249–261.*

Capps, L., Yirmiya, N. and Sigman, M. (1992) Understanding of simple and complex emotions in non-retarded children with autism. *Journal of Child Psychology and Psychiatry, 33,* 1169–1182.

Carr, E. G. (1979) Teaching autistic children to use sign language: Some research issues. *Journal of Autism and Developmental Disorders, 9 (4),* 345–359.

Carr, E. G. (1982) Sign language. In R. L. Koegel, A. Rincover and A. L. Egel (eds.) *Educating and Understanding Autistic Children.* New York: College Hill Press.

Carr, E. G. and Durand, V. M. (1985) Reducing behaviour problems through functional communication training. *Journal of Applied Behaviour Analysis, 18,* 111–126.

Changeux, J.-P. (1985) *Neuronal Man: The Biology of Mind.* New York: Pantheon.

Charlop, M. H. and Walsh, M. E. (1986) Increasing autistic children's spontaneous verbalisations of affection: An assessment of time delay and peer modelling procedures. *Journal of Applied Behaviour Analysis, 19,* 307–314.

Chess, S. (1977) Follow-up report on autism and congenital rubella. *Journal of Autism and Childhood Schizophrenia, 7,* 68–81.

Chess, S., Korn, S. J. and Fernandez, P. B. (1971) *Psychiatric Disorders of Children with Congenital Rubella.* New York: Brunner/Mazel.

Chugani, H. T., and Phelps, M. E. (1986), Maturational changes in cerebral function in infants determined by FDG position emission tomography. *Science, 231,* 840–843.

Cialdella, P. and Mamelle, N. (1989) An epidemiological study of infantile autism in a French Department (Rhaene): a research note. *Journal of Child Psychology and Psychiatry, 30,* 165–175.

Cicchetti, D. and Sroufe, L. A. (1978) An organizational view of affect: illustration from the study of Down's syndrome infants. In M. Lewis and Rosenblum, L. A. (eds) *The Development of Affect* pp.309–350. New York: Plenum.

Clark, P. and Rutter, M. (1981) Autistic children's responses to stucture and to interpersonal demands. *Journal of Autism and Developmental Disorders, 11,* 201–217.

Clements, J. (1987) *Severe Learning Disability and Psychological Handicap.* Chichester: John Wiley and Sons.

Coggins, T. E. and Frederickson, R. (1988) Brief report: The communicative role of a highly repeated utterance in the conversations of an autistic boy. *Journal of Autism and Developmental Disorders, 18,* 687–694.

Cohen, D., Donnellan, A. and Paul, R. (eds.) (1987) *The Handbook of Autism and Pervasive Developmental Disorders.* New York: Wiley.

Cohen, D.J., Carparulo, B.K., Gold, J.R., Waldo, M.C., Shaywitz, B.A., Ruttenberg, B.A. and Rimland, B. (1978) Agreement in diagnosis: clinical assessment and behaviour rating scales for pervasively disturbed children. *Journal of the American Academy of Child Psychiatry, 17,*589–603.

Cohen, I. L., Brown, W. T., Jenkins, E. C., Krawczun, M. S., French, J. H., Raguthu, S., Wolf-Schein, E. G., Sudhalter, V., Fisch, G. and Wisniewski, K. (1989) Fragile-X syndrome in females with autism. *American Journal of Medical Genetics, 34,* 302–303.

Cohen, I. L., Campbell, M., Posner, D., Small, A. M., Triebel, D. and Anderson, L. T. (1980) Behavioral effects of haloperidol in young autistic children. *Journal of the American Academy of Child Psychiatry,* 19: 655–677.

Cohn, J. F. and Tronick, E. Z. (1983) Three-month-old infants' reaction to simulated maternal depression. *Child Development, 54,* 185–193.

Comings, D.E. (1986) The genetics of Rett Syndrome: the consequences of a disorder where every case is a new mutation. *American Journal of Medical Genetics, 24,* 383–88.

Comings, D. E. (1990) *Tourette Syndrome and Human Behaviour*, Duarte: Hope Press.

Condon, W. S. (1975) Multiple response to sound in dysfunctional children. *Journal of Autism and Childhood Schizophrenia, 5*, 3–56.

Condon, W. S. and Sander, L. (1974) Neonate movement is synchronised in adult speech. *Science, 183*, 99–101.

Courchesne, E. (1989) Neuroanatomical substems involved in infantile autism. The implications of cerebellar abnormalities. In G. Dawson (ed), *Autism: Nature, Diagnosis and Treatment.* New York: Guilford Press.

Courchesne, E., Hesselink, J. R., Jernigan, T. L. and Yeung-Courchesne, R. (1987) Abnormal neuroanatomy in a non-retarded person with autism: unusual findings with magnetic resonance imaging. *Archives of Neurology, 44*, 335–341.

Courchesne, E., Yeung-Courchesne, R., Press, G. A., Hesselink, J. R. and Jernigan, T. L. (1988) Hypoplasia of cerebellar vermal lobules VI and VII in autism. *New England Journal of Medicine, 318*, 1349–1354.

Creak, M. (1964) Schizophrenic syndrome in childhood: Further progress report at a working party. *Developmental Medicine and Child Neurology, 6*, 530–535.

Creasey, H., Rumsey, J. M., Schwartz, M., Duara, R., Rapoport, J. L. and Rapoport, S. I. (1986) Brain morphometry in autistic men as measured by volumentric computerised tomography. *Archives of Neurology, 43*, 669–672.

Critchley, M. and Henson, R.A. (eds) (1977) *Music and the Brain: Studies in the Neurology of Music.* London: Heinemann.

Cummins, R. A. (1988) *The Neurologically Impaired Child: Doman-Delacato Techniques Reappraised.* London: Croom Helm.

Cunningham, M. A. (1968) A comparison of the language of psychotic and non-psychotic children who are mentally retarded. *Journal of Child Psychology and Psychiatry, 9*, 229–244.

Curcio, F. (1978) Sensorimotor functioning and communication in mute autistic children. *Journal of Autism and Childhood Schizophrenia, 8*, 281–292.

Dahlgren, S. O. and Gillberg, C. (1989) Symptoms in the first two years of life: A preliminary population study of infantile autism. *European Archives of Psychiatry and Neurological Sciences, 238*, 169–174.

Damasio, A. R. and Maurer, R. G. (1978) A neurological model for childhood autism. *Archives of Neurology, 35*, 777–786.

Damasio, A. R. and Van Hoesen, G. W. (1983) Emotional disturbances associated with focal lesions of the limbic frontal lobe. In K. M. Heilman and E. Valenstein (eds.), *Clinical neuropsychology.* New York: Oxford University Press.

Damasio, H., Maurer, R. G., Damasio, A. R. and Chui, H. C. (1980) Computerised tomographic scan findings in patients with autistic behaviour. *Archives of Neurology, 37*, 504–510.

Davis, W. B., Gfeller, K. E. and Thaut, M. H. (eds.) (1992) *An Introduction to Music Therapy: Theory and Practice.* Dubuque, Indiana: William C. Brown Publishers.

Dawson, G. (ed) (1989) *Autism: Nature, Diagnosis and Treatment.* New York: Guilford.

Dawson, G. and Adams, A. (1984) Imitation and social responsiveness in autistic children. *Journal of Abnormal Child Psychology, 12*, 209–226.

Dawson, G. and Fischer, K. W. (1994) *Human Behavior and the Developing Brain.* New York: The Guilford Press.

Dawson, G. and Galpert, L. (1990) Mothers' use of imitative play for facilitating social responsiveness and toy play in young autistic children. *Development and Psychopathology, 2*, 151–162.

Dawson, G., Hill, D., Spencer, A., Galpert, L., and Watson, L. (1990) Affective exchanges between young autistic children and their mothers. *Journal of Abnormal Child Psychology, 18*, 335–345.

Dawson, G. and Lewy, A. (1989a) Arousal, attention, and the socioemotional impairments of individuals with autism. In G. Dawson (ed), *Autism: Nature, Diagnosis, and Treatment.* New York: Guilford, 49–74.

Dawson, G. and Lewy, A. (1989b) Reciprocal subcortical-cortical influences in autism: The role of attentional mechanisms. In G. Dawson (ed), *Autism: Nature, Diagnosis, and Treatment.* New York: Guilford, 144–173.

Dawson, G. and McKissick, F. C. (1984) Self recognition in autistic children. *Journal of Autism and Developmental Disorders, 14*, 383–394.

DeCasper, A. and Fifer, W. (1980) Of human bonding: Newborns prefer mother's voices. *Science*, 208: 1174.

Delacato, C. H. (1974) *The Ultimate Stranger: The Autistic Child.* New York: Doubleday and Co.

Demb, H. B. and Weintraub, A. G. (1989) A five year follow-up of preschool children diagnosed as having an atypical pervasive developmental disorder. *Journal of Developmental and Behaviour Paediatrics, 10,* 292–298.

DeMyer, M. K., Mann, N. A., Tilton, J. R. and Loew, L. H. (1967) Toy-play behaviour and use of body by autistic and normal children as reported by mothers. *Psychological Reports, 21,* 973–981.

Deutsch, S. I. (1986) Rationale for the administration of opiate antagonists in treating infantile autism. *Journal of Mental Deficiency Research, 90,* 631–635.

Dewey, J. (1934) *Art As Experience.* New edition, 1980. New York: Perigree.

DiLavore, P. C., Lord, C., and Rutter, M. (1995) The pre-linguistic autism diagnostic observation schedule. *Journal of Autism and Developmental Disorders, 25 (4),* 355–379.

Donaldson, M. (1978) *Children's Minds.* London: Fontana/Collins.

Donaldson, M.L. (1995) *Children with Language Impairments: An Introduction.* London: Jessica Kingsley Publishers.

Dore, J. (1983) Feeling, form and intention in the baby's transition to language. In R. Golnikoff (ed) *The Transition from Pre-Linguistic Communication.* Hillsdale, NJ: Lawrence Erlbaum Associates.

DSM (1987) *DSM-III-R: Diagnostic and Statistical Manual of Mental Disorders (Third Edition-Revised)* Washington, DC: American Psychiatric Association.

Durig, A. (1993) The microsociology of autism. Internet::/ /ftp.syr.edu/information/autism/microsocialogy of autism.txt.

Duboule, D. (1994) *Guidebook to the Homeobox Genes.* New York: Oxford University Press.

Dvorkin, J. M. (1994) Considerations of developmental issues in choosing interventions for resistance in music therapy. *British Journal of Music Therapy, 8 (1),* 5–6.

Echelard Y., Epstein D.J., St-Jaques B., Shen L., Mohler J., McMahon J.A. and McMahon A.P. (1993) Sonic hedgehog, a member of a family of putative signaling molecules, is implicated in the regulation of CNS polarity. *Cell, 75,* 1417–1430.

Edgerton, C-L. (1994) The effect of improvisational music therapy on the communicative behaviours of autistic children. *Journal of Music Therapy, 31 (1),* 31–62.

Eikeseth, S. and Lovaas, O. I. (1992) The autistic label and its potentially detrimental effect on the child's treatment. *Journal of Behaviour Therapy and Experimental Psychiatry, 23,* 151–157.

Eisenberg, L. and Kanner, L. (1956) Early infantile autism. *American Journal of Orthopsychiatry, 26,* 556–566.

Ellis, D. (ed) (1986) *Sensory Impairment in Mentally Handicapped People.* Beckenham: Croom Helm.

Emde, R. N. (1983) The prerepresentational self and its affective core. *Psychoanalytic Study of the Child, 38,* 165–192. New Haven, CT: Yale University Press.

Emde, R. N. (1990) Mobilizing fundamental modes of development: empathic availablility and therapeutic action. *Journal of American Psychoanalytic Association, 38 (4),* 880–913.

Eriksson, A. and DeChateau, P. (1992) Brief report: A girl aged two years and seven months with autistic disorder videotaped from birth. *Journal of Autism and Developmental Disorders, 22,* 127–129.

Evans, J. R. (1986) Dysrhythmia and disorders of learning and behaviour. In J. R. Evans and M. Clynes (eds.) *Rhythm in Psychological, Linguistic and Musical Processes.* Springfield, IL: Charles C. Thomas, pp.249–274.

Evans, J. R. and Clynes, M. (eds) (1986) *Rhythm in Psychological, Linguistic and Musical Processes.* Springfield, IL: Charles C. Thomas.

Evans, R. and Clifford, A. (1976) Captured for consideration – using videotape as an aid to the treatment of the disturbed child. *Child: Care, Health and Development, 2,* 129–137.

Fay, W.H. (1993) Infantile autism. In D. Bishop and K. Mogford (eds) *Language Development in Exceptional Circumstances.* Hillsdale, NJ: Lawrence Erlbaum Associates.

Fein, D., Humes, M., Kaplan, E., Lucci, D. and Waterhouse, L. (1984) The question of left hemisphere dysfunction in infantile autism. *Psychological Bulletin, 95,* 258–281.

Fein, D., Pennington, B, Markowitz, P., Braverman, M., and Waterhouse, L. (1986) Toward a neuropsychological model of infantile autism: Are the social defects primary? *Journal of American Academy of Child Psychiatry, 25 (2),* 198–212.

Fein, D., Pennington, B. and Waterhouse, L. (1987) Implications of Social Deficits in Autism for Neurological Dysfunction. In E. Schopler and G. B. Mersibov (eds.) *Neurobiological Issues in Autism.* New York: Plenum Press, ISBN 0-306-42451-7, pp.127–144.

Fein, D., Waterhouse L., Lucci D., Pennington B. and Humes M. (1985) Handedness and cognitive functions in pervasive developmental disorders. *Journal of Autism and Developmental Disorders, 15,* 323–334.

Fein, D., Waterhouse, L., Lucci, D. and Snyder, D. (1985) Cognitive Subtypes in Developmentally Disabled Children: A Pilot Study. *Journal of Autism and Developmental Disorders, 15,* 77–95.

Fein, G.G. (1981) Pretend play: an integrative review. *Child Development, 52,* 1095–1118.

Feldstein, S., Konstantareas, M., Oxman, J. and Webster, C. D. (1982) The chronography of interactions with autistic speakers: An initial report. *Journal of Communication Disorders, 15,* 451–460.

Fernald, A. (1985) Four-month-old infants prefer to listen to motherese. *Infant Behaviour and Development, 8,* 181–195.

Field, T. M. and Fox, N., (eds.) (1985) *Social Perception in Infants.* Norwood, N.J.: Ablex.

First, M. B., Frances, A., Widiger, T. A., Pincus, H. A. and Davis, W. W. (1992) DSM-IV and behaviour assessment. *Behavioural Assessment, 14,* 297–306.

Fisch, B., Marcus, J., Hans, S.L., Auerbach, J.G. and Perdue, S. (1992) Infants at risk for schizophrenia: sequelae of a genetic neurointegrative defect. *Archives of General Psychiatry, 49,* 221–35.

Fish, B., Shapiro, T. and Campbell, M. (1966) Long term prognosis and the response of schizophrenic children to drug therapy: A controlled study of trifluoperazine. *American Journal of Psychiatry, 123,* 32–39.

Folstein, S. and Rutter, M. (1977) Infantile autism: A genetic study of 21 twin pairs. *Journal of Child Psychology and Psychiatry, 18,* 297–231. Ref on twins study.

Forinash, M. and Gonzalez, D. (1989) Phenomenology as research in music therapy. *Music Therapy, 8 (1),* 35–46.

Fraiberg, S. (1980) *Clinical Studies in Infant Mental Health: The First Year of Life.* London: Tavistock.

Franco, F. and Wishart, J. G. (1994) The use of pointing and other gestures by young children with Down syndrome. *American Journal on Mental Retardation 100,* 160–182

Franzen, E. A. and Myers, R. E. (1973) Neural control of social behaviour: Prefrontal and anterior temporal cortex. *Neuropsychologia, 11,* 141–157.

Freeman, B. J., Ritvo, E. R., Guthrie, D., Schroth, P. and Ball, J. (1978) The behaviour observation scale for autism: initial methodology, data analysis and preliminary findings on 89 children. *Journal of the American Academy of Child Psychiatry, 17,* 576–588.

Freeman, B. J., Ritvo, E. R. and Schroth, P. C. (1984) Behaviour assessment of the syndrome of autism: behaviour observation system. *Journal of the American Academy of Child Psychiatry, 23,* 588–594.

Freitag, G. (1970) An experimental study of the social responsiveness of children with autistic behaviours. *Journal of Experimental Child Psychology, 9,* 436–453.

Friedman, E. (1969) The 'Autistic Syndrome' and phenylketonuria. *Schizophrenia, 1,* 249–261.

Frith, U. (1989) *Autism: Explaining the Enigma.* Oxford: Basil Blackwell.

Gaffney, G. R., Kuperman, S., Tsai, L. and Minchin, S. (1989) Forebrain structure in infantile autism. *Journal of the American Academy of Child and Adolescent Psychiatry, 28,* 534–537.

Garber, H. J. and Ritvo, E. R. (1992) Magnetic resonance imaging of the posterior fossa in autistic adults. *American Journal of Psychiatry, 149,* 245–247.

Gardner, R. L. and Stern, C. D. (1993) Integration in development. In C. A. R. Boyd and D. Noble (Eds.) *The Logic of Life:The Challenge of Integrative Physiology,* pp.63–88 Oxford: Oxford University Press.

Garfin, D. G. and Lord, K. (1986) Communication as a social problem in autism. In E. Schopler and G. Mesibov (Eds.), *Social Behaviour in Autism.* New York: Plenum Press.

Garreau, B., Jouve, J., Bruneau, N., Muh, J. P. and LeLord, G. (1988) Urinary homovanillic acid levels of autistic children. *Developmental Medicine and Child Neurology, 30,* 93–98.

Gaston, E. T. (1968) Man and music. In E. T. Gaston (ed) *Music in Therapy.* New York: Macmillan.

George, M. S., Costa, D. C., Kouris, K., Ring, H. A. and Ell, P. J. George, M. S., Costa, D. C., Kouris, K., Ring, H. A. and Ell, P. J. (1992) Cerebral blood flow abnormalities in adults with infantile autism. *The Journal of Nervous and Mental Disease, 180,* 413–417.

Geschwind, N. and Galaburda, A. (1985) Cerebral lateralization: Biological mechanisms, associations, and pathology: I, II, III. A Hypothesis and Program for Research. *Archives of Neurology, 42,* 428–459, 521–552, 634–654.

Ghaziuddin, M., Tsai, L. Y. and Ghaziuddin, N. (1992) Brief report: A comparison of the diagnostic criteria for Asperger Syndrome. *Journal of Autism and Developmental Disorders, 22,* 643–649.

Gillberg, C. (1984) Infantile Autism and other childhood psychoses in a Swedish urban region. Epidemiological aspects. *Journal of the of Child Psychology and Psychiatry, 25,* 35–43.

Gillberg, C. (1988) The neurobiology of infantile autism. *Journal of the of Child Psychology and Psychiatry, 29,* 257–266.

Gillberg, C. (1988b) The role of the endogenous opioids in autism and possible relationships to clinical features. In L. Wing (ed) *Aspects of Autism: Biological Research.* London: Gaskell.

Gillberg, C. (1989) (ed) *Diagnosis and Treatment of Autism.* New York: Plenum.

Gillberg, C. (1990) Do children with autism have March birthdays? *Acta Psychiatrica Scandinavica, 82,* 152–156.

Gillberg, C. (1991a) The Emanuel Miller Memorial Lecture: Autism and autistic-like conditions: subclasses among disorders of empathy. *Journal of Child Psychology and Psychiatry, 33,* 813–842.

Gillberg, C. (1991b) The treatment of epilepsy in autism. *Journal of Autism and Developmental Disorders, 21,* 61–77.

Gillberg, C. (1992) Subgroups in autism: Are there behavioural phenotypes typical of underlying medical conditions? *Journal of Intellectual Disability Research, 36,* 201–214.

Gillberg C.and Coleman M. (1992a) *The Biology of the Autistic Syndromes,* (2nd edition). London: MacKeith Press.

Gillberg, C. and Coleman, M. (1992b) The Biology of the Autistic Syndromes, (2nd edn.) *Clinics in Developmental Medicine, 126.* London: MacKeith Press.

Gillberg, C., Ehlers, S., Schaumann, H., Jakobsson, G., Dahlgren, S. O., Lindblom, R., Bågenholm, A., Tjuus, T. and Blinder, E. (1990) Autism under age 3 years: a clinical study of 28 cases referred for autistic symptoms in infancy. *Journal of Child Psychology and Psychiatry, 31,* 921–934.

Gillberg, C., Hagberg, B., Witt-Engerstrom, I. and Eriksson, I. (1990) CSF beta-endorphin in childhood neuropsychiatric disorders. *Brain and Development, 12,* 88–92.

Gillberg, C., Persson, E. and Wahlström, J. (1986) The autism-fragile-X syndrome (AFRAX) A population-based study for ten boys. *Journal of Mental Deficiency Research, 30,* 27–39.

Gillberg, C. and Schauman, H. (1982) Social Class and Infantile Autism. *Journal of Autism and Developmental Disorders, 12,* 223–228.

Gillberg, C. and Steffenburg, S. (1987) Outcome and prognostic factors in infantile autism and similar conditions: a population based study of 46 cases followed through puberty. *Journal of Autism and Developmental Disorders, 17,* 273–87.

Gillberg, C., Steffenburg, S. and Schaumann, H. (1991) Autism: Epidemiology: Is autism more common now than 10 years ago? *British Journal of Psychiatry, 158,* 403–409.

Gillberg, C., Terenius, L. and Lonnerholm, G. (1985) Endorphin activity in childhood psychosis. *Archives of General Psychiatry, 42,* 780–783.

Gillberg, I. C. and Gillberg, C. (1989) Asperger Syndrome – Some epidemiological considerations: A research note. *Journal of the of Child Psychology and Psychiatry, 30,* 631–638.

Goldfarb, W. (1961) *Childhood Schizophrenia.* Cambridge, Mass.: Harvard University Press.

Goldman-Rakic, P. S. (1987) Development of cortical circuitry and cognitive function. *Child Development, 58,* 601–22.

Grafman, J., Litvan, I., Massaquoi, S., Stewart, M., Sirigu, A. and Hallett, M. (1992) Cognitive planning deficit in patients with cerebellar atrophy. *Neurology, 42,* 1493–1496.

Gram, L. F. and Rafaelsen, O. J. (1972) Lithium treatment of psychiatric children and adolescents: a controlled clinical trial. *Acta Psychiatrica Scandinavica, 48,* 253–260.

Grieser, D. L. and Kuhl, P. K. (1988) Maternal speech to infants in a tonal language: Support for universal prosodic features in motherese. *Developmental Psychology, 24,* 14–20.

Grigsby, J. P., Kemper, M. B. and Hagerman, R. J. (1987) Developmental Gerstmann syndrome without aphasia in fragile-X syndrome. *Neuropsychologia, 25,* 881–891.

Groden, G. and Baron, M. G. (eds.) (1988) *Autism: Strategies for Change: A Comprehensive Approach to the Education and Treatment of Children with Autism and Related Disorders.* New York: Gardner Press.

Grotstein, J. (1980) Primitive mental states. *Contemporary Psychoanalysis, 16,* 479–546.

Hagberg, B. (1989) Rett syndrome: clinical peculiarities, diagnostic approach, and possible cause. Pediatric Neurology, 5: 75–83.

Hagberg, B. (ed) (1993) *Rett Syndrome – Clinical and Biological Aspects.* London: Mac Keith Press (Clinics in Developmental Medicine, No. 127).

Hagberg, B., Aicardi, J., Dias, K., and Ramos, O. (1983) A progressive syndrome of autism, dementia, and loss of purposeful hand use in girls: Rett syndrome: a report of 35 cases. *Annals of Neurology, 14,* 471–479.

Hagberg, B. and Gillberg, C. (1993) Rett variants – Rettoid phenotypes. In B. Hagberg, (ed) *Rett Syndrome – Clinical and Biological Aspects.* (pp.40–60) London: Mac Keith Press (Clinics in Developmental Medicine, No.127).

Hagberg, B., Naidu, S. and Percy, A.K. (1992) Tokyo Symposium on Rett Syndrome: neurobiological approach. *Brain and Development, 14* (supplement), S151–153.

Hagerman, R. J. and McKenzie, P. (eds.) (1992) *International Fragile X Conference Proceedings.* Spectra, Colorado.

Halliday, M. A. K. (1975) *Learning How to Mean.* London: Arnold.

Hammes, J. G. W. and Langdell, T. (1981) Precursors of symbol formation and childhood autism. *Journal of Autism and Developmental Disorders, 11,* 331–346.

Happé, F. (1994) *Autism: An Introduction to Psychological Theory.* London: UCL Press.

Harris, P. (1989) *Children and Emotion.* New York: Basil Blackwell.

Harris, S. L., Handleman, J. S., Gordon, R., Kristoff, B., and Fuentes, F. (1991) Changes in cognitive and language functioning of preschool children with autism. *Journal of Autism and Developmental Disorders, 21 (3),* 281–290.

Hauser, S., DeLong, G. and Rosman, N. (1975) Pneumographic findings in the infantile autism syndrome: A correlation with temporal lobe disease. *Brain, 98,* 667–688.

Heal, M. and Wigram, T. (1993) *Music Therapy in Health and Education.* London: Jessica Kingsley.

Heal, M. (1994) The development of symbolic function in a young woman with Down's syndrome. In D. Dokter (ed) *Arts Therapies and Clients with Eating Disorders,* Ch. 18. London: Jessica Kingsley, pp 279–294.

Heal Hughes, M. (1995) A comparison of mother–infant interactions and the client–therapist relationship. In T. Wigram, B.Saperston, and R. West (eds.) *The Art and Science of Music Therapy: A Handbook.* Chur, Switzerland: Harwood Academic Publishers, 296–308.

Hebb, D.O. (1949) *The Organization of Behaviour.* New York: Wiley.

Heilman, K. M. and Satz, P. (eds.) (1983) *Neuropsychology of Human Emotion.* London: Guildford Press.

Hermelin, B. and O'Connor, N. (1970) *Psychological Experiments with Autistic Children.* Oxford: Pergamon Press.

Hermelin, B. and O'Connor, N. (1985) Logico-affective states and non-verbal language. In E. Schopler and G. Mesibov (eds) *Communication Problems in Autism.* New York: Plenum Press.

Herold, S., Frackowiak, R. S., Le Couteur, A., Rutter, M. and Howlin, P. (1988) Cerebral blood flow and metabolism of oxygen and glucose in young autistic adults. *Psychological Medicine, 18,* 823–831.

Hertzig, M. E., Snow, M. E., New, E. and Shapiro, T. (1990) DSM-III and DSM-III-R Diagnosis of autism and pervasive developmental disorder in nursery school children. *Journal of the American Academy of Child and Adolscent Psychiatry, 29,* 123–126.

Hier, D. B., LeMay, M. and Rosenberger, P. B. (1979) Autism and unfavourable left–right asymmetries in the Brain. *Journal of Autism and Developmental Disorders, 9,* 153–159.

Hobson, R. F. (1985) *Forms of Feeling: The Heart of Psychotherapy.* London: Tavistock/Routledge.

Hobson, R. P. (1983) The autistic child's recognition of age-related features of people, animals and things. *British Journal of Developmental Psychology, 1,* 343–352.

Hobson, R. P. (1984) Early childhood autism and the question of egocentrism. *Journal of Autism and Developmental Disorders, 14,* 85–104.

Hobson, R. P. (1986a) The autistic child's appraisal of expressions of emotion. *Journal of Child Psychology and Psychiatry, 27,* 321–342.

Hobson, R. P. (1986b) The autistic child's appraisal of expressions of emotion: A further study. *Journal of Child Psychology and Psychiatry, 27,* 671–680.

Hobson, R. P. (1987) Childhood autism: a once and future theory. *Medical Research Council News,* 9–10.

Hobson, R. P. (1989) Beyond cognition: A theory of autism. In G. Dawson (ed), *Autism: New Perspectives on Diagnosis, Nature and Treatment.* New York: Guilford, 22–48.

Hobson, R. P. (1990a) On the origins of self and the case of autism. *Development and Psychopathology, 2,* 163–182.

Hobson, R. P. (1990b) Concerning knowledge of mental states. *British Journal of Medical Psychology, 63,* 199–213.

Hobson, R. P. (1990c) On acquiring knowledge about people and the capacity to pretend: Response to Leslie (1987) *Psychological Review, 97,* 114–121.

Hobson, R. P. (1991) Against the theory of 'theory of mind'. *British Journal of Developmental Psychology, 9,* 33–51.

Hobson, R. P. (1993a) *Autism and the Development of Mind.* Hove/Hillsdale: Laurence Erlbaum Association.

Hobson, R. P. (1993b) Through feeling and sight to self and symbol. In U. Neisser (ed) *The Perceived Self: Ecological and Interpersonal Sources of Self-Knowledge.* New York: Cambridge University Press, pp.254–279.

Hobson, R. P., Ouston, J. and Lee, A. (1988a) What's in a face? The case of autism. *British Journal of Psychology, 79,* 411–453.

Hobson, R.P., Ouston, J. and Lee, A. (1988b) Emotion recognition in autism: coordinating faces and sounds. *Psychological Medicine, 18N, 911–23.*

Hogg, J. (1991) Developments in further education for adults with profound intellectual and multiple disabilities. In J. Watson (ed) *Innovatory Practice and Severe Learning Difficulties.* (Meeting Educational Special Needs: A Scottish Perspective, Volume 1, Series Editors, G. Lloyd and J. Watson) Edinburgh: Moray House Publications.

Holroyd, S., Reiss, A. L. and Bryan, R. N. (1991) Autistic features in Joubert Syndrome: genetic disorder with agenesis of the cerebellar vermis. *Biological Psychiatry, 29,* 287–294.

Horowitz, B., Rumsey, J. M., Grady, C. L. and Rapoport, S. I. (1988) The cerebral metabolic landscape in autism: intercorrelations of regional glucose utilization. *Archives of Neurology, 28,* 775–785.

Hoshino, Y., Kumashiro, H., Yashima, Y., Tashibana, R. and Watanabe, M. (1982) The epidemiological study of autism in Fukushima-Ken. *Folia Psychiatrica Neurological Japan, 36,* 115–124.

Howat, R. A. (1995) Elizabeth: a case study of an autistic child in individual music therapy. In T. Wigram, B. Saperston and R. West (eds.) *The Art and Science of Music Therapy: A Handbook.* Chur: Harwood Academic Publishers, 238–260.

Howlin, P. (1989) Changing approaches to communication and training with autistic children. *British Journal for Disorders of Communication, 24,* 151–168.

Howlin, P. and Rutter, M. (1987) *Treatment of Autistic Children.* Chichester: Wiley.

Howlin, P., Wing, L. and Gould, J. (1995) The recognition of autism in children with Down Syndrome: implications for intervention and some speculations concerning pathology. *Developmental Medicine and Child Neurology, 37,* 406–14.

Howlin, P. and Yates, P. (1989) Treating autistic children at home. A London based programme. In Gillberg C., (ed) *Diagnosis and Treatment of Autism.* New York: Plenum, 307–322.

Hubley, P. and Trevarthen, C. (1979) Sharing a task in infancy. In I. Uzgiris (ed), *Social Interaction During Infancy, New Directions for Child Development.* San Francisco: Jossey-Bass, 4: 57–80.

Hugh, J. H. and Rosenthal, T. L. (1981) Therapeutic videotaped playback. In Fryrear, J.L. and Fleshman, B. (eds.), *Videotherapy in Mental Health.* Illinois: Charles C Thomas.

Hulse, W. C. (1954). Dementia infantilis. *Journal of Nervous and Mental Disease, 119,* 471–477.

Hurtig, R., Ensrud, S. and Tomblin, J. B. (1982) The communicative function of question production in autistic children. *Journal of Autism and Developmental Disorders, 12,* 57–69.

Hutt, C., Hutt, S. J., Lee, D. and Ounsted, C. (1964) Arousal and childhood autism. *Nature, 204,* 908–909.

Hutt, C. and Ounsted, C. (1966) The biological significance of gaze aversion with particular reference to the syndrome of infantile autism. *Behavioural Science, 11,* 346–356.

ICD-9 (1978) *Mental Disorders: Glossary and Guide to their Classification in accordance with the Ninth Revision of the International Classification of Diseases.* Geneva: World Health Organization.

ICD-10 (1987) *International Classification of Diseases; Draft of Chapter V: Mental and Behavioural Disorders.* Geneva: World Health Organization.

ICD-10 (1993) *International Classification of Diseases.* Geneva: World Health Organization.

Imbert, M., (1985) Physiological underpinnings of perceptual development. In J. Mehler and R. Fox (eds.), *Neonate Cognition.* Hillsdale, N.J.: Erlbaum.

Itard, J. M. G. (1801) *The Wild Boy of Aveyron.* Trans. G. and M. Humphrey (1932), New York: Appleton-Century-Crofts.

Izard, C. E. (1993) Four systems for emotion activation: Cognitive and noncognitive processes. *Psychological Review, 100,* 68–90.

Jarrold, C., Boucher, J. and Smith, P. K. (1994) Executive function deficits and the pretend play of children with autism: A research note. *Journal of Child Psychology and Psychiatry, 35,* 1473–1482.

Jarrold, C., Smith, P. K., Boucher, J. and Harris, P. (1994) Comprehension of pretense in children with autism. *Journal of Autism and Developmental Disorders, 24,* 433–455.

Jenson, W. R. and Young, K. R. (1985) Childhood autism: Developmental considerations and behavioral interventions by professionals, families and peers. In R. J. McMahon and R. DeV. Peters (eds.) *Childhood Disorders: Behavioral and Developmental Approaches.* New York; Brunner/Mazel.

Johnson, M. H. and Morton, J. (1991) *Biology and Cognitive Development: The Case of Face Recognition.* Oxford: Basil Blackwell.

Jordan, R. (1993) The nature of linguistic and communication difficulties of children with autism. In D. J. Messer and G. J. Turner (eds.) *Critical Influences on Child Language Acquisition and Development.* New York: St. Martin's Press.

Junck, L., Gilman, S., Rothley, J. R., Betley, A. T., Koeppe, R. A. and Hichwa, R. D. (1988) A relationship between metabolism in frontal lobes and cerebellum in normal subjects studied with PET. *Journal of Cerebral Blood Flow and Metabolism, 8,* 774–782.

Kagan, J. (1982) The emergence of self. *Journal of Child Psychology and Psychiatry, 23,* 363–381.

Kanner L. (1943) Autistic Disturbances of Affective Contact. *Nervous Child, 2,* 217–250.

Kanner, L. (1946) Irrelevant and metaphorical language in early infantile autism. *American Journal of Psychiatry, 103,* 242–245.

Kanner, L. (1949) Problems of nosology and psychodynamics of early infantile autism. *American Journal of Orthopsychiatry, 19,* 416–426.

Kanner, L. (1973) *Childhood Psychosis: Initial Studies and New Insights.* Washington, D.C.: V.H. Winston and Sons.

Kanner L. and Eisenberg L. (1956) Early infantile autism: 1943–1955. *American Journal of Orthopsychiatry, 26,* 55–65.

Kasari, C., Sigman, M., Mundy, P. and Yirmiya, N. (1988) Caregiver interactions with autistic children. *Journal of Abnormal Child Psychology, 16,* 45–56,

Kasari, C., Sigman, M., Mundy, P. and Yirmiya, N. (1990) Affective sharing in the context of joint attention interactions of normal, autistic and mentally retarded children. *Journal of Autism and Developmental Disorders, 20,* 87–101.

Kaufman, B. N. and Kaufman, S. (1976) *To Love is to be Happy With.* Human Horizons Series. London: Souvenir Press.

Kaufman, B. N. (1981) *A Miracle to Believe In.* New York: Ballantine Books.

Kerr, A. M. (1995) Early clinical signs in the Rett disorder. *Neuropediatrics, 26,* 67–71.

Kitahara, K. (1983/84) *Daily Life Therapy, Volumes 1, 2 and 3.* Tokyo: Musashino Higashi Gakuen School.

Kleiman, M. D., Neff, S. and Rosman, N. P. (1990) The brain in infantile autism: Is the cerebellum really abnormal? *Annals of Neurology, 28,* 422 (Abstract).

Klin, A., Volkmar, F.R., Sparrow, S.S., Cicchetti, D.V. and Rourke, B.P. (1995) Validity and neuropsychological characterization of Asperger Syndrome: convergence with nonverbal learning disabilities syndrome. *Journal of Child Psychology and Psychiatry, 6,* 7, 1127–40.

Klinnert, M.D., Campos, J.J., Sorce, J.F., Emde, R.N., and Svejda, M. (1983) Emotions as behavior regulators: social referencing in infancy. In R. Plutchik and H. Kellerman (eds) *Emotion: Theory, Research and Experience, Volume Two.* New York: Academic Press.

Knight, C. (1991) Developing communication through interaction. In J. Watson (ed) *Innovatory Practice and Severe Learning Difficulties.* (Meeting Educational Special Needs: A Scottish Perspective, Volume 1, Series Editors, G. Lloyd and J. Watson) Edinburgh: Moray House Publications.

Knight, C. and Watson, J. (1990) *Intensive Interaction Teaching at Gogarburn School.* Edinburgh: Moray House College.

Konstantareas, M. M., Hauser, P., Lennox, C. and Homatidis, S. (1986) Season of birth in infantile autism. *Child Psychiatry and Human Development, 17,* 53–65.

Konstantareas, M. M., Webster, C. D. and Oxman, J. (1979) Manual language acquisition and its influence on other areas of functioning in four autistic and autistic-like children. *Journal of Child Psychology and Psychiatry, 20,* 337–350.

Konstantareas, M. M., Zajademan, H., Homatidis, S. and McCabe, A. (1988) Maternal speech to verbal and higher functioning versus nonverbal and lower functioning autistic children. *Journal of Autism and Developmental Disorders, 18,* 647–656.

Kraemer, G. W. (1992) A psychobiological theory of attachment. *Behavioural and Brain Sciences, 15 (3),* 493–541.

Krug, D. A., Arick, J. and Almond, P. (1980) Behaviour checklist for identifying severly handicapped individuals with high levels of autistic behaviour. *Journal of Child Psychology and Psychiatry, 21,* 221–229.

Kubicek, L. F. (1980) Organization in two mother–infant interactions involving a normal infant and his fraternal twin brother who was later diagnosed as autistic. In T. Field, S. Goldberg, D. Stein and A. Sostek (Eds.), *High Risk Infants and Children: Adult and Peer Interactions.* New York: Academic Press.

Kugiumutzakis, J. E. (1993) Intersubjective vocal imitation in early mother–infant interaction. In J. Nadel and L. Camaioni (Eds.) *New Perspectives in Early Communicative Development.* London: Routledge.

Landry, S. H. and Loveland, K. A. (1989) The effect of social context on the functional communication skills of autistic children. *Journal of Autism and Developmental Disorders, 19,* 283–299.

Langer, S. (1953) *Form and Feeling.* London: Routledge.

Latchford, G. (1989) *Towards an Understanding of Profound Mental Handicap.* Unpublished PhD Thesis, University of Edinburgh.

Lecourt, E. (1991) Off-beat music therapy: A psychoanalytic approach to autism. In K. E. Bruscia (ed) *Case Studies in Music Therapy.* Phoenixville, PA: Barcelona Publishers, pp.73–98.

Le Couteur, A., Rutter, M., Lord, C., Rios, P., Robertson, S., Holdgrafer, M. and McLennen, J. D. (1989) Autism diagnostic Interview: a stadnardised, investigator-based instrument. *Journal of Autism and Developmental Disorders, 19,* 363–387.

Lee, C. (1995) The analysis of therapeutic improvisatory music. In A. Gilroy and C. Lee (eds) *Art and Music Therapy and Research.* London: Routledge.

Lees, A. J. (1985) *Tics and Related Disorders* (Clinical Neurology and Neurosurgery Monographs, 7). Edinburgh: Churchill Livingstone.

LeLord, G., Muh, J. P., Barthèlèmy, C., Martineau, J., Garreau, B. and Callaway, E. (1981) Effects of pyridoxine and magnesium on autistic symptoms. Initial Observations. *Journal of Autism and Developmental Disorders, 11,* 219–230.

Lesch, M. and Nyhan, W. L. (1969) A familial disorder with uric acid metabolism and central nervous system function. *American Journal of Medicine, 36,* 561–570.

Leslie, A. M. (1987) Pretense and representation: The origins of 'Theory of Mind'. *Psychological Review, 94,* 412–426.

Leslie, A. M. (1991) The theory of mind impairment in autism: Evidence for a modular mechanism of development? In A. Whiten (ed), *Natural Theories of Mind: Evolution, Development and Simulation of Everyday Mindreading.* Oxford: Basil Blackwell.

Leslie, A. M. and Frith, U. (1988) Autistic children's understanding of seeing, knowing and believing. *British Journal of Developmental Psychology, 6,* 315–324.

Leslie, A. M. and Happé, F. (1989) Autism and ostensive communication: The relevance of metarepresentation. *Development and Psychopathology, 3,* 205–213.

Levinge, A. (1990) 'The use of I and me': music therapy with an autistic child. *Journal of British Music Therapy, 4 (2),* 15–18.

Lewis, V. and Boucher, J. (1988) Spontaneous, instructed and elicited play in relatively able autistic children. *British Journal of Developmental Psychology, 6,* 325–339.

Liddle, P. F. (1992) PET Scanning and schizophrenia: What progress? *Psychological Medicine, 22,* 557–560.

Lillard, A. S. (1993) Pretend play skills and the child's theory of mind. *Child Development, 64,* 348–371.

Locke, J.L. (1993) *The Child's Path to Spoken Language.* Cambridge MA: Harvard University Press.

Locke, J. L. (1994) *The Child's Path to Spoken Language.* Cambridge, Mass.: Harvard University Press.

Lord, C., Rutter, M., Goode, S., Heemsbergen, J., Jordan, H., Mawhood, L. and Schopler, E. (1989) Autism diagnostic observation schedule: A standardized observation of communicative and social behaviour. *Journal of Autism and Developmental Disorders, 19,* 185–212.

Lotter, V. (1966) Epidemiology of autistic conditions in young children. I. Prevalence. *Social Psychiatry, 1,* 124–137.

Lotter (1967) *The Prevalence of the Autistic Syndrome in Children.* London: University of London Press.

Lovaas, O. I. (1978) Parents as Therapists for Autistic Children. In Rutter M. and Schopler E. (eds.), *Autism: A Reappraisal of Concepts and Treatment.* New York: Plenum Press.

Lovaas, O. I. (1987) Behavioural treatment and normal educational and intellectual functioning in young autistic children. *Journal of Consulting and Clinical Pschology, 55 (1),* 3–9.

Loveland, K. and Laundry, S. (1986) Joint attention in autistic and language delayed children. *Journal of Autism and Developmental Disorders, 16,* 335–350.

Loveland, K. A, Laundry, S. H, Hughes, S. O., Hall, S. K. and McEvoy, R. E. (1988) Speech acts and the pragmatic deficits of autism. *Journal of Speech and Hearing Research, 31,* 593–604.

Lowe, M., (1975) Trends in the development of representational play in infants from one to three years – An observational study. *Journal of Child Psychology and Psychiatry, 16,* 33–47.

Luria, A. R. (1969) *The Mind of a Mnemonist.* (Trans. L. Solotaroff; Foreword by J. Bruner) London: Jonathan Cape.

Lynch, M. P., Oller, D. K., Steffens, M. L., Buder, E. H. (1995) Phrasing in prelinguistic vocalizations. *Developmental Psychobiology, 28,* 3–25.

Lyon, G. and Gadisseux, J.-F. (1991) Structural abnormalities of the brain in developmental disorders. In M. Rutter and P. Casaer (Eds.) *Biological Risk Factors for Psychosocial Disorders.* (pp.1–19) Cambridge: Cambridge University Press.

Lyons, J. (1977) *Semantics.* Volume Two. London: Cambridge University Press.

MacKinnon, P. C. B., and Greenstein, B. (1985) Sexual differentiation of the brain. In F. Falkner and J. M. Tanner (Eds.) *Human Growth. A Comprehensive Treatise. Vol. 2,* Postnatal Crowth; Neurobiology. (pp.437–468) New York: Plenum.

Mahlberg, M. (1973) Music therapy in the treatment of an autistic child. *Journal of Music Therapy, 10 (4),* 189–193.

Mahler, M. S. (1952) On child psychosis and schizophrenia. Autistic and symbolic psychoses. *Psychoanalytic Study of the Child, Vol. 7.* New York: International Universities Press, 286–305.

Mahler, M. S. (1968) *On Human Symbiosis and the Vicissitudes of Individuation. Infantile Psychosis.* New York: International Universities Press.

Mahoney, G., Fors, S. and Wood, S. (1990) Maternal directive behavior revisited. *American Journal of Mental Retardation, 94,* 398–406.

Main, M. and Goldwyn, R. (1984) Predicting rejection of her infants from mother's representation of her own experience. Implications for the abused–abusing intergenerational cycle. *International Journal of child Abuse and Neglect, 8,* 203–217.

Main, M. (1994) A move to the level of representation in the study of attachment organisation: implications for psychoanalysis. Annual Research Lecture to the British Psychoanalytic Society, London.

Maranto, C. D. (ed) (1993) Music Therapy: International Perspectives. Pipersville, Pennsylvania: Jeffrey Books.

Marchant, R., Howlin, P., Yule, W. and Rutter, M. (1974) Graded change in the treatment of the behaviour of autistic children. *Journal of Child Psychology and Psychiatry 15,* 221–227.

Martineau, J., Barthèlèmy, C., Cheliakine, C. and LeLord, G. (1988) An open middle-term study of combined B6-Mg in a subgroup of autistic children selected on their sensitivity to this treatment. *Journal of Autism and Developmental Disorders, 18,* 583–591.

Massie, H. N. (1978a) The early natural history of childhood psychosis. *Journal of the American Academy of Child Psychiatry, 17,* 29–45.

Massie, H. N. (1978b) Blind ratings of mother–infant interaction in home movies of pre-psychotic and normal infants. *American Journal of Psychiatry, 135,* 1371–1374.

Matthews, W. S. (1977) Modes of transformation in the initiation of fantasy play. *Developmental Psychology, 13,* 212–216.

McEachin, S.J., Smith, T., and Lovaas, I.O. (1993) Long-term outcome for children with autism who receive early intensive behavioural treatment. *American Journal of Mental Retardation, 97 (4),* 359–372, discussion 373–391.

McHale, S. M. (1983) Social interactions of autistic and non-handicapped children during free play. *American Journal of Orthopsychiatry, 53,* 81–91.

McHale, S. M., Simeonson, R. J. Marcus, L. M. and Olley, G. J. (1980) The social and symbolic quality of autistic children's communication. *Journal of Autism and Developmental Disorders, 10,* 299–310.

McNeill, D. (1992) *Hand and Mind: What Gestures Reveal About Thought.* Chicago: University of Chicago Press.

Mehler, J. and Fox, R. (1985) *Neonate Cognition: Beyond the Blooming Buzzing Confusion.* Hillsdale, N.J.: Erlbaum.

Meisels, S. J. and Shonkoff, J. P. (eds.) (1990) *Handbook of Early Childhood Intervention.* Cambridge: Cambridge University Press.

Melchior, J. C., Dyggve, H. V. and Gylstorff, H. (1965) Pneumo-encephalographic examination of 207 mentally retarded patients. *Danish Medical Bulletin, 12,* 38–42.

Meltzer, D., Bremer, J., Hoxter, S., Wedddell, D. and Wittenberg, I. (1975) *Explorations in Autism. A Psycho-Analytical Study.* Clunie Press

Meltzoff, A. N. (1985) The roots of social and cognitive development: Models of man's original nature. In T.M. Field and N.A. Fox (eds.), *Social Perception in Infants.* Norwood, NJ: Ablex, 1–30.

Merjanian, P. M., Bachevalier, J., Crawford, H. and Mishkin, M. (1986) Socioemotional disturbances in the developing rhesus monkey following neonatal limbic lesions. *Society for Neuroscience Abstracts, 12,* 23.

Mesibov, G. B., Troxler, M. and Boswell, S. (1988) Assessment in the classroom. In E. Schopler and G. B. Mesibov (eds.) *Diagnosis and Assessment in Autism.* New York: Plenum, pp.261–270.

Meyer, L.B. (1994) Emotion and meaning in music. In R. Aiello (ed) *Musical Perceptions,* Ch. 1, 3–39.

Mishkin, M. (1982) A memory system in the monkey. *Philosophical Transactions of the Royal Society of London, Series B, 298,* 85–95.

Mishkin, M. and Appenzeller, T. (1987) The anatomy of memory. *Scientific American, 256,* 80–9.

Muller, P. and Warwick, A. (1993) The effects of maternal involvement in therapy. In M. Heal and A. Wigram (eds.) *Music Therapy in Health and Education.* London and Philadelphia: Jessica Kingsley, 214–254.

Mundy, P., Kasari, C. and Sigman, M. (1992) Nonverbal communication, affect sharing and intersubjectivity. *Infant Behaviour and Development, 15,* 377–81.

Mundy, P. and Sigman, M. (1989) Specifying the nature of the social impairment in autism. In G. Dawson (ed), *Autism: New Perspectives on Diagnosis, Nature and Treatment.* New York: Guilford, 3–21.

Mundy, P., Sigman, M. and Kasari, C. (1990) A longitudinal study of joint attention and language development in autistic children. *Journal of Autism and Developmental Disorders, 20,* 115–129.

Mundy, P., Sigman, M. and Kasari, C. (1994) Joint attention, developmental level and symptom presentation in autism. *Development and Psychopathology, 6 (3),* 389–401.

Mundy, P., Sigman, M., Ungerer, J. and Sherman, T. (1986) Defining the social deficits of autism. The contribution of non-verbal communication measures. *Journal of Child Psychology and Psychiatry, 27,* 657–669.

Mundy, P., Sigman, M., Ungerer, J., and Sherman, T. (1987) Non-verbal communication and play correlates of language development in autistic children. *Journal of Autism and Developmental Disorders 17 (3),* 349–364.

Murakami, J. W., Courchesne, E., Press, G., Yeung-Courchesne, R. and Hesselink, J. R. (1989) Reduced cerebellar hemisphere size and its relationship to vermal hypoplasia in autism. *Archives of Neurology, 46,* 689–694.

Murphy, G. and Wilson, B. (eds)(1985) *Self-Injurious Behaviour.* London: British Institute for Mental Handicap.

Murray, E. A. and Mishkin, M. (1985) Amygdalectomy impairs cross-modal association in monkeys. *Science, 228,* 604–606.

Murray, L. (1988) Effects of post-natal depression on infant development: Direct studies of early mother–infant interactions. In I. Brockington and R. Kumar (eds.), *Motherhood and Mental Illness, Vol. 2.* Bristol: John Wright.

Murray, L. (1992) The impact of postnatal depression on infant development. *Journal of Child Psychology and Psychiatry, 33 (3),* 543–561.

Murray, L. and Trevarthen, C. (1985) Emotional regulation of interactions between two-month-olds and their mothers. In T. Field and N. Fox (eds.), *Social Perception in Infants.* Norwood, N.J.: Ablex.

Myers, R. E. (1975) Role of prefrontal and anterior temporal cortex in social behavior and affect in monkeys. *Acta Neurobiologiae Experimentalis, 32,* 567–579.

Nadel, J. (1986) *Imitation et Communication entre Jeunes Enfants.* Paris: PUF.

Nadel, J. (1992) Imitation et communication chez l'enfant autiste et le jeune enfant prélangagier. In J. Hochman and P. Ferrari (eds.) *Imitation et Identification chez l'Enfant Autiste.* Paris: Bayard.

Nadel, J. and Fontaine, A. M. (1989) Communicating by imitation: A developmental and comparative approach to transitory social competence. In B. Schneider, G. Attili, J. Nadel and R. Weissberg (eds.) *Social Competence in Developmental Perspective.* Dordrecht: Kluwer.

Nadel, J. and Peze, A. (1993) Immediate imitation as a basis for primary communication in toddlers and autistic children. In J. Nadel and L. Camioni (eds.) *New Perspectives in Early Communicative Development.* London: Routledge.

Nadel-Brulfert, J. and Baudonnière, P.M. (1982) The social function of reciprocal imitation in 2-year-old peers. *International Journal of Behavioral Development, 5,* 95–109.

Neisser, U. (ed) (1993) *The Perceived Self: Ecological and Interpersonal Sources of Self-Knowledge.* New York: Cambridge University Press.

Newport, E. L. and Meier, R. P. (1985) The acquisition of American Sign Language. In D. E. Slobin (ed), *The Crosslinguistic Study of Language Acquisition. Vol. I: The Data.* Hillsdale, N.J.: Erlbaum.

Nicholich, L. (1977) *Beyond sensor motor intelligence: assessment of symbolic maturity through analysis of pretend play.* Merrill-Palmer Quarterly, 23: 89–99.

Nielsen, J. B., Friberg, L., Lou, H., Lassen, N.A. S. and Sam, I. L. (1990) Immature pattern of brain activity in Rett syndrome. *Archives of Neurology, 47,* 98–986.

Nomura, Y., Segawa, M. and Higurashi, M. (1985) Rett syndrome – An early catecholamine and indolamine deficient disorder? *Brain and Development, 7 (3),* 334–341.

Nordoff, P. and Robbins, C. (1968) *The Second Book of Play-Songs.* Bryn Mawr, Pennsylvania: Theodore Presser Co.

Nordoff, P. and Robbins, C. (1971a) *Therapy in Music for Handicapped Children.* London: Gollancz.

Nordoff, P. and Robbins, C. (1971b) *Music Therapy in Special Education.* New York: John Day Company.

Nordoff, P. and Robbins, C. (1977) *Creative Music Therapy.* (Including case studies on audio cassette) New York: John Day Company. (Out of print. Available from The Nordoff-Robbins Music Therapy Centre, London).

Nowell, M. A., Hackney, D. B., Muraki, A. S. and Coleman, M. (1990) Varied MR appearance of autism: fifty-three paediatric patients have the full autistic syndrome. *Magnetic Resonance Imaging, 8,* 811–816.

O'Rahilly, R. and Müller, F. (1987) *The Embryonic Human Brain: An Atlas of Developmental Stages.* New York: Wiley-Liss.

O'Rahilly, R. and Müller, F. (1994) *The Embryonic Human Brain: An Atlas of Developmental Stages.* New York: Wiley-Liss;.

Ohta, M. (1987) Cognitive disorders of infantile autism: A study of employing the WISC, spatial relationship conceptualization and gesture imitations. *Journal of Autism and Developmental Disorders, 17,* 45–62.

Oppenheim, R. W. (1984) Cellular interactions and the survival and maintenance of neurons during development. In S. C. Sharma (ed) *Organizing Principles of Neural Development.* (pp.49–80) New York: Plenum.

Ornitz, E. M. (1983) The functional neuroanatomy of infantile autism. *International Journal of Neuroscience, 19,* 85–124.

Ornitz, E. M., Guthrie, D. and Farley, A. H. (1977) The early development of autistic children. *Journal of Autism and Child Schizophrenia, 7,* 207–229.

Ornitz, E. M. and Ritvo, E. R. (1968) Perceptual inconstancy in early infantile autism: The syndrome of early infant autism and its variants including certain cases of childhood schizophrenia. *Archives of General Psychiatry, 18,* 76–98.

Ozonoff, A., Pennington, B. F. and Rogers, S. (1991) Executive function deficits in high-functioning autistic individuals: Relationship to a theory of mind. *Journal of Child Psychology and Psychiatry, 32,* 1081–1105.

Ozonoff, S., Rogers, S. J. and Pennington, B. F. (1991) Asperger's Syndrome: Evidence of an Empirical Distinction from High-Functioning Autism. *Journal of Child Psychology and Psychiatry, 32,* 1107–1122.

Panksepp, J. (1979) A neurochemical theory of autism. *Trends in the Neurosciences, 2,* 174–177.

Panksepp, J. and Sahley, T. L. (1987) Possible brain opioid involvement in disrupted social intent and language development in autism. In E. Schopler and E. B. Mesibov (eds.) *Neurobiological Issues in Autism.* New York: Plenum Press, 357–372.

Papoudi, D. I. (1993) Interpersonal Play and Communication between Young Autistic Children and their Mothers. PhD Thesis, The University of Edinburgh.

Papousek, H. (1967) Experimental studies of appetitional behaviour in human newborns and infants. In H. W. Stevenson, E. H. Hess and H. L. Rhinegold (eds), *Early Behaviour, Comparative and Developmental Approaches.* New York: Wiley.

Papousek, H., and Papousek, M. (1979) The infant's fundamental adaptive response sysstem in social interaction. In E. B. Thoman (ed), *Origins of the Infant's Social Responsiveness.* Hillsdale, NJ: Lawrence Erlbaum.

Papousek, M. and Papousek, H. (1981) Musical elements in infants' vocalization: Their significant for communication, cognition and creativity. In L. P. Lipsitt (ed), *Advances in Infancy Research, Vol. 1.* Norwood, N.J.: Ablex.

Papousek, M., Papousek, H. and Bornstein, M. H. (1985) The naturalistic vocal environment of young infants: On the significance of homogeneity and variability in parental speech. In T. M. Field and N. Fox (eds), *Social Perception in Infants.* Norwood, N.J.: Ablex.

Parks, S. L. (1983) The assessment of autistic children: A selective review of available instruments. *Journal of Autism and Developmental Disorders, 13,* 255–267.

Pavlicevic, M. (1990) Dynamic interplay in clinical improvisation. *Journal of British Music Therapy 4 (2),* 5–9.

Pavlicevic, M. (1995) Interpersonal processes in clinical improvisation: towards a subjectively objective systematic definition. In T. Wigram, B. Saperston and R. West (eds), *The Art and Science of Music Therapy: A Handbook.* Chur, Switzerland: Harwood Academic Publishers, 167–178.

Pavlicevic, M. and Trevarthen, C. (1989) A musical assessment of psychiatric states in adults. *Psychopathology, 22 (6),* 325–334.

Payne, H. (1993) Directory of arts therapies research. In H. Payne (ed) *Handbook of Inquiry in the Arts Therapies: One River, Many Currents.* London and Philadelphia: Jessica Kingsley, 231–250.

Pedersen, I. N. (1992) Music therapy with autistic clients. In *Proceedings of the British Society for Music Therapy/Association of Professional Music Therapists Conference, 'Music Therapy in Health and Education'.* London: British Society for Music Therapy.

Perner, J., Frith, U., Leslie, A. M. and Leekam, S. R. (1989) Exploration of the autistic child's theory of mind: Knowledge, belief, and communication. *Child Development, 60,* 689–700.

Philippart, M. (1990) The Rett syndrome in Males. *Brain and Development, 122,* 33–36.

Piaget, J. (1954) *The Construction of Reality by the Child.* New York: Basic Books.

Piaget, J. (1962) *Play, Dreams, and Imitation in Childhood.* New York: Norton.

Piontelli, A. (1992) *From Fetus to Child.* London: Routledge.

Piven, J., Berthier, M., Starkstein, S., Nehme, E., Pearlson, G. and Folstein, S. (1990) Magnetic resonance imaging evidence for a defect of cerebral cortical development in autism. *American Journal of Psychiatry, 147,* 734–739.

Piven, J., Tsai, G., Nehme, E., Coyle, J. T., Chase, G. A. and Folstein, S. E. (1991) Platelet serotonin, a possible marker for familial autism. *Journal of Autism and Developmental Disorders, 21,* 51–60.

Priestley, M. (1994) *Essays on Analytical Music Therapy.* Phoenixville, PA: Barcelona Publishers.

Prior, M. and Cummins, R. (1992) Questions about facilitated communication and autism. *Journal of Autism and Developmental Disorders, 22,* 331–337.

Prior, M. R., Tress, B., Hoffman, W. L. and Boldt, D. (1984) Computed tomography study of children with classic autism. *Archives of Neurology 431,* 482–484.

Prizant, B. M. and Schuler, A. L. (1987) Facilitating communication: Language approaches. In D. J. Cohen and A. M. Donnellan (eds), *Handbook of Autism and Pervasive Developmental Disorders.* New York: Wiley.

Quill, K., Gurry, S. and Larkin, A. (1989) Daily Life Therapy: A Japanese model for educating children with autism. *Journal of Autism and Developmental Disorders, 19,* 625–635.

Rapin, I. and Allen, A. (1983) Developmental language disorders; nosological considerations. In U. Kirk (ed) *Neuropsychology of Language, Reading and Spelling.* London: Academic Press. Reber, S. A. (1985) The Penguin Dictionary of Psychology. London: Penguin.

Reber, S.A. (1985) *The Penguin Dictionary of Psychology.* London: Penguin.

Reddy, V. (1991) Playing with others' expectations; teasing and mucking about in the first year. In A. Whiten (ed) *Natural Theories of Mind: Evolution, Development and Simulation of Everyday Mindreading.* Oxford: Blackwell, pp.143–158.

Reiss, A. L. (1988) Carbellar Hypoplasia and Autism. *New England Journal of Medicine, 319,* 1152–1153, (Letter).

Reiss, A. L., Aylward, E., Freund, L., Joshi, P. and Bryan, R. N. (1991) Neuroanatomy of fragile X sysndrome: the posterior fossa. *Annals of Neurology, 29,* 26–32.

Repp, A. S. (1983) *Teaching the Mentally Retarded.* Prentice-Hall, Englewood Cliffs N.J.

Rett, A. (1966) Öber ein eigenartiges hirnatrophiches Syndrom bei Hyperammonmie im Kindersalter. *Weiner Medizinsche Wochenschrift, 116,* 723–726.

Rheingold, H., Hay, D. and West, M. (1976) Sharing in the second year of life. *Child Development, 83,* 898–913.

Richardson, J.S. and Zaleske, W.A. (1983) Naloxone and self-mutilation. *Biological Psychiatry, 18,* 99–101.

Richer, J. (1978) The partial communication of culture to autistic children: an application of human ethology. In M. Rutter and E. Schopler (eds) *A Reappraisal of Concepts and Treatment.* New York: Plenum Press.

Richer, J. (1983) Development of social avoidance in autistic children. In A. Oliverio and M. Zappella (eds) *The Behaviour of Human Infants.* London and New York: Plenum.

Ricks, D. M. (1975) Vocal communication in pre-verbal normal and autistic children. In N. O'Connor (ed) *Language, Cognitive Deficits and Retardation.* London: Butterworth.

Ricks, D. M. (1979) Making sense of experience to make sensible sounds: Experimental investigations of early vocal communication in pre-verbal autistic and normal children. In M. Bullowa (ed) *Before Speech. The Beginning of Interpersonal Communication.* Cambridge: Cambridge University Press.

Ricks, D. M. and Wing, L. (1975) Language, communication and the use of symbols in normal and autistic children. *Journal of Autism and Childhood Schizophrenia, 5,* 191–221.

Riguet, C. B., Taylor, N. D., Benaroya, S. and Klein, L. S. (1981) Symbolic play in autistic, Down's, and normal children of equivalent mental age. *Journal of Autism and Developmental Disorders, 11,* 439–448.

Rimland, B. (1964) *Infantile Autism.* New York: Appleton-Century-Crofts.

Rimland, B. (1971) The differentiation of childhood psychoses: An analysis of checklists for 2,218 psychotic children. *Journal of Autism and Childhood Schizophrenia, 1,* 161–174.

Ritvo, E. R., Freeman, B. J., Pingree, C., Mason-Brothers, A., Jorde, L. B., Jensen, W. R., McMahon, W. M., Petersen, P. B., Mo, A., and Ritvo, A. (1990) The UCLA-University of Utah epidemiologic survey of autism: prevalence. *American Journal of Psychiatry, 146,* 194–199.

Ritvo, E. R., Freeman, B. J., Scheibel, A. B., Duong, T., Robinson, H., Guthrie, D. and Ritvo, A. (1986) Lower Purkinje cell counts in the cerebella of four autistic subjects: Initial findings of the UCLA-NSAC autopsy research report. *American Journal of Psychiatry, 143,* 862–866.

Robarts, J. Z. (1994) Towards autonomy and a sense of self: the individuation process in music therapy in relation to children and adolescents suffering from early onset anorexia nervosa. In D. Dokter (ed) *Arts Therapies and Clients with Eating Disorders.* London: Jessica Kingsley Publishers, 229–246.

Robarts, J. Z. and Sloboda, A. (1994) Perspectives on music therapy with people suffering from anorexia nervosa. *Journal of British Music Therapy 8 (1),* 7–14.A.

Robbins, C. (1993) The creative processes are universal. In M. Heal and T. Wigram (ed) *Music Therapy in Health and Education.* London and Philadelphia: Jessica Kingsley, pp.7–25.

Rogers, P. (1993) Research in music therapy with sexually abused clients. In H. Payne (ed) *Handbook of Inquiry in the Arts Therapies: One River, Many Currents.* London and Philadelphia: Jessica Kingsley, pp.196–217.

Rogers, P. J. (1994) Sexual abuse and eating disorders: A possible connection indicated through music therapy? In D. Dokter (ed) *Arts Therapies with Clients with Eating Disorders.* London: Jessica Kingsley, pp.262–278.

Rogers, P. J. (1995) Music therapy research: A European perspective. *British Journal of Music Therapy, 10 (2).*

Rogers, S. J. and Pennington, B. F. (1991) A theoretical approach to the deficits in infantile autism. *Development and Psychopathology, 3,* 137–162.

Rogoff, B. (1990) *Apprenticeship in Thinking.* New York: Oxford University Press.

Rönnqvist, L. and von Hofsten, C. (1992) Varieties and determinants of finger movements in neonates. Poster, *Vth European Conference on Developmental Psychology.* Seville, Spain.

Rosenblatt, D. (1977) Developmental trends in infant play. In B. Tizard and D. Harvey, (eds.), *Biology of Play.* London: Heineman, 34–44.

Rumsey, J. M., Duara, R., Grady, C., Rapoport, J. L., Margolin, R. A., Rapoport, S. I., and Cutler, N. R. (1985) Brain metabolism in autism: resting cerebral glucose utilization rates as measured with positron emission tomography. *Annals of Neurology, 28,* 775–785.

Ruttenberg, B. A., Dratman, M. L., Fraknoi, J. and Wenar, C. (1966) An Instrument for Evaluating Autistic Children. *Journal of the American Academy of Child Psychiatry, 5,* 453–478.

Ruttenberg, B. A., Kalish, B I., Wenar, C. and Wolf, E. G. (1977) *Behaviour Rating Instrument for Autistic and Other Atypical Children* (Revised Edition). Philadelphia: Developmental Center for Autistic Children.

Rutter, M. (1966) Behavioural and cognitive characteristics of a series of psychotic children. In J.K. Wing (ed), *Early Childhood Autism,* 51–81.

Rutter, M. (1968) Concepts of autism. A review of research. *Journal of Child Psychology and Psychiatry, 9,* 1–25.

Rutter, M. (1978) Diagnosis and definition of childhood autism. *Journal of Autism and Childhood Schizophrenia, 8,* 139–161.

Rutter, M. (1983) Cognitive deficits in the pathogenesis of autism. *Journal of Child Psychology and Psychiatry, 24,* 513–531.

Rutter, M. (1985) Infantile autism and other pervasive developmental disorders. In M. Rutter and L. Hersov (eds), *Child and Adolescent Psychiatry: Modern Approaches.* Oxford: Blackwell Scientific, 545–566.

Rutter, M. (1991) Autism as a genetic disorder. In P. McGuffin and R. Murray (eds) *The New Genetics of Mental Illness.* (pp.225–244) Oxford: Butterworth-Heinemann.

Rutter, M., Bartak, L. and Newman, S. (1971) Autism – A central disorder of cognition and language? In M. Rutter (ed) *Infantile Autism: Concepts, Characteristics and Treatment.* London: Churchill Livingstone.

Rutter, M., Le Couteur, A., Lord, C., MacDonald, H., Rios, P. and Folstein, S. (1988) Diagnosis and subclassification of autism: Concepts and instrument development. In E. Schopler and G. B. Mesibov (eds.), *Diagnosis and Assessment in Autism.* New York: Plenum, 239–259.

Rutter, M. and Schopler, E. (1987) Autism and Pervasive Developmental Disorders: Conceps and Diagnostic Issues. *Journal of Autism and Developmental Disorders, 17,* 159–186.

Rutter, M. and Schopler, E. (eds.) (1978) *Autism: A Reappraisal of Concepts and Treatment.* New York: Plenum Press.

Sandman, C. A., Datta P. C., Barron J., Hoehler F. K., Wiliams C., and Swanson J. M. (1983) Naloxone attenuates self-injurious behaviour in developmentally disabled clients. *Applied Research in Mental Retardation, 4,* 5–12.

Saperston, B. (1973) The use of music in establishing communication with an autistic mentally retarded child. *Journal of Music Therapy 10,* 184–188.

Saperston, B. (1982) Case study: Timmy. In D. W. Paul (ed) *Music Therapy for Handicapped Children: Emotionally Disturbed.* Washington DC: Office of Special Education and the National Association for Music Therapy, pp.42–57.

Scaife, M. and Bruner, J. S. (1975) The capacity for joint visual attention in the infant. *Nature 253,* 265–6.

Schain, R. J. and Freedman, D. X. (1961) Studies on 5-hydroxyindole metabolism in autistic and other mentally retarded children. *Journal of Pediatrics, 58,* 315–320.

Schonfelder, T. (1964) Uber fruhkindlische antriebsstrorungen. *Acta Paedopsychiatrica, 31,* 112–129.

Schopler, E. (1992) Editorial comment on Prior and Cummins. *Journal of Autism and Developmental Disorders, 22,* 337.

Schopler, E. and Mesibov, G. B. (1987) (eds) *Neurobiological Issues in Autism.* New York: Plenum.

Schopler, E., Mesibov, G. B., and Baker, A. (1982) Evaluation of treatment for autistic children and their parents. *Journal of the American Academy of Child Psychiatry, 21,* 262–267.

Schopler, E., Mesibov, G. B., DeVellis, R, and Short, A. (1981) Treatment outcome for autistic children and their families. In P. Mittler (ed), *Frontiers of Knowledge in Mental Retardation. Volume 1. Special Educational and Behavioral Aspects.* Baltimore: University Park Press, pp.293–301.

Schopler, E., Mesibov, G. B., Shigley, R H., and Bashford, A. (1984) Helping autistic children through their parents: The TEACCH model. In E. Schopler and G.B. Mesibov (eds.), *The Effects of Autism on the Family*. New York: Plenum Press, pp.65–81.

Schopler, E. and Olley, J. G. (1982) Comprehensive educational services for autistic children: The TEACCH model. In C. R Reynolds and T. R Gutkin (eds.), *Handbook of School Psychology*. New York: Wiley, pp.629–643.

Schopler, E. and Reichler, R J. (1971) Developmental therapy by parents with their autistic child. In M. Rutter (ed), *Infantile Autism: Concepts, Characteristics, Treatment*. London: Churchill-Livingstone, pp.206–227.

Schopler, E. and Reichler, R. J. (1979) *Individualized Assessment and Treatment of Autistic and Developmentally Disabled Children, Vol. 1, Psychoeducational Profile, (2nd Edition)*, Austin, Texas: Pro-Ed.

Schopler, E., Reichler, R. J., DeVellis, R. F. and Kock, K. (1980) Toward objective classification of childhood autism: Childhood Autism Rating Scale (CARS) *Journal of Autism and Developmental Disorders, 10*, 91–103.

Schopler, E., Reichler, R. J. and Lansing, M. (1980) *Individualized Assessment and Treatment of Autistic and Developmentally Disabled Children, Vol. 2, Teaching Strategies for Parents and Professionals*, Dallas, Texas: Pro-Ed.

Schore, A. N. (1994) *Affect Regulation and the Origin of the Self: The Neurobiology of Emotional Development*. Hillsdale, NJ: Erlbaum.

Schreibman, L. (1988) Autism, Developmental Clinical Psychology and Psychiatry, 15, Sage Publications, Newbury Park, ISBN 0-8039-2809-2.

Sears, W. (1968) Processes in music therapy. In E.T. Gaston (ed) *Music in Therapy*. New York: Macmillan.

Segawa, M. (1992) Possible lesions of the Rett syndrome: opinions of contributors. *Brain and Development, 14, (Supplement)*, S149–S150.

Selfe, L. (1978) *Nadia: A Case of Extraordinary Drawing Ability in an Autistic Child*. London: Academic Press.

Shapiro,T., Frosch, E. and Arnold, S. (1987) Communicative interaction between mothers and their autistic children: Application for a new instrument and changes after treatment. *Journal of the American Academy of Child and Adolescent Psychiatry, 26*, 485–490.

Shapiro, T., Sherman, M, Calamari, G. and Kock, D. (1987) Attachment in autism and other developmental disorders. *Journal of the American Academy of Child and Adolescent Psychiatry, 26*, 480–484.

Sherwin, A. C. (1953) Reactions to music of autistic (schizophrenic) children. *American Journal of Psychiatry, 109*, 823–831.

Shuttleworth, J. (1989) Psychoanalytic theory and infant development. In Miller, L., Rustin, M., Rustin, M. and Shuttleworth, J. (Eds.) *Closely Observed Infants*. London: Duckworth., 22–51.

Siegel, B., Vukicevic, J. and Spitzer, R. L. (1990) Using signal detection methodology to revise DSM-III-R: reanalysis of the DSM-III-R National Field Trials for autistic disorder. *Journal of Psychiatric Research, 24*, 293–311.

Sigman, M. (1989) The application of developmental knowledge to a clinical problem: The study of childhood autism. In D. Cicchetti (ed), *Rochester Symposium on Developmental Psychopathology, Vol.1: The emergence of a discipline*. Hillsdale, NJ: Erlbaum, 165–187.

Sigman, M. and Mundy, P. (1989) Social attachments in autistic children. *Journal of the American Academy of Child and Adolescent Psychiatry, 28*, 74–81.

Sigman, M., Mundy, P., Sherman, T. and Ungerer, J. (1986) Social interactions of autistic, mentally retarded and normal children and their caregivers. *Journal of Child Psychology and Psychiatry, 27*, 647–656.

Sigman, M. and Ungerer, J. (1981) Sensorimotor skills and language comprehension in autistic children. *Journal of Abnormal Child Psychology, 9*, 149–165.

Sigman, M. and Ungerer, J. A. (1984a) Cognitive and language skills in autistic, mentally retarded and normal children. *Developmental Psychology, 20*, 293–302.

Sigman, M. and Ungerer, J. A. (1984b) Attachment behaviours in autistic children. *Journal of Autism and Developmental Disorders, 14*, 231–244.

Simmeonson, R. J., Olley, G. J. and Rosenthal, S. L. (1987) Early intervention for children with autism. In M. J. Guralnick and F. C. Bennett (eds) *The Effectiveness of Early Intervention for At-Risk and Handicapped Children.* New York: Academic Press.

Sinason, V. (1992) *Mental Handicap and the Human Condition: New Approaches from the Tavistock.* London: Free Association Books.

Singer, W. (1987) Activity-dependent self-organization of synaptic connections as a substrate of learning. In J.-P. Changeux and M. Konishi (eds.), *The Neural and Molecular Bases of Learning.* New York: Wiley.

Singer, W. and Raushecker, J. P. (1982) Central core control of developmental plasticity in the kitten visual cortex. II Electrical activation of mesencephalic and diencephalic projections. *Experimental Brain Research, 41,* 199–215.

Singer, W., Tretter, F. and Yinon, W. (1982) Central gating of developmental plasticity in kitten visual cortex. *Journal of Physiology, 324,* 221–237.

Sloman, L. (1991) Use of medication in pervasive developmental disorder. *Pediatric Clinics of North America, 14,* 165–182.

Smalley, S. L., Tanguay, P. E., Smith, M. and Guitierrez, G. (1992) Autism and Tuberous Sclerosis. *Journal of Autism and Developmental Disorders, 22,* 339–355.

Smeijsters, H. and Hurk, P. van den (1993) Research and practice in the music therapeutic treatment of a client with symptoms of anorexia nervosa. In M. Heal and A. Wigram (eds) *Music Therapy in Health and Education.* London and Philadelphia: Jessica Kingsley, 255–263.

Smeijsters, H., Rogers, P., Kortegaard, H-M., Lehtonen, K., Scanlon, P., (eds.) (1995) *The European Music Therapy Research Register Vol. II.* The Netherlands: The Stichting Muziektherapie Foundation.

Snow, M. E., Hertzig, M. E. and Shapiro, T. (1987) Expression of emotion in young autistic children. *Journal of the American Academy of Child and Adolescent Psychiatry, 26,* 836–838.

Söderbergh, R. (1986) Acquisition of spoken and written language in early childhood. In I. Kuroz, G. W. Shugar and J. H. Danks (eds), *Knowledge and Language.* Amsterdam: North Holland.

Sparling, J. W. (1991) Brief report: A prospective case report of infantile autism from pregnancy to four years. *Journal of Autism and Developmental Disorders, 21,* 229–236.

Spelke, E. (1985) *Perception of Unity, Persistence and Identity: Thoughts on Infants' Conceptions of Objects.* Hillsdale, NJ: Erlbaum.

Sperry, R. W. (1963) Chemoaffinity in the orderly growth of nerve fiber patterns and connections. *Proceedings of the National Academy of Sciences, USA, 50,* 703–710.

Squire, L.R. (1986) Mechanisms of memory. *Science, 232,* 1612–19.

Statistical Yearbook, (39th edn), UN, New York, 1994.

Steffenberg, S. (1991) Neuropsychiatric Assessment of Children with Autism: A Population-Based Study. *Developmental Medicine and Child Neurology, 33,* 495–511.

Steffenberg, S. and Gillberg, C. (1986) Autism and Autistic-like Conditions in Swedish Rural and Urban Areas: A Population Study. *British Journal of Psychiatry, 149,* 81–87.

Stern, D. N. (1974a) Mother and infant at play: the dyadic interaction involving facial, vocal and gaze behaviours. In M. Lewis and L.A. Rosenblum (eds) *The Effect of the Infant on Its Caregiver.* New York: Wiley.

Stern, D. N. (1974b) The goal and structure of mother–infant play. *Journal of the American Academy of Child Psychiatry, 13,* 402–421.

Stern, D. N. (1977) *The First Relationship: Infant and Mother.* Cambridge MA: Harvard University Press.

Stern, D. N. (1985) *The Interpersonal World of the Infant.* New York: Basic Books.

Stern, D. N. (1994) One way to build a clinically relevant baby. *Infant Mental Health Journal 15 (1)* Spring.

Stern, D. N. and Gibbon, J. (1980) Temporal expectancies of social behaviors in mother–infant play. In E. Thoman (ed), *Origins of Infant Social Responsiveness.* New York: Erlbaum.

Stern, D. N., Hofer, L., Haft, W. and Dore, J. (1985). Affect attunement: The sharing of feeling states between mother and infant by means of inter-modal fluency. In Field, T.M. and Fox, N.A. (eds) *Social Perception in Infants.* pp.249–268 Norwood, NJ: Ablex.

Stern, D. N., Spieker, S. and MacKain, K. (1982) Intonation contours as signals in maternal speech to prelinguistic infants. *Developmental Psychology, 18,* 727–735.

Stevens, E. and Clark, F. (1969) Music therapy in the treatment of autistic children. In *Journal of Music Therapy, 6*, 93–104.

Stewart-Clarke, A. and Hevey, C. (1981) Longitudinal relations in repeated observations of mother–child interaction from one to two-and-a-half years. *Developmental Psychology, 97*, 127–145.

Stone W. L., Hoffman E. L., Lewis S. E., and Ousley O. Y. (1994) Early Recognition of Autism: Parental Reports vs. Clinical Observation. *Archives of Pediatric and Adolescent Medicine, 148*, 174–179.

Stone, W.L., Lemanek, K.L., Fishel, P.T., Fernandez, M.C. and Altemeier, W.A. (1990) Play and imitation skills in the diagnosis of autism in young children. *Pediatrics, 86*, 267–72.

Strain, P. S. (1987) Comprehensive evaluation of interventions for young autistic children. *Topics in Early Childhood Education, 7*, 97–110.

Strain, P. S., Jamieson, B. and Hoyson, M. (1986) Learning experiences.... An alternative program for preschoolers and parents. A comprehensive service system for the mainstreaming of autistic-like preschoolers. In C. J. Meisel (ed) *Mainstreaming Handicapped Children: Outcomes Controversies and New Directions.* Hillsdale, NJ: Erlbaum.

Sugiyama, T. and Abe, T. (1989) The prevalence of autism in Nagoya, Japan: A Total Population Study. *Journal of Autism and Developmental Disorders, 19*, 87–96.

Szatmari, P., Bertolucci, G. and Bremner, R. (1989) Asperger's Syndrome and autism: comparisons on early history and outcome. *Developmental Medicine and Child Neurology, 31*, 130–6.

Szatmari, P., Tuff,L., Finlayson, M.A.J. and Bartolucci G. (1990) Asperger's syndrome and autism: Neurocognitive aspects. *Journal of the American Academy of Child and Adolescent Psychiatry, 29*, 130–136.

Tager-Flusberg, H. (1981) On the nature of linguistic functioning in early infantile autism. *Journal of Autism and Developmental Disorders, 11*, 45–56.

Tager-Flusberg, H. (1989) A psycholinguistic perspective on language development in the autistic child. In G. Dawson (ed) *Autism: Nature, Diagnosis and Treatment.* New York: Guilford Press.

Tanoue, Y., Oda, S., Asano, F. andKawashima, K. (1988) Epidemiology of infantile autism in Southern Ibaraki, Japan: Difference in prevalence in birth cohorts. *Journal of Autism and Developmental Disorders, 18*, 155–166.

Tantam, D. (1988) Lifelong eccentricity and social isolation. I. Psychiatric, social and forensic aspects. *British Journal of Psychiatry, 153*, 777–782.

Tantam, D. (1991) Asperger Syndrome in adulthood. In U. Frith (ed) *Autism and Asperger Syndrome.* Cambridge: Cambridge University Press.

Thatcher, R. W., Walker, R. A. and Giudice, S. (1987) Human cerebral hemispheres develop at different rates and ages. *Science, 236*, 1110–1113.

Thaut, M. H. (1980) *Music Therapy as a Treatment Tool for Autistic Children.* Unpublished Master's thesis. Michigan State University.

Thaut, M. H. (1983) A music therapy treatment model for autistic children. *Music Therapy Perspectives, 1*, 7–13.

Thaut, M. H. (1987) Visual versus auditory (musical) stimulus preferences in autistic children: A pilot study. *Journal of Autism and Developmental Disorders 17*, 425–432.

Thaut, M. H. (1988) Measuring musical responsiveness in autistic children: A comparative analysis of improvised musical tone sequences of autistic, normal and mentally retarded individuals. *Journal of Autism and Developmental Disorders, 18*, 561–571.

Thaut, M. H. (1992) Music therapy with autistic children. In W. B. Davis, K. E. Gfeller and M. H. Thaut (eds.) *An Introduction to Music Therapy: Theory and Practice.* Dubuque, Indiana: William C. Brown Publishers, 180–196.

Tiergerman, E. and Primavera, L. (1981) Object manipulation: An interactional strategy with autistic children. *Journal of Autism and Developmental Disorders, 11*, 427–438.

Tiergerman, E. and Primavera, L. (1984) Imitating the autistic child: Facilitating communicative gaze behaviour. *Journal of Autism and Developmental Disorders, 14*, 27–38.

Tilton, J. R. and Ottinger, D. R. (1964) Comparison of the toy play behaviour of autistic, retarded and normal children. *Psychological Reports, 15*, 967–975.

Tinbergen, N. and Tinbergen, E. A. (1983) *'Autistic' Children: New Hope for a Cure.* London: Allen and Unwin.

Tingey, C. (1989) *Implementing Early Intervention.* Baltimore: Paul Brookes Publishing.

Toigo, D. A. (1992) Autism: integrating a personal perspective in music therapy practice. *Music Therapy Perspectives, 10,* 13–20.

Tomasello, M. and Farrar, M. J. (1986) Joint attention and early language. *Child Development, 57,* 1454–1463.

Tomasello, M., Kruger, A. C. and Ratner, H. H. (1993) Cultural learning. *Behavioral and Brain Sciences 16,* 3, 495–552.

Tredgold, R. F. and Soddy, K. (1956) *A Textbook of Mental Deficiency.* London: Balliere, Tindal and Cox.

Trehub, S. E., Chang, Hsing-Wu (1977) Infants' perception of temporal grouping in auditory patterns. *Child Development, 48,* 1666–1670.

Trehub, S. E., Schneider, B. A., Thorpe, L. A., Judge, P. (1991) Observational measures of auditory sensitivity in early infancy. *Developmental Psychology, 27 (1),* 40–49.

Trehub, S. E., Thorpe, L. A. (1989) Infants' perception of rhythm: Categorization of auditory sequences by temporal structure. *Canadian Journal of Psychology, 43 (2),* 217–229.

Trehub, S.E., Thorpe, L.A. and Trainor, L.J. (1990) Rules for listening in infancy. In J. Enns (ed) *The Development of Attention: Research and Theory.* Amsterdam: Elsevier.

Trevarthen, C. (1979) Communication and cooperation in early infancy. A description of primary intersubjectivity. In M. Bullowa (ed) *Before Speech: The Beginnings of Human Communication.* London: Cambridge University Press.

Trevarthen, C. (1980) The foundations of intersubjectivity: development of interpersonal and cooperative understanding of infants. In D. Olson (ed), *The Social Foundations of Language and Thought: Essays in Honor of J.S. Bruner.* New York: W.W. Norton.

Trevarthen, C. (1984) Emotions in infancy: Regulators of contacts and relationships with persons. In K. Scherer and P. Ekman (eds.), *Approaches to Emotion.* Hillsdale, NJ: Erlbaum.

Trevarthen, C. (1985) Facial expressions of emotion in mother–infant interaction. *Human Neurobiology, 4,* 21–32.

Trevarthen, C. (1986) Form, significance and psychological potential of hand gestures of infants. In J. L. Nespoulos, P. Perron and A. Roch Lecours (eds.), *The Biological Foundation of Gestures: Motor and Semiotic Aspects.* Cambridge, MA: MIT Press.

Trevarthen, C. (1987a) Sharing makes sense: Intersubjectivity and the making of an infant's meaning. In R. Steele and T. Threadgold (eds.), *Language Topics: Essays in Honour of Michael Halliday.* Amsterdam and Philadelphia: John Benjamins.

Trevarthen, C. (1987b) Brain development. In R. L. Gregory and O. L. Zangwill (eds.), *Oxford Companion to the Mind.* Oxford, New York: Oxford University Press, 101–110.

Trevarthen, C. (1989) Development of early social interactions and the affective regulation of brain growth. In C. von Euler, H. Forssberg and H. Lagercrantz (eds) *Neurobiology of Early Infant Behaviour.* (Wenner-Gren Center International Symposium Series, Vol 55) Basingstoke: Macmillan/New York: Stockton Press.

Trevarthen, C. (1990a) Signs before speech. In T. A. Sebeok and J. Umiker-Sebeok (eds.), *The Semiotic Web,* 1989. Berlin, New York, Amsterdam: Mouton de Gruyter, 689–755.

Trevarthen, C. (1990b) Growth and education of the hemispheres. In C. Trevarthen (ed), *Brain Circuits and Functions of the Mind: Essays in Honour of Roger W. Sperry* (pp.334–363). New York: Cambridge University Press.

Trevarthen, C. (1992) An infant's motives for speaking and thinking in the culture. In A. H. Wold (ed) *The Dialogical Alternative* (Festschrift for Ragnar Rommetveit) Oslo/Oxford: Scandanavian University Press/Oxford University Press.

Trevarthen, C. (1993a) The function of emotions in early infant communication and development. In J. Nadel and L. Camaioni (eds) *New Perspectives in Early Communicative Development.* London: Routledge.

Trevarthen, C. (1993b) The self born in intersubjectivity: an infant communicating. In U. Neisser (ed) *Ecological and Interpersonal Knowledge of the Self.* New York: Cambridge University Press.

Trevarthen, C. (1993d) Human Emotions and Why We Need Them. Lecture to The Squiggle Foundation, London, February 14th, 1993.

Trevarthen, C. (1996) Lateral assymetries in infancy: implications for the development of the hemispheres. *Neuroscience and Biobehvioral Reviews* (in press).

Trevarthen, C. and Aitken, K. J. (1994) Brain development, infant communication, and empathy disorders: Intrinsic factors in child mental health. *Development and Psychopathology, 6,* 599–635.

Trevarthen, C. and Burford, B. (1995) The central role of parents: how they can give power to a motor impaired child's acting, experiencing and sharing. *European Journal of Special Needs Education, 10 (2),* 138–148.

Trevarthen, C. and Hubley, P. 1978. Secondary Intersubjectivity: Confidence, confiding and acts of meaning in the first year. In A. Lock (ed) *Action, Gesture and Symbol.* London: Academic Press.

Trevarthen, C. and Logotheti, K. (1987) First symbols and the nature of human knowledge. In J. Montangero, A. Tryphon and S. Dionnet (eds) *Symbolism and Knowledge.* Cahier No. 8. Geneva: Jean Piaget Archives Foundation.

Trevarthen, C. and Marwick, H. (1986) Signs of motivation for speech in infants, and the nature of a mother's support for development of language. In B. Lindblom and R. Zetterstrom (eds) *Precursors of Early Speech.* Basingstoke, Hampshire: Macmillan, 279–308.

Tronick, E. Z., Als, H., Adamson, L., Wise, S. and Brazelton, T. B. (1978) The infant's response to entrapment between contradictory messages in face-to-face interaction. *Journal of the American Academy of Child Psychiatry, 17,* 1–13.

Tsai, L. Y. (1982) Handedness in autistic children and their families. *Journal of Autism and Developmental Disorders, 12,* 421–423.

Tsai, L. Y., Jacoby, C. G. Stewart, M. A. and Beisler, J. M. (1982) Unfavorable left–right asymmetries of the brain and autism: A question of methodology. *British Journal of Psychiatry, 140,* 312–319.

Tustin, F. (1981) *Autistic States in Children.* London: Routledge and Kegan Paul.

Tustin, F. (1986) *Autistic Barriers in Neurotic Patients.* London: Karnac.

Tustin, F. (1994) Autistic children assessed as not brain-damaged. *Journal of Child Psychotherapy, 20 (10),* 209–225.

Ungerer, J. A. and Sigman, M. (1981) Symbolic play and language comprehension in autistic children. *Journal of the American Academy of Child Psychiatry, 20,* 318–337.

Van Rees, S. and Biemans, H. (1986) *Open-closed-open: An Autistic Girl at Home.* Video by Stichting Lichaamstaal, Scheyvenhofweg 12, 6093 PR Heythuysen The Netherlands.

Varley, C., Kolff, C., Trupin, E. and Reichler, R. J. (1980) Hemodialysis as a treatment for infantile autism. *Journal of Autism and Developmental Disorders, 10,* 399–404.

Volkmar, F. R. (1992) Child Disintegrative Disorder: Issues for DSM-IV. *Journal of Autism and Developmental Disorders, 22,* 625–642.

Volkmar, F.R. (1994) Childhood disintegrative disorder. *Child and Adolescent Psychiatric Clinic of North America, 3,* 199–229.

Volkmar, F.R. and Cohen, D.J. (1989) Disintegrative disorder or 'late onset' autism? *Journal of Child Psychology and Psychiatry, 30,* 717–24.

Volkmar, F. R. and Cohen, D. J. (1991) Comorbid association of autism and schizophrenia. *American Journal of Psychiatry, 148,* 1705–1707.

Volkmar, F. R. and Mayes, L. (1990) Gaze behaviour in autism. *Development and Psychopathology, 2,* 61–69.

Volkmar, F. R. and Nelson D. S. (1990) Seizure disorders in autism. *Journal of the American Academy of Child and Adolescent Psychiatry, 29,* 127–129.

Volterra, V. (1981) Gestures, signs and words at two years: When does communication become language? *Sign Language Studies, 33,* 351–362.

von der Mahlsberg, C. and Singer, W. (1988) Principles of cortical network organization. In P. Rakic and W. Singer (eds) *Neurobiology of Neocortex.* New York: Wiley.

Walker, E.F., Grimes, K.E., Davis, D.M. and Smith, A.J. (1993) Childhood precursors of schizophrenia: facial expressions of emotion. *Americal Journal of Psychiatry, 150,* 1654–60.

Walker, M. (1980) *The Revised Makaton Vocabulary.* Published by the author. London: St George's Hospital.

Wallin, N. L. (1991) *Biomusicology: Neurophysiological, Neuropsychological and Evolutionary Perspectives on the Origins and Purposes of Music.* Stuyvesant, New York: Pendragon Press.

Wang P. P, Bellugi U. (1993) Williams syndrome, Down syndrome, and cognitive neuroscience. *American Journal of Diseases of Children, 147,* 1246–1251.

Warwick, A. (1995) Music therapy in the education service: research with autistic children and their mothers. In T. Wigram, B. Saperston and R. West (eds) *The Art and Science of Music Therapy: A Handbook.* 209–225.

Watters, R. G. and Watters, W. E. (1980) Decreasing self-stimulatory behaviour with physical exercise in a group of autistic boys. *Journal of Autism and Childhood Schizophrenia, 6*, 175–191.

Weinberg, M. K. and Tronick, E. Z. (1994) Beyond the face: An empirical study of infant affective configurations of facial, vocal, gestural, and regulatory behaviors. *Child Development, 65*, 1503–1515.

Weinberger, D. R. (1987) Implications of normal development for the pathogenesis of schizophrenia. *Archives of General Psychiatry, 44*, 660–669.

Welch, M. G. (1983) Retrieval from autism through mother–child holding therapy. In N. Tinbergen and E. A. Tinbergen (eds) *'Autistic' Children: New Hope for a Cure.* London: Allen and Unwin.

Wenar, C. and Ruttenberg, B. A. (1976) The use of BRIACC for evaluating therapeutic effectiveness. *Journal of Autism and Developmental Disorders, 10*, 379–387.

Wetherby, A. M. (1986) Ontogeny of communicative functions in autism. *Journal of Autism and Developmental Disorders, 16*, 295–316.

Wetherby, A. M. and Prutting, C. A. (1984) Profiles of communicative and cognitive social abnormalities in autistic children. *Journal of Speech and Hearing Research, 27*, 364–377.

Wheeler, B. (ed) (1995) *Music Therapy Research: Quantitative and Qualitative Perspectives.* Phoenixville, PA: Barcelona Publishers.

Wigram, T. (1995) A model of assessment and differential diagnosis of handicapped children through the medium of music. In T. Wigram, B. Saperston, and R. West (eds) *The Art and Science of Music Therapy: A Handbook.* Chur, Switzerland: Harwood Academic Publishers, 181–193.

Williams D. (1992) *Nobody Nowhere: The Remarkable Autobiography of an Autistic Girl.* London: Doubleday.

Wiltshire, S. (1987) *Drawings.* (Foreword by Lorraine Cole) London: Dent.

Wiltshire, S. (1989) *Cities* (Foreword by Oliver Sacks; Introduction by Anthony Clare) London: Dent.

Wing L. (1981) Asperger's Syndrome: A clinical account. *Psychological Medicine, 11*, 115–130.

Wing, L. (1969) The handicaps of autistic children – a comparative study. *Journal of Child Psychology and Psychiatry, 10*, 1–40.

Wing, L. (1976) Diagnosis, clinical description and prognosis. In L. Wing (ed) *Early Childhood Autism: Clinical, Educational and Social Aspects.* New York: Pergamon Press.

Wing, L. (1980a) Childhood autism and social class: A question of selection. *British Journal of Psychiatry, 137*, 410–417.

Wing, L. (1980b) Sex ratios in early childhood autism and related conditions. *Psychiatry Research, 5*, 129–137.

Wing, L. and Gould, J. (1979) Severe Impairments of Social Interaction and Associated Abnormalities in Children: Epidemiology and Classification. *Journal of Autism and Developmental Disorders, 9*, 11–29.

Wing, L., Gould, J., Yeates, S. and Brierly, L. (1977) Symbolic play in severely mentally retarded and in autistic children. *Journal of Child Psychology and Psychiatry, 18*, 167–178.

Wing, L., Yeates, S., Brierly, L. and Gould, J. (1976) The prevalence of early childhood autism: Comparison of administrative and epidemiological studies. *Psychological Medicine, 6*, 89–100.

Winnicott, D. W. (1952) Psychoses and child care. In *Through Paediatrics to Psycho-Analysis.* London: Hogarth Press, pp.219–228.

Winnicott, D. W. (1965) The theory of the parent–infant relationship. In *The Maturational Processes and the Facilitating Environment.* London: Karnac.

Winnicott, D. W. (1971) *Playing and Reality.* New York: Penguin.

Wishart, J.G. (1991) Taking the intiative in learning: a developmental investigation of children with Down Syndrome. *International Journal of Disability, Development and Education, 38*, 27–44.

Wishart, J. G. and Bower, T. G. R. (1984) Spatial relations and object concept: A normative study. In L. P. Lipsitt and C. Rovee-Collier (eds.), *Advances in Infancy Research, Vol. 3.* Norwood, NJ: Ablex.

Wolff, P. H., Garner J., Paccia J. and Lappen J. (1989) The Greeting Behaviour of Fragile-X Males. *American Journal of Mental Retardation, 93*, 406–411.

Wolff, S. and Chess, S. (1964) A behavioural study of schizophrenic children. *Acta Psychiatrica Scandinavica, 40*, 438–466.

Wulff, S. B. (1985) The symbolic and object play of children with autism: A review. *Journal of Autism and Developmental Disorders, 15*, 139–148.

Yirmiya, N., Kasari, C., Sigman, M. and Mundy, P. (1989) Facial expressions of affect in autistic, mentally retarded and normal children. *Journal of Child Psychology and Psychiatry, 30,* 725–735.

Zappella, M. (1992) Hypomelanosis of Ito is common in autistic syndromes. *European Child and Adolescent Psychiatry, 1,* 170–177

Zappella, M., Chiarucci, P., Pinassi, D., Fidanzi, P. and Messeri, P. (1991) Parental bonding in the treatment of autistic behaviour. *Ethology and Sociobiology, 12,* 1–11.

Zilbovicius, M., Garreau, B., Tzourio, N., Mazoyer, B., Bruck, B., Martinot, J-L., Raynaud, C., Samson, Y., Syrota, A. and Lelord, G. (1992) Regional Cerebral Blood Flow in Childhood Autism: A SPECT Study. *American Journal of Psychiatry, 149,* 924–930.

Zuckerkandl, V. (1976) *Man the Musician.* Princeton: Bollingen.

Glossary

ABC: The Autism Behaviour Checklist (see p.17).

ADI: The Autism Diagnostic Inventory (see p.18).

ADOS: The Autism Diagnostic Observation Schedule (see p.18).

Adreno-Cortico-Trophic Hormone (ACTH): A hormone produced in the anterior pituitary gland of the brain that stimulates the adrenal gland with a range of effects, including release of sex hormone.

AFRAX (Autism with Fragile-X Syndrome): The combination of the Fragile-X syndrome with a behavioural profile sufficient for a diagnosis of autism.

Agenesis: Absence, failure of formation or lack of development of a particular structure.

Amygdala: A pair of almond-shaped nuclei, one near the tip of each temporal lobe of the brain. They are part of the limbic system and a key component in emotional regulation in learning and communication.

Anomalous Dominance: As used by Geschwind and Galaburda, this term denotes any handedness patterns other than strong right-handedness.

Antagonist: A substance which blocks or reduces the activity of another substance, such as a drug or a natural neurotransmitter or hormone.

Anterior: Found towards the front of a structure in the body.

Aphasia: Impairment or absence of language.

Arnold-Chiari I: A congenital abnormality resulting in the cerebellum and caudate developing with extension down into the region of the upper spinal column.

Asperger's sydrome: A condition, similar to high functioning autism, characterised by marked social impairments and extremely circumscribed interests, clumsiness, performance difficulties on cognitive testing and executive function problems, but no simple 'metacognitive', or model-of-mind, problems (see p.27).

Atrophy: Physical wasting of a tissue or organ.

Basal Ganglia: A forebrain region consisting of a number of structures which include the caudate, putamen and globus pallidus. They are important in regulation of movement patterns.

Batten's Syndrome (Infantile Neural Seroid Lipofuscinosis): A genetic disorder which can now be identified antenatally by a genetic marker. On initial presentation, up to the third year, it is often confused with autism or Rett's syndrome. Loss of head control and abnormal postures make differential diagnosis easier in older children.

Bipolar Affective Disorder: A term used interchangeably with manic-depressive psychosis to indicate a specific psychiatric disorder.

BOS: The Behaviour Observation Scale for Autism (see p.16).

BRIACC: The Behaviour Rating Instrument for Autistic and Atypical Children (see p.16).

BSE: The Behavioural Summarised Evaluation (see p.17).

CARS: The Childhood Autism Rating Scale.

Caudate: A pair of tadpole-shaped structures which make up part of the basal ganglia.

Cerebellum: A large hindbrain structure situated under the rear portion of the cerebral cortex at the back of the head. It is important in motor control and planning, and in simple learning. It consists of two large hemispheres on left and right and a narrow middle region, the vermis.

Cerebral Cortex: The gray, cell-rich layer, approximately three millimetres thick, which covers the entire surface of the cerebral hemispheres.

CHAT: The Checklist for Autism in Toddlers – an 18 month screening test for detection of precursor behaviours for autism (see p.19).

Childhood Disintegrative Disorder: Another name for Heller's syndrome, originally callled dementia infantilis. A condition with early normal development until during the second year, followed by loss in language and cognitive skills.

Chromosomes: Structures in the cell nucleus containing DNA (deoxyribose nucleic acid), the physical genetic code which determines the inherited biochemical makeup of the individual and directs development of the body and all its components.

Computerised Axial Tomography (CAT): An X-ray procedure which allows pictures to be made of deep brain structures from outside the head. This technique differentially images denser structures. It is less effective in imaging deeper structures of the midbrain and the cerebellum than it is in revealing tissues of the cerebral hemispheres.

Congenital: Present at birth, thus reflecting the influence of genetic, conceptual, pregnancy or labour and delivery factors.

Corpus Callosum: The principal fibre bridge which links equivalent areas of the cortex of the two cerebral hemispheres.

Dandy-Walker: A condition in which the child has hydrocephalus (accumulation of fluid in the cavities of the brain), enlargement of the brain and abnormalities in the formation of the cerebellum.

Declive: Part of the central vermis of the cerebellum.

Dopamine: A neurotransmitter from cells found principally in the caudate and putamen of the basal ganglia and in the substantia nigra nucleus of the brainstem.

Down's Syndrome: A genetic developmental disorder which results from the presence of an extra copy of chromosome 21.

DSM III-R: the classification system for behavioural and emotional disorders used by the American Psychiatric Association between 1987 and 1994.

DSM IV: The most recent classification system for behavioural and emotional disorders used by the American Psychiatric Association introduced at the beginning of 1995.

Dyskinesias: Difficulty in performance of voluntary movements.

Dyslexia: A significant difficulty with or impairment in reading ability when reading is compared to other aspects of psychological functioning. Dylsexia can be of various types and have a variety of causes.

Dysphasia: Difficulty with the production of comprehensible speech.

Echolalia: Copying or repeating the content and/or intonation patterns of another person's speech.

Egocentrism: Being unable to think of situations from any perspective other than than one's own.

Endorphin: A range of naturally produced opium-like substances found in the brain that act as neurotransmitters and affect natural pain control.

Epilepsy: A range of chronic disorders that cause excessive neural discharge, either in restricted areas or more extensively in the brain, resulting in impairment in the functioning of those structures which are affected. Manifested as 'fits', which can affect emotions, consciousness, movement or perception in different combinations.

Ethology: The study of animal behaviour and communication in the natural environment.

Executive Function: The ability to plan complex cognitive tasks (such as the 'Wisconsin Card Sorting Test' or the 'Tower of Hanoi'). This ability is interfered with by dysfunction in the frontal lobes of the brain.

Familial: Present in several members of the same family group.

Fenfluramine: A medication used as an antagonist to the neurotransmitter serotonin to reduce the concentration of seratonin in the fluids of the central nervous system, blood and urine.

Folium: A portion of the cerebellar vermis.

Form E1/2: The standardised scale developed by Rimland in San Diego for characterisation of the typical developmental patterns seen in autism (see p.15).

Fragile-X Syndrome: A genetic disorder resulting in developmental delay and autism in a significant number of those possessing the defect, in which there is an over-replication (repetition) of a small section of genetic substance near the tip of the X-chromosome. The cause of this fault and the mode of action of the disorder are uncertain.

Haemodialysis: Removal of water and soluble substances from the blood by diffusion through a semipermeable membrane in a dialysis machine.

Haloperidol: A medication which acts as a virtually pure antagonist or blocking agent for the D2 dopamine receptor.

Heller's Syndrome: See Childhood Disintegrative Psychosis.

Hippocampus: A paired structure in the temporal lobe of the brain forming part of the limbic system. It is involved in emotion and is essential for the laying down of short term memories.

Homovanillic Acid (HVA): A substance, the end product of chemical treatment of the transmitter dopamine in the body, which can be detected in brain fluids and urine.

5-Hydroxyindoleacetic Acid (5-HIAA): A substance which is the end product of serotonin breakdown within the body.

Hydrocephalus: An increase of fluid pressure in the brain which can result from a number of factors, such as increased production of fluid, decreased absorption of fluid, or some blockage within the ventricular system – the fluid filled cavaties inside the brain.

Hypomelanosis of Ito: A condition of unknown cause which results in depigmented spots or pale streaks on the skin, best seen under ultraviolet light. This skin condition is often associated with skeletal and eye abnormalities, and there are central nervous system defects in approximately 50 per cent of cases.

Hypoplasia: Underdevelopment of a structure, normally due to a decrease in the number of cells.

Hypotonia: Significantly reduced muscle tone or resting muscle tension.

IBSE: The Infant Behavioural Summarised Evlauation (see p.19).

ICD 9: The World Health Organization classification system for diseases in use between 1980 and 1994.

ICD 10: The World Health Organization classification system for diseases in use from 1995 (a draft version of part of the psychiatric systems was introduced in 1987).

Inter-Rater Reliability: A measure of the extent of agreement between independent observers who are rating the same phenomenon using an agreed rating system.

Intramuscular: Within a muscle.

Insula: An oval region of the cerebral cortex to the side of the lenticular nucleus of the basal ganglia.

In utero: during foetal development inside the womb.

Joubert's Syndrome: A recessive genetic disorder resulting in hypoplasia or agenesis of the cerebellar vermis with mental retardation, ataxia, hypotonia and abnormal breathing and eye movements.

Kleinian School: the psychoanalytic group who base their ideas on the work of the analyst Melanie Klein (see Chapter 12).

Lacanian School: The Psychoanalytic group who base their ideas on the work of the French analyst Lacan (see Chapter 12).

Lenticular Nucleus: A paired nucleus of the basal ganglia situated between the caudate and the thalamus.

Limbic System: A group of brain tissues between the brain stem and the neocortex. The principal components of this system include hippocampus, mammillary bodies, septum, olfactory bulbs, fornix and cingulate gyrus. They are important in emotions and in regulation of consciousness and learning.

Lithium: An alkali metal chemical element, used in the the stabilisation of manic-depressive patients.

Magnetic Resonance Imaging (MRI): A brain imaging technique which differentially images structures with high water content. Clear diagnostic imaging of cerebellar and midbrain structures is possible with this technique.

Mammillary Bodies: Paired structures in the limbic system.

Melanin: A black pigment, found in the nerve cells of the substantia nigra of the brain stem, and in skin, hair and the retina of the eye. It is not present in the newborn but appears towards the end of the first year and increases steadily until puberty.

Motor Stereotypies: Constant, involuntary repetition of meaningless gestures or movements.

Naloxone: A short-acting, intramuscularly injected substance that blocks endorphin receptor binding sites (i.e. it is an endorphin 'antagonist').

Naltrexone: A long-acting, orally administered blocker of endorphin receptor binding sites.

Neocortex: The grey matter layer covering the surface of the cerebral hemispheres, not including limbic cortex.

Neurofibromatosis (von Recklinghausen's Disease): A genetic (autosomal dominant) disorder of skin and nerve tissue with small pigmented skin lesions (often called *cafe-au-lait* spots) which may develop into abnormal tissue masses along the course of peripheral nerves.

Olivary Nucleus: A paired structure in the brainstem with ascending connections into the cerebellum.

Olivo-Ponto-Cerebellar Degeneration: A progressive disorder of movement control with onset in adult life. Accompanied by degeneration of the cerebellum, olivary nuclei and pons.

Paraldehyde: A medication sometimes used to control severe epileptic seizures, normally given by intramuscular injection.

Parietal Cortex: A region of the cerebral cortex which lies beneath the parietal bone of the skull at the back and side of the head.

Peripheral Nerves: Nerves passing between the central nervous system (brain and spinal cord) and the sense organs, glands and muscles of the body.

Pertubation: Interference with the normal development of a function.

Posterior: Towards the back of the structure in question.

Phenothiazines: A group of medications used primarily in the treatment of schizophrenia.

Phenylketonuria (PKU): A genetic disorder resulting from lack of a single gene that normally codes for the enzyme required for the body to process phenylalanine, an amino acid which is present in most foodstuffs. Affected individuals, unless given a special diet with low levels of phenylalanine present with developmental delay and often with autism. Routine neonatal screening with the Guthrie test has virtually eliminated this as a cause of autism in the UK.

PL-ADOS: The Preschool Autism Diagnostic Observations Schedule (see p.19).

Positron Emission Tomography (PET): A method for imaging blood flow through the brain which allows the investigator to identify structures in which there is an increase or decrease of blood flow during particular activities, and to locate structures with abnormal levels of cell activity.

Proto-conversation: Preverbal communicative interactions between infants and their caregivers which exhibit many of the affective, prosodic and intentional components observed in verbal conversations between adults.

Purine Autism: Autism consequent on abnormalities in purine metabolism.

Purkinje Cells: Large cells found in a single layer at the junction of the molecular and granular layers of the cerebellum.

Receptive: Concerned with comprehension of the communicative messages of others. Also applied to cells or membrane structures that are affected by messenger substances released by other cells.

Refrigerator Parenting: The term used by Kanner during the period when he felt autism to be psychogenic, or environmentally caused, to describe the cold, emotionless patterns of behaviour shown by parents which he felt caused autistic behaviour in their children.

Rett's Syndrome: A condition, presumed to be genetic, which is found only in females. It is characterised by slow head growth, loss of speech and loss of functional hand use after normal progress in early infancy, progressive muscle wasting and abnormal breathing. Electrical activity of the brain (EEG) is abnormal, and there is frequently late-onset epilepsy.

Rubella: The virus of German measles, resulting in a high incidence of developmental abnormalities in children born to women who contract the virus in the early months of pregnancy.

Serotonin: A neurotransmitter, found in high levels in the hypothalamus, midbrain and caudate nucleus.

Testosterone: The male sex hormone.

Thalamus: A group of nuclei in the diencephalon inside the cerebral hemispheres the cells of which transmit impulses to and from the cerebral cortex. Contains nuclei that convey information from the sensory receptors to the cortex.

Theory of Mind: A philosophical concept of the understanding one has that another person has an individual perspective on states of affairs, that this consciousness depends in part on information which they may have that is not available to oneself, and *vice versa*.

Tuber: A portion of the central vermis of the cerebellum.

Tuberous Sclerosis: Potato-like tissue masses in the brain caused by abnormal cell migration and clustering in development.

Ventricular Dilatation: Expansion of the ventricular system or cavities of the brain, commonly caused by raised pressure of brain fluids (see 'Hydrocephalus').

Vermis: The midline portion of the cerebellum, between the two cerebellar hemispheres.

William's Syndrome: A condition involving hypocalcaemia (low calcium levels) with characteristic physical and behavioural features, including an enlarged cerebellum, extreme sensitivity to certain noises (hyperacusis), learning disability, spatial problems and relatively good verbal ability.

Subject Index

Author Index